MIDSTREAM:
MY LATER LIFE

Helen Keller and Sieglinde

MIDSTREAM

My Later Life

by

HELEN KELLER

GREENWOOD PRESS, PUBLISHERS
WESTPORT, CONNECTICUT

The Library of Congress cataloged this book as follows:

Keller, Helen Adams, 1880–1968.
　　Midstream: my later life.　New York, Greenwood Press,
1968 [ᶜ1929]

　　xxiii, 362 p.　port.　22 cm.

　I. Title.

HV1624.K4A17　1968　　　362.4'0924　(B)　　　68–8063

Library of Congress　　　　　[2]

HV
1624
.K4
A17
1968

Reprinted in 1968 by Greenwood Press, Inc.,
51 Riverside Avenue, Westport, Conn. 06880

Library of Congress catalog card number 68-8063

ISBN 0-8371-0127-1

Printed in the United States of America

10 9 8 7 6 5 4 3 2

TO

ANNE SULLIVAN

WHOSE LOVE

IS

THE STORY OF MY LIFE

"There be many shapes of mystery;
And many things God brings to be,
    Past hope or fear.
And the end men looked for cometh not,
And a path is there where no man thought.
    So hath it fallen here."

—EURIPIDES.

FOREWORD

SOMEWHERE in the course of her book Miss Keller
speaks of the "sacrosanct privacy to which tradition
and the necessities of concentrated thinking entitle
writers and artists." It is something she has never
known. Since she was seven years old, when she was
hailed as "a most extraordinary little individual,"
"a mental prodigy," and "an intellectual phenom-
enon," whose achievements were "little short of a
miracle," whose progress was "a sort of triumphant
march—a series of dazzling conquests," the great
megaphones of publicity have followed her, trumpet-
ing truth and untruth with equal fury, even when the
truth alone was more wonderful than all the embel-
lishments heated imaginations could add to it.

Helen Keller was born, a perfectly healthy and
normal child, in Tuscumbia, Alabama, on June 27,
1880. At the age of eighteen months she was stricken
with a severe illness, the exact nature of which is not
known. It left her deaf and blind; as a result
of the deafness she soon became dumb also.
For five years she remained imprisoned. Then,
through Dr. Alexander Graham Bell, to whom her
father appealed because he knew Dr. Bell's interest

in the deaf, a deliverer was sent to her in the person of a twenty-year-old graduate of the Perkins Institution for the Blind at Boston, Mass., a girl by the name of Anne Mansfield Sullivan. From the day of Miss Sullivan's arrival on March 3, 1887, the story of Miss Keller's life reads like a fairy tale. Within a month the teacher had presented the gift of language to her little pupil, an achievement in itself so miraculous that fifty years earlier no one had believed it possible. Until Dr. Samuel Gridley Howe proved through the education of Laura Bridgman that their minds could be reached and shown how to reach out, the totally blind and deaf were classified with idiots and left alone.

Since Laura's education numbers of those afflicted as she was have been placed in communication with the world. Some of them have shown considerable natural ability, but Helen Keller is to-day, as she has always been, incomparably the greatest among them. She is the only one who has ever been received, without apology, into the world of the seeing. In a college for normal girls to which she was admitted reluctantly and without favour she won a degree *cum laude* in the same length of time it took her classmates to win theirs. She has learned to speak—the first deaf-blind person in America of whom this was true. She has acted in vaudeville and in motion pictures; she has lectured in every state in the Union except

Florida,[1] and in many parts of Canada; she has written books of literary distinction and permanent
value; she has, since her graduation from college,
taken an active part in every major movement on
behalf of the blind in this country, and she has
managed to carry on a wide correspondence in English, French, and German, and to keep herself informed by means of books and magazines in those
three languages.

Two years ago she laid down—temporarily—her
work for the American Foundation for the Blind,
thinking to go quietly to her home on Long Island,
and there with her teacher, Mrs. Macy,[2] her secretary, Miss Thomson, and her Great Dane, Sieglinde,
review the part of her life which had elapsed since
her sophomore year at Radcliffe College when *The
Story of My Life,* which is the story of her childhood and young girlhood, was published.

I think she had not realized how difficult it would
be to isolate herself. She could stop sending letters
out, but she could not stop them coming in, nor could
she head off the beggars who swarmed to her door.
Few people realize what is expected—nay, what is
demanded—of her. Not a day passes without urgent
and heartbreaking appeals from all over the world.
They come by letter and in person—from the blind,
the deaf, the crippled, the sick, the poverty-stricken,

---

[1]Since this was written Miss Keller has also lectured in Florida.
[2]Formerly Miss Anne Mansfield Sullivan.

and the sorrow-laden. In addition to these, there are, of course, requests for pictures, autographs, testimonials, and explanations of what she thinks of reincarnation or prohibition. But the majority of Miss Keller's letters and the majority of her callers come with distressing pleas for help. "Oh, Miss Keller, you, with your unparalleled opportunities! You, with your wealthy friends!"

The letters were turned over to Miss Thomson and Miss Keller sat down—it must be confessed without special enthusiasm, for she has never been greatly interested in herself—to continue the story of her life. Almost immediately Miss Thomson was imperatively called away, and Mrs. Macy, who is nearly blind, and Miss Keller, who is quite blind, were left to struggle along as best they could.

They got their own meals, Mrs. Macy doing most of the cooking while Miss Keller washed the dishes, made the beds, did the dusting, and on Monday pricked out the laundry list in braille so she could check it when the clothes came back on Saturday. When the morning chores were done and the most insistent letters answered she turned to *Midstream*. Poignant, heartbreaking days out of the past swept over her; even to think of them was pain.

She had known for many years that she would one day have to write this book, and had, in preparation, jotted down in braille many fragmentary im-

pressions. Going over them was slow work. Never
believe one who tells you that the blind can read as
rapidly as the seeing. The swiftest finger cannot keep
up with the eye. It is not only much slower, but in-
finitely more laborious. The arm grows tired, the
ends of the fingers ache, and Miss Keller discovered
that the friction of years had worn down the
treacherous little dots to such an extent that in many
cases she could not make out what she had written.

Much of her material was not in braille. The letters from Mark Twain, Dr. Bell, William James,
and others were in hand- or typewriting. So was
most of the data on the blind except that which the
American Foundation for the Blind had put into
raised print. Numbers of articles and stray paragraphs of her own she had typed, thereby, since she
had at the same time destroyed her braille notes,
placing them forever beyond her own reach. All of
this Mrs. Macy, Miss Thomson, and I read to her
by means of the manual alphabet.

Miss Keller had not been long at work before
Mrs. Macy became ill. A temporary servant was
called in. Mrs. Macy became much worse. The doctors were grave. She had been abusing her eyes. They
had told her not to use them. Work on *Midstream*
stopped abruptly. Nervous and anxious, Miss Keller
paced the house and tramped the garden. She could
not read, she could not write, she could not even

think. It was not until Mrs. Macy was completely out of danger that the autobiography was resumed.

Most of the time Miss Keller composed in braille and revised in braille. Sometimes she composed directly on the typewriter, pricking notations at the top of the pages with a hairpin so she could keep track of them. Parts she was most uncertain about she kept in braille a long time, going over and over them. Often, as she mulled over what she had written, she decided to write it again, and sometimes the second or the third or the fourth version was better than the first.

The mass of material grew. Thousands of pages lay piled on the floor sprinkled through with thousands of directions: "Put this with what I have already written about the garden." . . . "Please see if the letter I had from Mr. Carnegie in 1913 will not fit in here." . . . "I think this quotation is right, but perhaps someone should verify it. It is not in raised print." . . . "These paragraphs may add a pleasant touch to what I have already written about Dr. Bell."

Under Miss Keller's direction, oral and written, the typed manuscript was rewritten with scissors and paste, Mrs. Macy, Miss Thomson, and I constantly spelling back to her pages, paragraphs, and chapters. As Miss Keller says, it was like putting a picture puzzle together, only it was not a puzzle one could hold in a tray; sometimes it seemed as big as the whole city of New York, and sometimes it seemed bigger than that. When we had finished we gave it to a typist to copy while Miss Keller set to writing connecting paragraphs for chapters that did not fit together and rewriting parts she did not like and trying frantically to catch up with the outside claims upon her. Once she left Forest Hills at eleven o'clock in the morning, delivered an address in Washington at four o'clock in the afternoon, returned immediately to Forest Hills where she arrived so late that the taxi drivers had gone to bed, walked home from the station, snatched a few hours' sleep, and went back to work the next morning at eight o'clock! They were heroic days.

Even yet the book was to her a thing of shreds and patches. Naturally, our work did not begin with page one and run through to the end the way the reader has it now. It was done in small units and with many interruptions. When the typist had finished, scissors and paste were once more brought out, and for the second time, under Miss Keller's direction, the manuscript was put together, after which it was spelled to her again three times from beginning to end while she made still further alterations. In galley proofs it was read to her once more and for the last time. To the end she was revising and rewriting. She has not yet read the book with her own fingers; she cannot do that until the braille edition is printed.

Of the content perhaps a word is necessary. The book is Miss Keller's. Doubts concerning the authenticity of her accomplishment have long since been laid to rest, even in Europe where for many years she was regarded as nothing more than a fine example of American exaggeration. It is only those who do not know her who suggest, now and then, that it is Mrs. Macy who tells her what to say. Miss Keller has convictions of her own, and a stubborn way of hanging on to them. In most instances they are not those of her teacher. Temperamentally she and Mrs. Macy are utterly different, and the word "utterly" is not carelessly used. Each has chambers in her mind that the other does not, cannot, penetrate. No one can be more surprised at some of the revelations in this book than the woman who has lived in daily association with Miss Keller for the last forty years.

There are people who think of Miss Keller as cut off from all that is unpleasant, living in a happy realm of ideality where everything is as it should be. This has never been true. Six months after she went to Alabama Mrs. Macy wrote, "From the beginning I have made it a practice to answer all Helen's questions to the best of my ability and at the same time truthfully."

Much has been made of the fact that in the education of Helen Keller Mrs. Macy followed the methods of Dr. Samuel Gridley Howe, who taught Laura Bridgman. It is true that they both used the manual alphabet as their means of communication, but it is also true that neither of them invented it. Mrs. Macy's method of presenting language to her pupil was unlike Dr. Howe's, as has been made clear in *The Story of My Life*. As for the difference in method after language was acquired, the statement of Mrs. Macy's I have just quoted, which was written when Miss Keller was seven years old and had been under instruction four months, may be contrasted with this from Dr. Howe in a letter to Laura when she was fifteen years old and had been under instruction for seven years: "Your mind is young and weak and cannot understand hard things, but by and by it will be stronger and you will be able to understand hard things." Laura had asked him about "God and heaven and souls and many questions."

It is annoying to a certain type of mind to have Miss Keller describe something she obviously cannot know through direct sensation. The annoyance is mutual. These sensations, whatever expert opinion on them may be, are as real to her as any others. Her idea of colour, to take only one instance, is built up through association and analogy. Pink is "like a baby's cheek or a soft Southern breeze." Gray is "like a soft shawl around the shoulders." Yellow is

"like the sun. It means life and is rich in promise."
There are two kinds of brown. One is "warm and
friendly like leaf mould." The other is "like the
trunks of aged trees with worm holes in them, or like
withered hands." Lilac, which is her teacher's
favourite colour, "makes her think of faces she has
loved and kissed." The warm sun brings out odours
that make her think of red. Coolness brings out
odours that make her think of green. A sparkling
colour brings to mind soap bubbles quivering under
her hand.

In her descriptions of San Francisco, to which objections are sure to be raised, she is not repeating
something she has been told. She is telling what she
has built up for herself out of the descriptions she
has read and those that have been spelled to her.
In what way her picture differs from ours we cannot say, for she has only our language to use in describing it. Mark Twain used to think that her im-
ages were more beautiful and gave his own experience with Niagara Falls and the Taj Mahal to prove
it. In his imagination before he saw them Niagara
Falls were "finer than anything God ever thought
of in the way of scenery," and the Taj Mahal was a
"rat hole" compared with what he thought it would
be. "I thank God," he said one day after Miss Keller
had described the face of a friend, "she can't see."

All that Miss Keller claims for her world is

that there is a workable correspondence between it
and ours, since she finds no incongruity in living in
both at the same time. William James was not surprised at this correspondence. I think few phil-
osophers are. They see only too clearly how much of
what we all know and feel has come to us not through
personal knowledge, but through the accumulated
experience of our ancestors and contemporaries as
it is handed down and given over to us in words. She
is, thinks Professor Pierre Villey, himself a blind
man, and a most careful observer, a dupe of words,
and her æsthetic enjoyment of most of the arts is "a
matter of auto-suggestion rather than perception."
He is right, but this is true of all of us.

It has been doubted that Miss Keller can enjoy
sculpture, since it is addressed to the eye, yet the
sculptor's own contact with his work is as much with
the hand as with the eye.

Her enjoyment of music has also been thrown
open to question. She has "listened" with her fingers
to the piano and the violin and various devices
have been contrived to make it possible for her to
"hear" an orchestra. Recently she has been listening
over the radio by placing her fingers lightly on a
sounding board of balsa wood. She can tell when the
announcer is talking and she has learned to recognize
station WEAF by the dogmatic staccato of the announcer's voice when he repeats the letters. She can

tell whether one or more instruments are playing, and very frequently can tell what the instruments are. The singing voice she sometimes confuses with the violin. The 'cello and the bass viol are likewise confused, but there is never a mistake in the rhythm or the general mood of the selection, though efforts have been made to trip her up on these two points.

Miss Keller's impressions of the world have come much as they do to anyone, only the mechanism is different. She reads with her fingers instead of her eyes and listens with her hands instead of her ears. Those who are familiar with the manual alphabet generally use it in talking to her. One who is accustomed to talking in this way talks with as little embarrassment as in any other. Those who do not know the manual alphabet talk with their mouths and Miss Keller listens by placing her fingers lightly on the lips. She talks with her mouth and is readily understood by anyone who has been with her a short time. Her voice is not normal, but to those of us who are used to it, it seems no more abnormal than that of a person with a marked foreign accent.

So far as tests have been able to determine, her sensory equipment is in no way, except perhaps in the sense of smell, superior to that of the normal person. She seems totally without the sense of direction which is so pronounced in some of the deaf blind. In her own home, which is not large, she frequently starts toward the opposite wall instead of the door, and orients herself by contact with the furniture. When the rugs are taken up she is completely bewildered and has to learn the whole pattern again. Her sense of distance is also poor. She does not know when she has reached the door until she has run into it, and in winter when the ground is covered with snow and ice her daily walk becomes a mighty adventure.

Much nonsense has been written about her; no doubt much more will be. She is perfectly aware of it, and also of the criticisms that have been levelled against her. No attack that has ever been made has been withheld from her. I think she has come to know that, in judging her, mistakes have been made on both sides. We have been trying to interpret what she feels in terms of what we feel, and she, whose greatest desire has always been, like that of most of the handicapped, to be like other people, has been trying to meet us half way. So it is that we find ourselves in the end where we were in the beginning, on opposite sides of a wall. Little bits have crumbled away, but the wall is still there, and there is no way to break it down.

Many have tried. She has been the subject of much scientific experimentation and philosophical speculation. This has caused a great deal of disturbance in learned minds, for she has a disconcerting way of upsetting nearly all preconceived theories about herself. Even William James went through this experience. No one has yet said the final word about her, except in one particular. William James did that when at the end of his consideration he said, "The sum of it is that you are a *blessing,* and I'll kill anyone who says you are not."

NELLA BRADDY.

CONTENTS

MIDSTREAM
MY LATER LIFE

MIDSTREAM:
MY LATER LIFE

Chapter I

TUNING IN

WHEN people are old enough to write their memoirs,
it is time for them to die, it seems to me. It would
save themselves and others a great deal of trouble
if they did. But since I have the indiscretion to be
still alive, I shall add to their burden by trying to
set down the story of my life since I was a sophomore at Radcliffe College.

During many years I have written detached notes
on whatever has interested me, in all kinds of moods,
under all kinds of circumstances. This desultory
manner of writing is temperamental with me. I like
it because it gives me a chance to chat and laugh
a little and be friendly along the way.

I shall not attempt to follow a continuous thread
of thought or give a special message in these pages.
I shall not pursue any one idea up and down the
labyrinths of the mind. It is my wish to jot down
fugitive thoughts and emotions, and let them bear

what they will. I have often been told that if I would put more such fleeting bits of life into words, I might add somewhat to the fund of sympathy, thought, and sincerity from which men draw strength to live. So if what grows out of my notes should not prove bright or fair, at least the seed is sweet—the seed of my friends' encouragement.

Since I have been at work upon this autobiography, I have frequently thought of the occupation which engaged the attention of my friend Colonel Roebling the latter years of his life. He was always a builder. In his young manhood he constructed the Brooklyn suspension bridge, and incidentally invalided himself by staying too long under water in one of the caissons. Years later when I visited him in Trenton, New Jersey, he showed me with much enthusiasm a picture which he was building out of little bits of paper. The picture represented a great river spanned by a noble bridge, between green hills; and the fleecy clouds of a summer day were reflected in the blue waters. Every tiny bit of paper was tinted and shaped to fit into the design. Great patience and ingenuity were required to assemble the thousands of bits that composed the landscape and the flowing river. From a little tray he painstakingly selected lights and shadows, leaves and ripples, and the bridge's flowing spans.

The process of shaping a book is not unlike

Colonel Roebling's picture-building. Into the tray
of one's consciousness are tumbled thousands of
scraps of experience. That tray holds you dismembered, so to speak. Your problem is to synthesize
yourself and the world you live in, with its mountains and streams, its oceans and skies, its volcanoes,
deserts, cities and people, into something like a coherent whole. The difficulty multiplies when you
find that the pieces never look the same to you two
minutes in succession. You pick them up, and find
that they are "sicklied o'er" with sentiment, with old
beliefs and relationships. With each new experience
you pass through, they undergo strange transmuta-
tions. I put together my pieces this way and that;
but they will not dovetail properly. When I succeed
in making a fairly complete picture, I discover
countless fragments in the tray, and I do not know
what to do with them. The longer I work, the more
important these fragments seem; so I pull the picture apart and start it all over again. I trace the
irregular lines of experience through the design, and
wonder at the queer conjunctions of facts and imaginings. My sense of the fitness of things demands
that there should be some degree of beauty in the
composition; but alas, I am driven finally to the
realization that the elements which went into the
shaping of my life were not as carefully tinted and
shaped as those in Colonel Roebling's picture. Per-

haps, to the eye of the Creator, there may be symmetry and purpose and fulfilment; but the individual perceives only fragments incongruously mingled together, and blank spaces which one feels should be filled by something noble, dramatic, or extraordinary.

The first part of *The Story of My Life* was written in the form of daily and fortnightly themes in English 22 at Radcliffe College under Professor Charles Townsend Copeland. I had no idea of publishing them and I do not remember how Mr. Bok became interested in them. I only know that one morning I was called out of my Latin class to meet Mr. William Alexander of the *Ladies' Home Journal*. If I remember rightly, Mr. Alexander said that Mr. Bok wished to publish *The Story of My Life* in monthly installments. I told him that it was out of the question, as my college work was all I could manage. His answer surprised me. "You have already written a considerable part of it in your themes."

"How in the world did you find out I was writing themes?" I exclaimed. He laughed and said it was his business to find out such things. He talked so optimistically about how easily the themes could be connected to form magazine articles that, without having a very clear idea of what I was doing, I signed an agreement to furnish the *Ladies' Home Journal* with *The Story of My Life* in monthly in-

stallments for three thousand dollars. At the moment
I thought of nothing but the three thousand dollars.
There was magic in those three words. In my imagination the story was already written. Indeed, it
had already found a sure place in "The Golden
Treasury of Literature." My happiness and conceit
knew no bounds. Everything went smoothly at first.
I had already written a number of themes which
Mr. Copeland had read and criticized. He had
also made suggestions which I was able to
use in the first chapter. But the day was not far
distant when I found that I had used all the suitable
themes. I was in deep water, and frightened out of
my wits. I was utterly inexperienced in the preparation of magazine articles. I did not know how to
cut my material to fit the given space. I had no idea
that the time limit was of such importance until
telegrams began to come, thick and fast, like greedy
birds to a cherry tree. Special delivery letters filled
the chorus of dismay: "We must have the next chapter immediately." "There is no connection between
page six and page seven. Wire the missing part."
Mr. Bok told me years afterwards that the
people in Dante's *Inferno* had a pleasant time of
it compared with what the staff of the *Ladies' Home
Journal* endured while my story was on its way. He
said he resolved then never again to start publishing a serial until he had the whole manuscript in his

hands; he told me a few years ago that he never had. When things were at the worst, my friend, Lenore Kinney, who had just married Philip Sidney Smith, a classmate of John Macy's, told me about Mr. Macy. She described him as extremely clever, and just the sort of knight errant to deliver me from the jaws of this dilemma. At that time, Mr. Macy was an English instructor at Harvard University. He had classes in Radcliffe also, but I did not know him. Lenore arranged for us to meet. I liked him; he was eager, intelligent, gentle. He understood my difficulties, and promptly set about relieving me of them. We went over the material I had accumulated, which was in the state of original chaos. Quickly and skillfully he brought the recalcitrant parts to order; and we constructed a tolerably coherent and readable chapter in a few hours. Mr. Bok hailed him as a *deus ex machina,* and from that time on the *Journal* got its "copy" in fairly good time.

Mr. Macy was a writer himself, with a keen, well-stored mind, and his advice was most precious to me. He was a friend, a brother, and an adviser all in one, and if this book is not what it should be, it is because I feel lonely and bewildered without his supporting hand.

Chapter II

YOUTH, OH, YOUTH

IN *The Story of My Life* I went quite fully into my struggle for admission to Radcliffe College. In these pages, therefore, I shall merely summarize my experiences and impressions.

I knew that there would be obstacles to conquer; but they only whetted my desire to try my strength by the standards of normal students. I thought that in college I should touch hands with girls who were interested in the same subjects that I was, and who were trying like me to hew out their own paths in life. I began my studies with enthusiasm. I entered the lecture halls in the spirit of the young men who gathered about Socrates and Plato. Here were cup-bearers "of the wine that's meant for souls" who would answer all the questions that perplexed me.

But soon I found that my great expectation had sprung from inexperience. I was reminded of the upright divisions between the shelves in the library in a house where I lived while attending the Gilman School for Girls. When my teacher and I first saw them she exclaimed, "What beautiful books! Just feel them." I touched the handsome volumes and

7

read some of the titles, which were so richly embossed that I could distinguish the letters. But when I tried to take one of them down I found that they were imitation books, all bound and lettered in gold to look like Chaucer, Montaigne, Bacon, Shakespeare, and Dante. That is the way I felt as the days in college passed, and my dreams faded into a rather drab reality.

Two insurmountable obstacles confronted me throughout my college course—lack of books in raised letters, and lack of time. Most of the required books Miss Sullivan read to me, spelling into my hand. Often when every one else in the house was asleep, she and I were busy with our books, trying to catch up with the day's reading. Generous friends like Mr. H. H. Rogers and Mr. William Wade would gladly have had the books specially made for me but often I could not find out from the professors what books I would need in time to have them transcribed. No such splendid service as that offered by the Red Cross was available for blind students twenty-five years ago. If it had been there would have been fewer shadows of discontent and more liberty in my work.

Books that were not in braille had to be read to me by means of the manual alphabet as rapidly as possible in order that I might keep up with the classes. I was a slow student and it tried my patience not to be able to read for myself the passages I especially wanted, as often as I pleased. Miss Sullivan was ever at my side, not only reading to me and spelling the lectures into my hand but looking up words in Latin, German, and French dictionaries. She was not familiar with any of these languages, and to this day I marvel how, with her imperfect sight, she accomplished such an arduous task.

Each volume in braille—and I remember especially "Othello," "A Winter's Tale," "Henry IV," "Henry V," and the *Sonnets,* parts of Livy and Tacitus, Plautus's plays, and the poetry of Catullus, selections from Pope, Dryden, Addison, and Steele, and the poets to whose divine songs I still withdraw from the discords of the world: Keats, Wordsworth, Browning, and Shelley—was a treasure island to me, and it was an inexpressibly sweet sense of independence I had preparing some lessons from pages over which I could sprawl my fingers and gather the material for a theme or an examination.

As I look back upon it, it seems to me that, my own special difficulties aside, we were all in too much of a hurry. It was like rushing through Europe on a summer holiday. I caught only fleeting gleams of the blaze and glory of Elizabethan literature, the satire and the wit of Swift, Johnson, and Goldsmith, and the splendour of the Nineteenth Century poets as they poured out their exuberant messages of spiritual power, cheer, and courage from nature, from men, and from the Divine Life breathing through all things. But in the harvest of my later years it is a delight to remember those wandlike touches of fancy, wisdom, and imagination by which my soul was set aflame!

The noble men and women of history and poetry moved and breathed before me vividly on the picture screen of time. Generals, kings, and Holy Alliances did not concern me much; I could not see what good could result from the ruthless destruction wrought by the Alexanders, Cæsars, and Napoleons, but my imagination glowed as I beheld Socrates fearlessly teaching the youth of Athens the truth and drinking the fatal cup rather than surrender. Columbus's sublime perseverance as he sailed chartless seas with an unfriendly crew quickened my sense of adventure in exploring and perhaps mapping a dark, soundless world. I had always loved Joan of Arc with a tender reverence, and her beautiful, tragic figure in Schiller's play, in English and French history, and in essays by men of widely different temperaments, her simple wisdom that cut through all entangling arguments, her undaunted faith in the midst of betrayal and cruelty, revealed to me new heights and glories of womanhood. She has remained very close to me—"One of the few whom God whispers in the ear."

With many an amazing scene the vast drama of
the ages unfolded before me—empires rising and
falling, old arts giving way to new ones, races
strangely fused out of the fragments of ancient peoples, heroic doers and thinkers pouring life and energy into the Dark Ages, scholars defying church
and state, taking the wanderer's staff in hand, suffering and perishing that paths might be cleared to
higher goals of truth. Fascinated, I watched how
new ideas appeared, waxed great, and waned. I
lost all sense of stability in earthly things, but I
was reassured by the thought that the mind of man
that unmakes what is made can also withdraw into
itself and find peace. This resource was the *elixir
vitae* I gained from another study that I took up
at Radcliffe College, philosophy.

I was so happily at home in philosophy, it alone
would have rendered those four difficult years worth
while. As a spring rain makes the fields greener, so
my inner world grew fair beneath the shower of new
ideas that fell from the magic words of the sages! I
had faith and imagination; but philosophy taught
me how to keep on guard against the misconceptions
which spring from the limited experience of one
who lives in a world without colour and without
sound. I gained strength for my groping belief from
thinkers who saw with their eyes, heard with their
ears, touched with their hands and perceived the

untrustworthiness of the senses even in the best equipped human being. Socrates's discourses on knowledge, friendship, and immortality I found intensely absorbing and stimulating, so full were they of truth and poetry in declaring that the real world exists only for the mind. Plato made me happily aware of an inner faculty—an "Absolute" which gives beauty to the beautiful, music to the musical, and truth to what we call true, and thus creates order and light and sound within us, no matter what calamity may afflict us in the outer world. I was delighted to have my faith confirmed that I could go beyond the broken arc of my senses and behold the invisible in the fullness of light, and hear divine symphonies in silence. I had a joyous certainty that deafness and blindness were not an essential part of my existence, since they were not in any way a part of my immortal mind.

But this idea was faith only until I came to Descartes's maxim, "I think, therefore I am." I realized, then, that my "absolute" was not merely a possession, but an instrument of happiness. I rose up actively on my little island of limitations and found other ways to bridge over the dark, silent void with concepts of a light-flooded, resonant universe. In other words, I used my inner senses with a stronger will to dominate the deaf, blind being groping its way through a welter of objects, sensations, and fragmentary impressions. Before this, through some obtuseness I had failed to "take hold" of the higher consciousness which enlarges life to infinity. But those five direct, emphatic words, "I think, therefore I am," waked something in me that has never slept since.

Kant and Emerson led me farther on the road to emancipation. I had often before felt bound by my lack of hearing and sight to such an extent that I doubted if I could ever have an adequate conception of what others saw and heard. My crippled senses and I seemed at times to be one and inseparable, and I could not see clearly how my ideas or testimony of things I touched could be taken seriously. I was told that nine tenths of the human being's impressions came to him through his eyes and ears, and I wondered if my friends and I would ever be able to understand each other. However lovingly our hearts might meet, there appeared to be an impassable gulf between us. The crowded experience of our so-different lives obstructed many of the natural channels of understanding. I thought I must seem almost like a ghost to the strong, confident senses that ruled the world, but when I penetrated into the immaterial realm which is the world of philosophy, I gained a cheerful, reconciling view of our situations. I apprehended the truth of what Kant said, that sensations without concepts are barren, and concepts without sensations are empty. I put more thought and feeling into my senses; I examined as I had not before my impressions arising from touch and smell, and was amazed at the ideas with which they supplied me, and the clues they gave me to the world of sight and hearing. For example, I observed the kinds and degrees of fragrance which gave me pleasure, and that enabled me to imagine how the seeing eye is charmed by different colours and their shades. Then I traced the analogies between the illumination of thought and the light of day, and perceived more clearly than I ever had the preciousness of light in the life of the human being. This way of thinking helped me later when critics of my writings asked, "But how can she know about life?" . . . "How can she know what it means to an adult person to lose his sight, and what kind of help he especially needs when she has not had his special experiences?" . . . "What right has she to write about landscapes she can't see?" and other questions that showed how little they knew of the foundations upon which I was building up closer associations with normal people.

Another shower of thoughts that refreshed my life-garden fell when I read in Kant that time and space are not fixed, immutable elements, but changeable ways of experiencing life. Like most people I had felt the spell of the senses to such a degree that the walls of time and space seemed very solid and inescapable, and that made it harder for me to sit still and wait when I wanted to be up and getting somewhere. But when I found that I could over-leap time and space, crowd years of remembrance into an hour, or lengthen an hour into eternity, I saw my true self as a free spirit throwing into the winds the bonds of body and condition and matter. With Emerson I read a great poem or listened to a sub-lime utterance, or held the perfection of a flower in my hand, and instantly I was over the walls of mortal life, speeding through the uplands of boundless beauty. It was in the joy of these new thoughts that I wrote *Optimism* and *The World I Live In*. For it was Emerson who revealed to me the romance in Kant's abstract words, and made it easier for me afterwards to read Swedenborg's discourses on time and space. I did not then know the importance of philosophy as a star in lonely hours and dark pas-sages of my life; and now it is a delight to recall how many times it has kept me happy in the face of per-plexing questions about my little world, and how often it has made as my own the pleasure of another in wonders beyond the reach of my two sealed senses!

It was a disappointment to me that I did not have closer contact with my professors. Most of them seemed as impersonal as victrolas. I never met Dean

Briggs, although I lived next door to him, nor did I ever meet Dr. Eliot. He signed my diploma, but so far as I know, this was the extent of his interest in me.

Among the four or five members of the faculty who took a personal interest in me were Professor Bartlett, who taught German, Dr. William Allan Neilson, who is now President of Smith College, Professor Royce, and Professor Charles T. Copeland. My teacher and I saw much of Dr. Neilson outside the college. He and his sweet sister invited us to tea sometimes, and their friendliness to us both was delightful. Dr. Neilson is a charming Scot with an irrepressible sense of humour and a spirited way of lecturing on the glories of Elizabethan literature. He was the only professor who learned the manual alphabet so that he might talk with me. I have not seen him as much as I would like in recent years, but his friendship has continued to this day.

Mr. Copeland was not a professor when I was at Radcliffe, but he was a great force. His power lay, I think, in an elusive charm difficult to put into words—the charm of a unique personality. They told me his voice was capable of conveying poignant emotion. I could follow it in the ebb and flow of my teacher's fingers. I never knew any one who could by a mere word or phrase express so much. His way of talking was often Carlylesque, and his wit was incisive. But even when he read our trivial themes and unimportant opinions there was a kindly tolerance beneath his whimsical mannerisms. He greatly lightened the dark ways of my understanding of composition, and his words of praise are among the most precious encouragements I have ever had in my work.

Professor Royce was so unfailingly detached that he seemed more like a statue of Buddha than a human being, but his serene nature, the kindness of his greetings, and the nobility of his social ideas, which he afterwards embodied in his book, *The Philosophy of Loyalty,* make me wish I might have known him better.

I enjoyed the history course under Professor Archibald Cary Coolidge, but I never talked with him. He was singularly shy. Once when I wanted to ask him a question Miss Sullivan stopped him just as he was leaving his desk. He was so frightened that she had to repeat the question twice. His answer was utterly incoherent, and he rushed out of the room as soon as he had given it. To me he never seemed a personality. His words came as out of a book read aloud, but few of my professors were so enlightening. After my undergraduate days he served on several missions—the American Peace Delegation, the American Economic Mission, and the American Relief Administration in Russia in 1921. It is no exaggeration to say that he outshone many of his more talked of compatriots.

The barrier of my physical handicap lay between me and my classmates. Only one of them learned to talk with me on her fingers, but they had many charming ways of showing their friendliness. At Mrs. Hogan's lunch room, where we ate sandwiches and chocolate éclairs they gathered around me and Miss Sullivan spelled their bright chatter into my hand. The girls made me vice-president of our class. If my work had not been so strenuous I should probably not have missed so much of the lighter side of the college life.

One of my classmates, Bertha Meckstroth, learned to write braille, and in her free moments copied Elizabeth Barrett Browning's *Sonnets from the Portuguese* for me. This was just before I graduated, and I never saw or heard from her afterwards. But I treasure the lovely deed as a precious memento of my college days.

Another episode I like to recall was a surprise my class planned for me. One day several girls invited me to go with them to see some jolly friends in Brookline. That was all they would tell me, and when we reached our destination, they were very mysterious. I began to sniff, and in a moment I realized that instead of a human habitation we were

entering a kennel, the abode of many Boston terriers.
The dogs gave us a royal welcome, and one ugly
beauty, heir of a noble pedigree, with the title of Sir
Thomas Belvedere, bestowed upon me his special
favour, planting himself resolutely at my feet, pro-
testing with his whole body if I touched any other
dog. The girls asked me if I liked him. I said I
adored him.

"Take him home then," they said. "He is our gift
to you."

Sir Thomas seemed to understand; for he began
spinning round and round me like a top. When he
had quieted down a little I told him I did not care
much for titles. He assured me that he had no ob-
jection to changing his name, and when I told him
that I was going to call him Phiz he rolled over
thrice by way of showing his approval. So we carried him happily back with us to Cambridge.

We were living at that time at 14 Coolidge Avenue,
in part of a house which had once been a fine man-
sion. It was picturesquely situated on a knoll, almost
hidden by great trees, facing Mt. Auburn Street,
and so far back that the trolley cars and traffic never
disturbed us. The home of James Russell Lowell was
near by. Dear Bridget kept house for us and was
always there to open the door and bid us welcome.

The land behind was utilized by a florist to raise
several crops of flowers in the season—pansies, mar-

guerites, geraniums, and carnations. The fragrance was heavenly, and when Italian women and children in bright-coloured dresses and shawls came to pick the flowers for the market, and waked us with their laughter and song it was like being in an Italian village. What an unusual scene it was in the heart of a busy city—women with their arms full of carnations—not mere pictures, but live women with the fresh colour of country life in their cheeks and large dark eyes and coils of black hair—and children carrying baskets of bright geraniums and chattering like birds—their happy voices and expressive gestures, and the whiffs of sweetness from the many flowers!

While we were in Cambridge we made the acquaintance of a number of students and young instructors at Harvard. Some of them learned the manual alphabet, which made real companionship possible, and we had no end of delightful times together. Among them was Philip Sidney Smith, who is now Chief Alaskan Geologist of the National Geological Survey in Washington. His wife, Lenore, was one of our most staunch friends, and she helped me in my studies or went with me to the lectures when Miss Sullivan was ill or tired. Then there was John Macy, who afterwards married my teacher,

and whose name remains forever a part of all that is
most precious in our lives.

What zest we had for life in those days! We
thought nothing of a ten mile tramp over country
roads or a forty mile ride on our tandems. Everything interested us—the autumn woods bright with
jewelled leaves and sparkling sunlight, the migrat-
ing birds, the squirrels gathering their winter stores,
the wild apple trees raining their fruit upon our
heads, the Medford marshes spangled with sapphire
pools and red cat-tails.

But my memories are not all of summer weather,
with the odours of meadow, field, and orchard floating out to us on balmy breezes. Winter, too, brought
its delights. On clear nights we used to go sleighing
in Shay's express wagon which had been put on run-
ners and filled with sweet-smelling hay. Patrick held
the prancing horses until we climbed in, but no
sooner were we seated than they sprang forward,
and we sped away, to the music of the sleigh bells, to
a universe of snow and stars!

And the homecoming! How inviting was the cosy
warmth that breathed in our faces as dear Bridget
opened the door for us, her sweet, patient face alight
with welcome! How good the smell of coffee and
muffins! How jolly the confusion of rushing about
and putting the supper on the table, everyone getting

in Bridget's way. But she only smiled the more, happy in our youth. I cannot think of Cambridge without thinking of Bridget's continual bestowal of herself in loving service to my teacher and me.

Many times during the long winter evenings we sat around an open fire with a circle of eager, imaginative students, drinking cider, popping corn, and joyously tearing to pieces society, philosophies, religions, and literatures. We stripped everything to the naked skeleton. Fortunately, the victims of our superior criticism were unaware of our scorn and even of our existence. We did not proclaim our opinions to the dull world, but enjoyed them the more keenly within the seclusion of our little circle. We were passionately independent. All of us were individualists, yet all of us responded to the altruistic movements of the time. We believed in the rising tide of the masses, in peace, and brotherhood, and "a square deal" for everybody. Each one of us had an idol around whom our theories revolved like planets around the sun. These idols had familiar names— Nietzsche, Schopenhauer, Karl Marx, Bergson, Lincoln, Tolstoi, and Max Stirner. We read Shelley, Whitman, and Swinburne. The more we read and discussed, the more convinced we were that we belonged to that choice coterie who rise in each age, and manage to attain freedom of thought. We felt that undoubtedly we were a group of modern pio-

neers who had risen above our materialistic surroundings. Despite a dismal dearth of inspiration,
we succeeded in living a life rich in thought and
spiritual experience. From our lofty, lonely heights
we looked down upon our fellow students with pity
akin to that which the angels feel for mortals. What
a wealth of wit and wisdom we lavished upon each
other! And the endless discussions that darkened
counsel! For each of us had a panacea to turn this
barren world into a paradise, and each defended his
special kingdom with argument flashed against
argument in true duelling fashion. Nonchalantly we
swept empires into the dust heap, and where they
had flourished we, with astounding ease, established
perfect democracies. In these democracies all the
inhabitants were to display great eagerness to leave
behind commonplace existence. Practical problems
were left to take care of themselves—as they are
in most Utopias.

Oh, young days, young days, what are you saying
to me out of the Long Ago? March winds off Fresh
Pond, a hat gone to the fishes! April showers
on the Concord road, two friends under one mackin-
tosh! May days in the Middlesex Fells, following the
delicate scent of the trailing arbutus! A hatless youth
spelling his gay talk into eager hands, unmindful of
wondering sedate folk taking their carriage exercise! It was a joy to feed the squirrels with nuts and

sit by the roadside and count the birds. They do not seem to be so many now, and they do not sing as merrily as they did when Carl imitated their liquid notes for me.

But I must move on. I must not appear to my reader an old woman living over again the events of her youth.

There was another side to my experience in Radcliffe College which I must present here if I am to remove some of the errors which have arisen with regard to my life in Cambridge and the details of my graduation. It has been said that praises and honours were showered upon Miss Sullivan and me by all who saw us grappling with our difficulties. I have before me a sympathetic article in French, which contains a description of the ceremony in which I received the degree of Bachelor of Arts.

Une foule immense emplissait ce jour-là le théâtre où avait lieu la fête du Collège. Plusieurs autres étudiantes allaient aussi recevoir des diplômes, mais toutes les attentions, tous les regards, tous les cœurs étaient fixés sur la gracieuse jeune fille . . . qui se tenait au premier rang au milieu de ses compagnes. Miss Sullivan, assise à côté d'elle, partageait naturellement l'heure de son triomphe, comme elle avait partagé les jours et les années de son pénible labeur . . . Lorsqu'on appela le nom d'Helen, maîtresse et élève, ou plutôt mère et fille spirituelles, la main dans la main, montèrent ensemble les dégrès de l'estrade. Au milieu de tonnerres d'applaudissements frénétiques qu'elle ne pouvait entendre, mais dont elle sentait résonner les échos, la jeune fille reçut le précieux diplôme portant cette mention spéciale—"Non seulement a subi avec succès les examens de tous grades universitaires, mais excelle en littérature anglaise."*

The words about my teacher are true. The best part of my success was having her by my side who had kept me steadfast to my purpose. But the rest of the account is the stuff that myths are made of. There were no huge crowds filling the hall that June afternoon. Only a few friends came especially to see me. My mother was prevented by illness from being with me on that occasion, and her disappointment was as bitter as my own. Dean Briggs delivered the usual commencement address, but he did not mention Miss Sullivan. In fact, none of the faculty spoke either to her or to me. When I received my diploma, I felt no "thunder of wild applause." It was nothing like the imposing, brilliant ceremony which has been pictured in some accounts of my college days. Several of the students, when they took off their caps and gowns,

---

*On that day an immense crowd filled the auditorium where the commencement exercises were held. Other students were to receive diplomas but all attention, all looks, all hearts were fixed on the lovely young girl who held first rank among her companions. Miss Sullivan, seated beside her, naturally shared the hour of her triumph as she had shared the days and years of her strenuous labour. When the name of Helen was called, mistress and pupil, or rather spiritual mother and daughter, hand in hand, mounted the steps. In the midst of thunders of frantic applause which she could not hear but of which she felt the echo, the young girl received the precious diploma carrying this special mention: "Not only has she passed successfully the university examinations, but she excels in English literature."

expressed indignation, and one sweet girl declared
that Miss Sullivan should have received a degree, too.
We had come in to our seats quietly that afternoon,
and we went out as soon as we could, caught a street
car and hastened away to the fragrant peace of the
lovely New England village packed with summer
time, where we were already settling down to live.
That evening I was gliding out on Lake Wollomonapoag in a canoe with some friends, forgetting my
weariness and the strange ways of the world in
dreams of beauty, the odours which the breezes
carried to me from unseen flowers, and starlit silence,
and little green hills sloping down to the water. May
it ever be thus, may I always return after the clamour
and agitation of eventful days to the great kindliness
of earth and sky and restful twilight!

Chapter III

MY FIRST YEARS IN WRENTHAM

THE French article from which I have quoted says that I was given a home in Wrentham by the public, who wished to honour me as the ancients did when they bestowed upon a victorious general an estate where he could live and enjoy his laurels:

Boston, la ville la plus intellectuelle l'Athenes des Etats Unis, a, au lendemain de ses examens offert cette maison en hommage à la jeune fille qui a remporte une victoire sans pareille de l'esprit sur la matière, de l'âme immortelle sur les sens.*

Others who have tried to describe the house without knowing it have added an extensive park and a wonderful garden. No such pomp and circumstance marked my triumphal entrance into the village of Wrentham. Miss Sullivan and I had already bought a small, old farmhouse, long and narrow, decidedly Puritanical in appearance, with a neglected field of seven acres. Miss Sullivan converted a dairy room

*Boston, the most intellectual city, the Athens of the United States, had on the day after the examinations offered this house in homage to the young girl who had won a victory without parallel of the spirit over matter, the immortal soul over the sense.

and two pantries into a study for me. The French article describes it as follows:

Helen Keller passe la plupart de ses journées dans son elegant cabine de travail, orné de bronzes et d'objets d'art offerts pars ses adorateurs, et dont les murs disparaissent du haut en bas sous des centaines et des centaines de gros volumes au pages blanches couvertes de points en relief—ses chers livres en Braille.*

As a matter of fact, the study was very simple. The only "works of art" were a plaster Venus di Milo which my foster-father, Mr. John Hitz, had given me, a bas-relief medallion of Homer, a gift from Dr. Jastrow of the University of Wisconsin, and some curios sent to me by friends from foreign countries. Only one wall "disappeared" behind large volumes of braille, and that did not mean hundreds of books. In most cases there were three, four, or five big volumes to a book. They were few enough in comparison with what I wanted, but to any one as hungry for ideas as I was any bit of honest thinking was a treasure trove. The chief attractions of the study were sunshine, the big eastern window full of plants I tended, and a glass door through which I could step out into a cluster of pines and sit alone with my thoughts and my dreams.

*Helen Keller passes the greater part of her days in her elegant workroom ornamented with bronzes and *objets d'art* presented by her admirers, with walls which from top to bottom disappear behind hundreds and hundreds of huge volumes with white pages covered with points in relief—her dear books in braille.

Miss Sullivan had a balcony built for me which opened out of my bedroom so that I could walk whenever I wanted to. The evergreens came so close to the railing I could lean over and feel their rustling music. It was on this balcony that I once "heard" the love song of a whippoorwill. I had been walking up and down for an hour or more, pausing every now and then to breathe the scented air of May. At the south end I could reach out and touch a wisteria vine which clung to the rail with long, tenacious fingers. At the opposite end I faced the garden and the apple trees, which were in full bloom, and oh, so heavenly sweet! I was standing under the wisteria vine with my thoughts far away when suddenly the rail began to vibrate unfamiliarly under my hands. The pulsations were rhythmical, and repeated over and over, exactly as I have felt a note repeated when I have placed my fingers on a singer's throat. All at once they ceased, and I felt the wisteria blossom ticking against my cheek like the pendulum of a fairy clock. I guessed that a breeze or a bird was rocking the vine. Then the rail began vibrating again. A queer beat came always before the rhythmical beats, like nothing I had ever felt before. I did not dare move or call, but Miss Sullivan had heard the sound and put out her hand through the window and touched me very quietly. I knew I must not speak.

She spelled, "That's a whippoorwill. He is standing on the corner post so close to you I believe you could touch him; but you must not—he would fly away and never come back."

Now that I knew he was saying "Whip-poor-will! Whip-poor-will" over and over I could follow the intonations exactly. The singing seemed joyous to my touch, and I could feel the notes grow louder and louder, faster and faster.

Miss Sullivan touched me again and spelled, "His lady-love is answering him from the apple trees. Apparently, she has been there all the time, hiding. Now they are singing a duet."

When the rail stopped vibrating she spelled, "They are both in the apple tree now singing under billows of pink and white blossoms."

We paid for this house in Wrentham and the alterations by selling some shares of sugar stock which Mr. J. P. Spaulding of Boston had given us about ten years before. I feel moved to say something here about one who took the most generous interest in us both at a time when we needed a strong friend.

I was nine years old, I think, when Elsie Leslie Lyde, the beautiful child actress who played "Little Lord Fauntleroy," introduced us to Mr. Spaulding. He was so tender and understanding, he won me at once, and from that day he was eager to do anything for our comfort or pleasure. He liked to come to the Perkins Institution when we stayed there, and join in our midday meal. He always brought a big box of roses, or fruits or candies. He took us for long drives, and Elsie accompanied us when she was not appearing at the theatre. She was a lovely, vivacious child, and Mr. Spaulding beamed with delight to see "his two darlings together." I was just learning to speak, and it distressed him very much because he could not understand what I said. I practised saying "Elsie Leslie Lyde" one day, and kept on until I cried; but I wanted Mr. Spaulding to hear me say it intelligibly, and I shall never forget his joy when I succeeded. Whenever I failed to articulate well, or there was too much noise for him to hear me, he would hug me and say, "If I can't understand you, I can always love you," and I know he did with a deep affection. Indeed, he was beloved by many people in every walk of life. Elsie called him "King John," and he was a king in spirit, royal and noble of heart.

Mr. Spaulding assisted my teacher and me financially for a number of years. He told us many times that he would provide for our future. But he died without making any provision for us in his will, and his heirs refused to continue the help he had given us. Indeed, one of his nephews said that we had taken advantage of his uncle when he was not in a condition to know his own mind!

I see I have again wandered far afield; but I

could not pass over in silence a rare and beautiful generosity which imposed no obligations upon us, nor asked anything in return, except the satisfaction of having us happy.

Somehow Mr. Spaulding seemed very near indeed when we threw open the doors and windows of our home—the first home of our own—to the June sunshine and started our new life full of bright hopes for the future.

On May 2, 1905, the year after my graduation, my teacher married John Macy. She had devoted the best years of her womanhood to me, and I had often longed to see her blessed with a good man's love; I felt the tenderest joy in their union. Dr. Edward Everett Hale, one of our oldest and closest friends, performed the ceremony in the sunny, flower-filled sitting room of our white farmhouse, and I stood beside my teacher. Lenore spelled the ceremony into my hand. My mother and a few close friends were present. Then Mr. and Mrs. Macy left for their wedding trip to New Orleans, and I went south with my mother for a visit. A few days later we were delightfully surprised to see Mr. and Mrs. Macy walking into the house! My cup ran over! It seemed like a dream, having them with me, revelling in the beauty of early summer in the Southland. The air was laden with the odour of magnolias, and they kept saying how heavenly the song of the mocking birds was—they called it their wedding music. When we were all back in Wrentham, I heard that several people thought I was jealous and unhappy, and one letter of condolence was actually inflicted upon me!

I wish I could engrave upon these pages the picture in my fingers that I cherish of those two friends —my teacher with her queenly mind and heart, strong and true, going direct to the core of the subject under discussion, her delight in beauty, her enthusiasm for large service and heroic qualities; her husband with his brotherly tenderness, his fine sensibilities, his keen sense of humour, and his curious combination of judicial severity and smiling tolerance. Since I was out of active life, they both strove to keep my narrow round pleasant and interesting. Both had a magical way of breaking up the monotony for me with bright comments and rapid, frequent reports of what I could not see or hear. And such a difference as there was in the way each talked! My teacher's comments on scenes and news and people were like nuggets of gold, lavishly spilled into my hands, while her husband put his words together carefully, almost as if he were writing a novel. He often said he wanted to write a novel, and certainly there was material for one in his brilliant conversation. His hands were seldom still, and even when he was not spelling to me I could tell by his gestures

whether he was arguing or joking or simply carrying on an ordinary conversation.

I cannot enumerate the helpful kindnesses with
which he smoothed my rugged paths of endeavour.
Once, when my typewriter was out of order, and I
was tired with the manual labour of copying, he sat
up all night, and typed forty pages of my manuscript,
so that they might reach the press in time.

Next to my teacher, he was the friend who discovered most ways to give me pleasure and gratify
my intellectual curiosity. He kept me faithfully in
touch with the chief happenings of the day, the discoveries of science, and the new trends in literature.
If he was particularly pleased with a book, he would
have Mr. John Hitz put it into braille for me, or
he would read it to me himself when he had time.

Not long after we moved to Wrentham Mr. Gilder
asked me to write a series of essays for the *Century*
about my ideas of the world around me. The essays
appeared in the magazine under the title, "Sense and
Sensibility," but as Jane Austen had used that title
for one of her books, I called them the *The World I
Live In* when they came out in book form. I do not
remember writing anything in such a happy mood
as *The World I Live In*. I poured into it everything
that interested me at one of the happiest periods of
my life—my newly discovered wealth of philosophy

and the feeling of the New England beauty which surrounded me. I had always revelled in the wonders of nature; but I had not dreamed what abundance of physical enjoyment I possessed until I sat down and tried to express in words the lacy shadows of little leaves, the filmy wings of insects, the murmur of breezes, the tremulous flutter of flowers, the soft-breathing breast of a dove, filaments of sound in the waving grass, and gossamer threads intertwining and unreeling themselves endlessly.

The next book I wrote was *The Song of the Stone Wall*. The idea of writing it came to me with the joy of spring while we were building up the old walls in our green field. In it I tried to image the men who had built the walls long ago. I dedicated the book to Dr. Edward Everett Hale because he, too, loved the old walls and the traditions that cling about them. Moreover, the zeal of the men who built them was upon his lips and their courage in his heart.

While I was writing these books Mr. Macy was always near by to help me. He criticized me severely when my work did not please him, and his praise was sweet when I wrote something he liked. We read the pages over and over, weeding out the chaff, until he thought I had done my best. "When one's best is not satisfactory," he would say, "there is nothing to do about it."

He had the art of pulling me out of a solemn or

discouraged mood with laughter that leaves the heart light and soothes the ruffled mind. I used to love to ramble or drive with him along the winding roads of Wrentham. With a gesture of delight he would point out a pond smiling like a babe on earth's breast, or a gorgeous bird on the wing, or a field full of sunshine and ripening corn, or we would sit together under the Great Oak on the edge of Lake Wollomonapoag while he read to me from one of Thoreau's books. There are no words to tell how dear he was to me or how much I loved him. Little incidents hardly noticed at the time but poignantly remembered afterwards crowd upon me as I write. On a still summer evening or by a winter fire, my thoughts still wander back to those days and dwell with sweet longing on the affection of those two friends sitting beside me in the library, their hands in mine, dreaming of a bright future of mutual helpfulness. I can never quite accustom myself to the bewildering vicissitudes of life, but, despite the shadows upon it, both my teacher and I feel that all that was loveliest in the Wrentham days is ours forever.

When we went to Wrentham to live I had in my mind a vision of a real farm, like my father's in Tuscumbia, Alabama, where I could live in the midst of the strong, abiding simplicity of homely things among trees and crops and animals.

The only animal we owned was Phiz, whom we carried with us from Cambridge. He died a year after we moved to Wrentham. We buried him at the end of the field under a beautiful white pine tree. I grieved for him a long time, and resolved never to have another dog. But everybody knows how, in the course of time, the proverbial other dog arrives. Kaiser was his name. He was a sturdy French bull terrier. A friend of Mr. Macy's presented him to the family. Having lived all the days of his three years with a man, Kaiser was at first inclined to assume a supercilious attitude towards women folk. He pondered over what we said to him, and usually decided that it might be ignored. We undertook to teach him he must obey in order to eat. But he found out quickly that apples could be used as a substitute for meat and bread. He learned to hold an apple between his paws and eat it with a good deal of gusto. But when he fully made up his mind that he could not maintain the fallacy of masculine superiority in an establishment where the feminine forces outnumbered the males three to one, he surrendered all the major points, also his pretence that he had a special fondness for apples, though to the end he retained a certain masculine swagger which was not unbecoming.

There is not much to tell about Kaiser. His fate confirms the story of modern civilization. He found food abundant and obtainable without exertion; therefore he took advantage of every opportunity to gourmandize. Both dogs and human beings find this a pleasant pastime, but they must make up their minds that sooner or later they will die of it.

A similar fate overtook some Rhode Island Reds, which we bought from Mr. Dilley, our next door neighbour, who was a bird fancier. I fed them myself, and they soon became very tame. It was fun to watch them, but after a while I noticed that they sat down to their meals, and it was very hard to get them to move about. Our neighbour was called to give advice. He declared that I had overfed them to such an extent that he doubted if Mr. Pierce, our marketman, would take them. I was so disappointed with the little gourmands I gave up the idea of ever trying to raise chickens again.

But it seemed a shame to waste the enclosure we had put up with so much trouble and expense. So we bought Thora, a beautiful brindle Dane. I knew it would be easier to raise puppies; and anyway I loved dogs better than chickens. In due time Thora's eleven puppies arrived. Of course I had not dreamed that there would be so many, or that they would be so mischievous.

I have not space to give a detailed account of the

upbringing of that family of Dane puppies. They were as temperamental as poets and musicians are supposed to be. There was one everybody singled out as the gem of the clan. We called her Sieglinde and lavished special care and affection upon her. Her colour was red gold, and her head was moulded on noble lines. Of all the dogs we have ever owned she was the most beautiful and intelligent, and I am not belittling my splendid Danish baron, Hans, nor my fascinating, perverse Scotch lassie, Darky, who are clamouring at the door of my study as I write.

In the meantime there was the barn—a fine, large barn with no living creature in it. It did not seem right that there should be no livestock to enjoy it. We began to read the advertisements in the Boston *Transcript*. We were surprised to find how many fine animals were without a comfortable home. The tears actually came to my eyes when I heard of a lady who was going abroad, and must leave her noble Great Dane to the mercy of strangers. She said that if some one who loved animals would only give Nimrod a home, she would part with him for seventy-five dollars, which was like giving him away. We wrote the lady that we should be glad to take Nimrod. It was arranged that Mr. Macy should meet her and Nimrod at the North Station in Boston. Mrs. Macy and I waited at home.

I have never seen such a huge dog. He was more like a young elephant than a dog. Mr. Macy insisted that he should be left out on the porch until we found out what his upbringing had been, but we could not think of such inhospitality to a stranger within our gates. The door was flung open, and Nimrod was invited to enter. There was a small table with a lamp on it near the door. In passing it, he knocked it over. Fortunately the lamp was not lighted—in those days we used kerosene—or I suppose the house would have been burned. As it was, the crash frightened the poor dog, so that he charged into the dining room, knocking Mr. Macy's supper off and the dishes all over the room. With great difficulty Mr. Macy succeeded in getting the terrified creature out to the barn. Family relations were somewhat strained that evening, and I did not learn much of what happened, except that the conductor on two trains had refused to let Nimrod on, and that he had caused a stampede in the waiting room of the station.

Thora would have nothing to do with him. She even growled at him when he tried to make friends with the puppies. Out in the field Nimrod seemed contented to be by himself; but somebody noticed that he was eating stones. There were too many stones in the field. Our distress was not caused by any regret over their disappearance, but we were concerned about Nimrod's digestion. We sent for our neighbour, Dr. Brastow, the state veterinarian. He controlled his feelings wonderfully when he gave us the report of his diagnosis.

"The dog," he said, "is about fourteen years old. He has no teeth, and very little sight. Probably he thinks the stones are bones. His former owner was, no doubt, too tender-hearted to have him put to sleep." However, we thought our friend rather heartless when he proposed to do forthwith that which had been left undone. Still it seemed best.

It was some time before we began to read the advertisements in the *Transcript* again. But inevitably history repeats itself. We had a marvellous, versatile gift of forgetting previous unfortunate ventures and joyously entering upon new ones. There is nothing to be said in favour of this gift, except that it lends spice to life. The day came when we felt that we must have a horse, and that very day we read a column of advertisements of wonderful horses which could be purchased for half or a third of what they would naturally sell for; but their owners were in various difficulties, and wanted to part with them for stated amounts. The horse we decided to buy was described as a spirited dark bay; weight, 1150 pounds; age, six years; gentle, fearless, broken to saddle, suitable for a lady to drive or ride.

We three innocents went to Boston to see the horse. The stable man said the owner was out of town, but he showed us the horse, and certainly the animal was a beauty. His coat was as smooth as satin and he held his head so high I could scarcely reach his ears. One of his feet was white, and there and then, with several endearing pats and caresses, I christened him Whitefoot. We paid for him on the spot, and it was arranged that a boy should ride him out to Wrentham. We learned afterwards that Whitefoot had thrown the boy three times on the way; but he never said a word to us. The next morning Mr. Macy hitched the horse to a light Democrat wagon we had, and started for the village. He had not got out of the driveway when Whitefoot began to give trouble. Mr. Macy jumped out to see if there was anything wrong with the harness. At that moment the Foxboro car passed the gate. The horse reared, and dashed across the lawn and out through the neighbour's gate. The wagon caught on a stone post and was smashed to kindling. Two days later a country man brought the horse home. He had found him in a wood road with scraps of harness still hanging to him.

We finally sold Whitefoot to a man in Attleboro who claimed to be a horse tamer. We learned a year or so later that Whitefoot had been the cause of the death of a cabman, and was pronounced crazy by the state veterinarian and shot.

It was a long time before we summoned up courage to try our luck with horses again. But we finally succeeded in getting what we wanted. King was an English-bred cob, a rich bay in colour. We used to say that he stepped as Queen Elizabeth danced, "high and disposedly." He was a horse tempered like finest steel—strong, patient, good-natured with common sense—the kind of horse erratic drivers should prize above pearls and rubies.

Our various enterprises with livestock having not only failed, but plunged us into deeper financial tribulations, we were advised to plant an apple orchard. This seemed just the thing. We bought a hundred choice three year nurslings and planted them according to the rules sent out by the United States Department of Agriculture. They prospered. The fifth year we were delighted to find a few apples on them. I knew how many apples each tree had, and almost daily I made a note of their size. The apple orchard was such a comfort to us that we were annoyed with ourselves for not having thought of it in the beginning.

All went well until one fateful summer afternoon when Ian Bittman, our Russian man of all work, came rushing up to my study where Mrs. Macy and I were reading. "Look! look! look, Madam! See, the wild cow have come," he cried.

We ran to the window, and in great excitement Ian pointed out five wonderful creatures disporting themselves through the orchard. Mrs. Macy could scarcely believe her eyes—they were wild deer—a great antlered buck, a doe, and three half-grown fawns! They were beautiful in the afternoon sunlight, skipping from tree to tree and stripping the bark with their teeth. Indeed, they were so graceful and lovely, it did not occur to one of us to chase them out of the orchard. We stood there fascinated until they had destroyed nearly every tree before we realized what had happened. That year Massachusetts paid thousands of dollars to farmers for the losses they had sustained from marauding deer. It never occurred to us to send the state a bill for our apple trees. The last time I visited the old place, I saw perhaps half a dozen of the trees we had planted, and which had escaped the sharp teeth of the invaders, grown to a goodly size, and bearing fruit each year.

I used to stay out of doors as much as possible and watch that most delightful form of progress—the preparation of the old garden for young plants, and the new vegetation which spread over it more and more. I found paths I could follow in my daily walk through the field, and explored the wood at the end of it which was to be the retreat of my happiest hours. All this was most pleasant to live through, but not much to write about. However, it indicates the sort of material I have for an autobiography. I have no great adventures to record, no thrilling romances, no extraordinary successes. This book contains simply the impressions and feelings which have passed through my mind. But perhaps, after all, our emotions and sensations are what are most worth relating, since they are our real selves.

As the seasons came round, I would run out to gather armfuls of flowers, or watch trees being pruned, or help bring in wood. There were some big elms and apple trees which Mr. Macy used to look after with pride, and they responded beautifully to his care. Every autumn I would put up a ladder against one of the ancient apple trees, climb as high as I could, hold to a branch, and shake down the rosy, fragrant fruit. Then I would descend, pick up the apples, and fill barrels with them for the winter. Those were delicious hours when my soul seemed to cast aside its earthly vesture, glide into the boughs and sing like the birds about me. I also walked a great deal. By following the wire which Mr. Macy had stretched along the field, I easily found my way to a pine wood, where I could sit and dream, or wander from tree to tree. In summer there were tall, bright grasses, timothy, and wonderful goldenrod and Queen Anne's lace. Altogether, it was the longest and most free walk—about a quarter of a mile—that I ever had by myself. These details may seem trivial, but without this bit of freedom and sunny solitude I could not have endured the exacting nature of my daily work. Occasionally some one took me for a "spin" on my tandem bicycle. There were long, delightful rides on the trolley cars through the New England woods. I remember with pleasure that no odour of gasoline marred the purity of the air.

As I look back, everything seems to have moved with the slowness of a woodland stream—no automobiles or aëroplanes or radios, no revolutions, no world wars. Such was our life in Wrentham, or something like it, between 1905 and 1911. For it seems so far away, I sometimes feel as if it were a sort of preëxistence—a dream of days when I wore another body and had a different consciousness. Yet I see it clear enough, all the more vivid because it was free from the external distractions which keep one's thoughts occupied with trivial things and leave no leisure for the soul to develop. Where gayety was infrequent, the simplest amusements had the perfume of heavenly joy. Where the surroundings were rural, and life monotonous, any beam that shone upon them was precious. Any flower discovered among the rocks and crannies or beside the brook had the rareness of a star. Small events were full of poetry, and the glory of the spirit lay over all.

OUR MARK TWAIN

ONE of the most memorable events of our Wrentham years was our visit to Mark Twain.

My memory of Mr. Clemens runs back to 1894, when he was vigorous, before the shadows began to gather. Such was the affection he inspired in my young heart that my love for him has deepened with the years. More than anyone else I have ever known except Dr. Alexander Graham Bell and my teacher, he aroused in me the feeling of mingled tenderness and awe. I saw him many times at my friend Mr. Lawrence Hutton's in New York, and later in Princeton, also at Mr. H. H. Rogers's and at his own home at 21 Fifth Avenue, and last of all at Stormfield, Connecticut. Now and then I received letters from him. We were both too busy to write often, but whenever events of importance in our lives occurred we wrote to each other about them.

I was fourteen years old when I first met Mr. Clemens—one Sunday afternoon when Miss Sullivan and I were the guests of Mr. and Mrs. Lawrence Hutton in New York. During the afternoon several celebrities dropped in, and among them Mr.

Clemens. The instant I clasped his hand in mine, I knew that he was my friend. He made me laugh and feel thoroughly happy by telling some good stories, which I read from his lips. I have forgotten a great deal more than I remember, but I shall never forget how tender he was.

He knew with keen and sure intuition many things about me and how it felt to be blind and not to keep up with the swift ones—things that others learned slowly or not at all. He never embarrassed me by saying how terrible it is not to see, or how dull life must be, lived always in the dark. He wove about my dark walls romance and adventure, which made me feel happy and important. Once when Peter Dunne, the irrepressible Mr. Dooley, exclaimed: "God, how dull it must be for her, every day the same and every night the same as the day," he said, "You're damned wrong there; blindness is an exciting business, I tell you; if you don't believe it, get up some dark night on the wrong side of your bed when the house is on fire and try to find the door."

The next time I saw Mr. Clemens was in Princeton during a spring vacation when we were visiting the Huttons in their new home. We had many happy hours together at that time.

One evening in the library he lectured to a distinguished company—Woodrow Wilson was present—on the situation in the Philippines. We listened breathlessly. He described how six hundred Moros—men, women, and children—had taken refuge in an extinct crater bowl near Jolo, where they were caught in a trap and murdered, by order of General Leonard Wood. A few days afterwards, Col. Funston captured the patriot Aguinaldo by disguising his military marauders in the uniform of the enemy and pretending to be friends of Aguinaldo's officers. Upon these military exploits, Mr. Clemens poured out a volcano of invective and ridicule. Only those who heard him can know his deep fervour and the potency of his flaming words. All his life he fought injustice wherever he saw it in the relations between man and man—in politics, in wars, in outrages against the natives of the Philippines, the Congo, and Panama. I loved his views on public affairs, they were so often the same as my own.

He thought he was a cynic, but his cynicism did not make him indifferent to the sight of cruelty, unkindness, meanness, or pretentiousness. He would often say, "Helen, the world is full of unseeing eyes, vacant, staring, soulless eyes." He would work himself into a frenzy over dull acquiescence in any evil that could be remedied. True, sometimes it seemed as if he let loose all the artillery of Heaven against an intruding mouse but even then his "resplendent vocabulary" was a delight. Even when his ideas were quite wrong, they were expressed with such lucidity, conviction, and aggressiveness that one felt impelled to accept them—for the moment at least. One is almost persuaded to accept any idea which is well expressed.

He was interested in everything about me—my friends and little adventures and what I was writing. I loved him for his beautiful appreciation of my teacher's work. Of all the people who have written about me he is almost the only one who has realized the importance of Miss Sullivan in my life, who has appreciated her "brilliancy, penetration, wisdom, character, and the fine literary competences of her pen."

He often spoke tenderly of Mrs. Clemens and regretted that I had not known her.

"I am very lonely, sometimes, when I sit by the fire after my guests have departed," he used to say. "My thoughts trail away into the past. I think of Livy and Susie and I seem to be fumbling in the dark folds of confused dreams. I come upon memories of little intimate happenings of long ago that drop like stars into the silence. One day everything breaks and crumbles. It did the day Livy died." Mr. Clemens repeated with emotion and inexpressible tenderness the lines which he had carved on her tombstone:

Warm summer sun,
Shine kindly here;
Warm Southern wind,
Blow softly here;
Green sod above,
Lie light, lie light;
Good night, dear heart,
Good night, good night.

The year after her death he said to me, "This has been the saddest year I have ever known. If it were not that work brings forgetfulness, life would be intolerable." He expressed regret that he had not accomplished more. I exclaimed, "Why, Mr. Clemens, the whole world has crowned you. Already your name is linked with the greatest names in our history. Bernard Shaw compares your work with that of Voltaire, and Kipling has called you the American Cervantes."

"Ah, Helen, you have a honeyed tongue; but you don't understand. I have only amused people. Their laughter has submerged me."

There are writers who belong to the history of their nation's literature. Mark Twain is one of them. When we think of great Americans we think of him. He incorporated the age he lived in. To me he symbolizes the pioneer qualities—the large, free, unconventional, humorous point of view of men who sail new seas and blaze new trails through the wilderness. Mark Twain and the Mississippi River are inseparable in my mind. When I told him that *Life on the Mississippi* was my favourite story of adventure, he said, "That amazes me. It wouldn't have occurred to me that a woman would find such rough reading interesting. But I don't know much about women. It would be impossible for a person to know less about women than I do."

After some badinage back and forth about women, Mr. Clemens's manner changed. A sadness came into his voice. "Those were glorious days, the days on the Mississippi. They will come back no more, life has swallowed them up, and youth will come no more. They were days when the tide of life was high, when the heart was full of the sparkling wine of romance. There have been no other days like them."

It was just after he had read my book *The World I Live In,* that he sent a note to Wrentham saying, "I command you all three to come and spend a few days with me in Stormfield."

It was indeed the summons of a beloved king. His carriage met us at Redding station. If my memory serves me, it was in February; there was a light snow upon the Connecticut hills. It was a glorious five mile drive to Stormfield; little icicles hung from the edges of the leaves and there was a tang in the air of cedar and pine. We drove rapidly along the winding country roads, the horses were in high spirits.

Mr. Macy kept reading signboards bearing the initials "M. T." As we approached the Italian villa on the very top of the hill, they told me he was standing on the verandah waiting. As the carriage rolled between the huge granite pillars, he waved his hand; they told me he was all in white and that his beautiful white hair glistened in the afternoon sunshine like the snow spray on the gray stones.

There was a bright fire on the hearth, and we breathed in the fragrance of pine and the orange pekoe tea. I scolded Mr. Clemens a little for coming out on the verandah without his hat; there was still a winter chill in the air. He seemed pleased that I thought about him in that way, and said rather wistfully, "It is not often these days that anyone notices when I am imprudent."

We were in the land of enchantment. We sat by the fire and had our tea and buttered toast and he insisted that I must have strawberry jam on my toast. We were the only guests. Miss Lyon, Mr. Clemens's secretary, presided over the tea table.

Mr. Clemens asked me if I would like to see the house, remarking that people found it more interesting than himself.

Out of the living room there was a large sunny, beautiful loggia, full of living plants and great jardinières filled with wild grasses, cat-tails, goldenrod, and thistles which had been gathered on the hills in the late fall. We returned through the living room to the dining room and out on to the pergola and back again to the house and into the billiard room, where Mr. Clemens said he spent his happiest hours. He was passionately fond of billiards, and very proud of the billiard table with which Mrs. H. H. Rogers had presented him. He said he would teach me to play.

I answered, "Oh, Mr. Clemens, it takes sight to play billiards."

"Yes," he teased, "but not the variety of billiards that Paine and Dunne and Rogers play. The blind couldn't play worse." Then upstairs to see Mr. Clemens's bedroom and examine the carved bed-posts and catch a glimpse of the view out of the great windows before darkness closed in upon us.

"Try to picture, Helen, what we are seeing out of these windows. We are high up on a snow-covered hill. Beyond, are dense spruce and firwoods, other snow-clad hills and stone walls intersecting the landscape everywhere, and over all, the white wizardry of winter. It is a delight, this wild, free, fir-scented place."

Our suite of rooms was next to his. On the mantelpiece, suspended from a candlestick, was a card explaining to burglars where articles of value were in the room. There had recently been a burglary in the house, and Mr. Clemens explained that this was a precaution against being disturbed by intruders.

"Before I leave you," he said, "I want to show you Clara's room; it is the most beautiful apartment in the house."

He was not content until he had shown us the servants' quarters, and he would have taken us to the attic if Miss Lyon had not suggested that we leave it for another day. It was obvious that Mr. Clemens took great satisfaction in his unusual house. He told us that it had been designed by the son of my life-long friend, William Dean Howells. Delightfully he pointed out that the architecture was exactly suited to the natural surroundings, that the dark cedars and pines, which were always green, made a singularly beautiful setting for the white villa. Mr. Clemens particularly enjoyed the sunlight that came through the great windows and the glimpse of field and sky that could be seen through them.

"You observe," he said to us, "there are no pictures on the walls. Pictures in this house would be an impertinence. No artist, going to this window and looking out, has ever equalled that landscape."

We stayed in our room till dinner was announced. Dinner in Mr. Clemens's house was always a function where conversation was important; yes, more important than the food. It was a rule in that house that guests were relieved of the responsibility of con-

versation. Mr. Clemens said that his personal experience had taught him that you could not enjoy your
dinner if the burden of finding something to say was
weighing heavily upon you. He made it a rule, he
said, to do all the talking in his own house, and expected when he was invited out that his hosts would
do the same. He talked delightfully, audaciously,
brilliantly. His talk was fragrant with tobacco and
flamboyant with profanity. I adored him because he
did not temper his conversation to any femininity.
He was a playboy sometimes and on occasions liked to
show off. He had a natural sense of the dramatic, and
enjoyed posing as he talked. But in the core of him
there was no make-believe. He never attempted to
hide his light under a bushel. I think it was Goethe
who said, "Only clods are modest." If that is true,
then in the world there was not less of a clod than
Mr. Clemens.

He ate very little himself, and invariably grew
restless before the dinner was finished. He would get
up in the midst of a sentence, walk round the table
or up and down the long dining room, talking all
the while. He would stop behind my chair, and ask
me if there was anything I wanted; he would sometimes take a flower from a vase and if I happened to
be able to identify it he showed his pleasure by
describing in an exaggerated manner the powers that
lie latent in our faculties, declaring that the ordinary

human being had not scratched the surface of his brain. This line of observation usually led to a tirade upon the appalling stupidity of all normal human beings. Watching my teacher spelling to me, he drawled, "Can you spell into Helen's left hand and tell her the truth?" Sometimes the butler called his attention to a tempting dish, and he would sit down and eat.

To test my powers of observation, he would leave the room quietly and start the self-playing organ in the living room. My teacher told me how amusing it was to see him steal back to the dining room and watch stealthily for any manifestations on my part that the vibrations had reached my feet. I did not often feel the musical vibrations, as I believe the floor was tiled, which prevented the sound waves from reaching me, but I did sometimes feel the chord vibrations through the table. I was always glad when I did, because it made Mr. Clemens so happy.

We gathered about the warm hearth after dinner, and Mr. Clemens stood with his back to the fire talking to us. There he stood—our Mark Twain, our American, our humorist, the embodiment of our country. He seemed to have absorbed all America into himself. The great Mississippi River seemed forever flowing, flowing through his speech, through the shadowless white sands of thought. His voice seemed to say like the river, "Why hurry? Eternity is long; the ocean can wait." In reply to some expression of our admiration for the spaciousness and the beauty of the room, which was a combination of living room and library, he said with more enthusiasm than was his wont, "It suits me perfectly. I shall never live anywhere else in this world."

He was greatly interested when we told him that a friend of ours, Mr. W. S. Booth, had discovered an acrostic in the plays, sonnets, and poems usually attributed to Shakespeare, which revealed the author to be Francis Bacon. He was at first sceptical and inclined to be facetious at our expense. He attacked the subject vigorously, yet less than a month elapsed before he brought out a new book, *Is Shakespeare Dead?* in which he set out, with all his fire, to destroy the Shakespeare legend, but not, he said in a letter to me, with any hope of actually doing it.

"I wrote the booklet for pleasure—*not* in the expectation of convincing anybody that Shakespeare did not write Shakespeare. And don't you," he warned me, "write in any such expectation. Shakespeare, the Stratford tradesman, will still be the divine Shakespeare to our posterity a thousand years hence."

When the time came to say good night, Mr. Clemens led me to my room himself and told me that I would find cigars and a thermos bottle with Scotch whiskey, or Bourbon if I preferred it, in the bathroom. He told me that he spent the morning in bed writing, that his guests seldom saw him before lunch time, but if I felt like coming in to see him about ten-thirty, he would be delighted, for there were some things he would like to say to me when my Guardian Angel was not present.

About ten o'clock the next morning, he sent for me. He liked to do his literary work in bed, propped up among his snowy pillows looking very handsome in his dressing gown of rich silk, dictating his notes to a stenographer. He said if doing my work that way appealed to me, I might have half the bed, provided I maintained strict neutrality and did not talk. I told him the price was prohibitive, I could never yield woman's only prerogative, great as the temptation was.

It was a glorious bright day, and the sun streamed through the great windows. Mr. Clemens said if I did not feel inclined to work after lunch (which was by way of sarcasm, as he had previously remarked that I did not look industrious, and he believed that I had somebody to write my books for me), he would take a little walk with us and show us the "farm." He said he would not join us at lunch, as his doctor had put him on a strict diet. He appeared, however, just as dessert was being served. He said he had smelt the apple pie and could not resist. Miss Lyon protested timidly.

"Oh, Mr. Clemens——"

"Yes, I know; but fresh apple pie never killed anybody. But if Helen says I can't, I won't." I did not have the heart to say he couldn't, so we compromised on a very small piece, which was later augmented by a larger piece, after a pantomimic warning to the others not to betray him.

I suspected what was going on, and said, "Come, let us go before Mr. Clemens sends to the kitchen for another pie."

He said, "Tell her I suspected she was a psychic. That proves she is."

He put on a fur-lined greatcoat and fur cap, filled his pockets with cigars, and declared himself ready to start on the walk. He led me through the pergola, stopping to let me feel the cedars which stood guard at every step.

"The arches were intended for ramblers," he said, "but unfortunately they haven't bloomed this winter. I have spoken to the gardener about it, and I hope the next time you come we shall have roses blooming for you." He picked out a winding path which he thought I could follow easily. It was a delightful path, which lay between rocks and a saucy little brook that winter had not succeeded in binding with ice fetters. He asked Mr. Macy to tell me there was a tall white building across an intervening valley from where we were standing. "Tell her it's a church.

It used to stand on this side of the brook; but the
congregation moved it last summer when I told them
I had no use for it. I had no idea that New England
people were so accommodating. At that distance it
is just what a church should be—serene and pure
and mystical." We crossed the brook on a little rustic
footbridge. He said it was a prehistoric bridge, and
that the quiet brown pool underneath was the one
celebrated in the Song of Solomon. I quoted the
passage he referred to: "Thine eyes like the fishpools
in Heshbon, by the gate of Bath-rabbim." It was a
joy being with him, holding his hand as he pointed
out each lovely spot and told some charming untruth
about it. He said, "The book of earth is wonderful.
I wish I had time to read it. I think if I had begun in
my youth, I might have got through the first chapter.
But it's too late to do anything about it now."

We wandered on and on, forgetful of time and
distance, beguiled by stream and meadow and seduc-
tive stone walls wearing their antumn draperies of
red and gold vines a little dimmed by rain and snow,
but still exquisitely beautiful. When we turned at
last, and started to climb the hill, Mr. Clemens
paused and stood gazing over the frosty New England valley, and said, "Age is like this, we stand on
the summit and look back over the distance and
time. Alas, how swift are the feet of the days of the
years of youth." We realized that he was very tired.

Mr. Macy suggested that he should return cross-lots and meet us on the road with a carriage. Mr. Clemens thought this a good idea, and agreed to pilot Mrs. Macy and me to the road, which he had every reason to suppose was just beyond that elephant of a hill. Our search for that road was a wonderful and fearsome adventure. It led through cowpaths, across ditches filled with ice-cold water into fields dotted with little islands of red and gold which rose gently out of the white snow. On closer inspection we found that they were composed of patches of dry goldenrod and huckleberry bushes. We picked our way through treacherously smiling cart roads. He said, "Every path leading out of this jungle dwindles into a squirrel track and runs up a tree." The cart roads proved to be ruts that ensnared our innocent feet. Mr. Clemens had the wary air of a discoverer as he turned and twisted between spreading branches of majestic pines and dwarfed hazel bushes. I remarked that we seemed to be away off our course. He answered, "This is the uncharted wilderness. We have wandered into the chaos that existed before Jehovah divided the waters from the land. The road is just over there," he asserted with conviction. "Yes," we murmured faintly, wondering how we should ever ford the roaring, tumbling imp of a stream which flung itself at us out of the hills.

There was no doubt about it. The road was just there "where you see that rail fence." Prophecy deepened into happy certainty when we saw Mr. Macy and the coachman waiting for us. "Stay where you are," they shouted. In a few seconds they had dismembered the rail fence and were transporting it over the field. It did not take them long to construct a rough bridge, over which we safely crossed the Redding Rubicon, and sure enough, there was the narrow road of civilization winding up the hillside between stone walls and clustering sumachs and wild cherry trees on which little icicles were beginning to form like pendants. Half way down the drive Miss Lyon met us with tearful reproaches. Mr. Clemens mumbled weakly, "It has happened again—the woman tempted me."

I think I never enjoyed a walk more. Sweet is the memory of hours spent with a beloved companion. Even being lost with Mr. Clemens was delightful, although I was terribly distressed that he should be exerting himself beyond his strength. He said many beautiful things about Stormfield, for instance, "It is my Heaven. Its repose stills my restlessness. The view from every point is superb and perpetually changes from miracle to miracle, yet nature never runs short of new beauty and charm." I hope the report is not true that he came to hate the place and feel that he had been defrauded of the society of his fellow men. But I can understand that a temperament like Mr. Clemens's would grow weary of the solitude.

The last evening of our visit we sat around a blazing log fire, and Mr. Clemens asked me if I would like to have him read me "Eve's Diary." Of course I was delighted.

He asked, "How shall we manage it?"

"Oh, you will read aloud, and my teacher will spell your words into my hand."

He murmured, "I had thought you would read my lips."

"I should like to, of course; but I am afraid you will find it very wearisome. We'll start that way anyhow, and if it doesn't work, we'll try the other way." This was an experience, I am sure, no other person in the world had ever had.

"You know, Mr. Clemens," I reminded him, "that we are going home to-morrow, and you promised to put on your Oxford robe for me before I went."

"So I did, Helen, and I will—I will do it now before I forget."

Miss Lyon brought the gorgeous scarlet robe which he had worn when England's oldest university conferred upon him the degree of Doctor of Letters. He put it on, and stood there in the fire light the embodiment of gracious majesty. He seemed pleased that I was impressed. He drew me towards him and kissed me on the brow, as a cardinal or pope or feudal monarch might have kissed a little child.

How I wish I could paint the picture of that evening! Mr. Clemens sat in his great armchair, dressed in his white serge suit, the flaming scarlet robe draping his shoulders, and his white hair gleaming and glistening in the light of the lamp which shone down on his head. In one hand he held "Eve's Diary" in a glorious red cover. In the other hand he held his pipe. "If it gets in the way," he said, "I'll give it up, but I feel embarrassed without it." I sat down near him in a low chair, my elbow on the arm of his chair, so that my fingers could rest lightly on his lips. Mr. Macy lighted his cigar, and the play began. Everything went smoothly for a time. I had no difficulty getting the words from his lips. His pleasant drawl was music to my touch, but when he began gesticulating with his pipe, the actors in the drama got mixed up with the properties and there was confusion until the ashes were gathered into the fireplace. Then a new setting was arranged. Mrs. Macy came and sat beside me and spelled the words into my right hand, while I looked at Mr. Clemens with my left, touching his face and hands and the book, following his gestures and every changing expression. As the reading proceeded, we became utterly absorbed in the wistful, tender chronicle of our first parents. Surely the joy, the innocence, the opening mind of childhood are among life's most sacred mysteries, and if young Eve laughs she makes creation all the sweeter for her Heaven-born merriment. The beauty of Mr. Clemens's voice, when Eve sighed her love, and when Adam stood at her grave grieving bitterly saying "wheresoever she was, there was Eden" caused me to weep openly, and the others swallowed audibly. Every one of us felt the yearning homesickness in that cry of pain.

To one hampered and circumscribed as I am it was a wonderful experience to have a friend like Mr. Clemens. I recall many talks with him about human affairs. He never made me feel that my opinions were worthless, as so many people do. He knew that we do not think with eyes and ears, and that our capacity for thought is not measured by five senses. He kept me always in mind while he talked, and he treated me like a competent human being. That is why I loved him.

Perhaps my strongest impression of him was that of sorrow. There was about him the air of one who had suffered greatly. Whenever I touched his face his expression was sad, even when he was telling a funny story. He smiled, not with the mouth but with his mind—a gesture of the soul rather than of the face. His voice was truly wonderful. To my touch, it was deep, resonant. He had the power of modulating it so as to suggest the most delicate shades of meaning and he spoke so deliberately that I could get almost every word with my fingers on his lips. Ah, how sweet and poignant the memory of his soft slow speech playing over my listening fingers. His words seemed to take strange lovely shapes on my hands. His own hands were wonderfully mobile and changeable under the influence of emotion. It has been said that life has treated me harshly; and sometimes I have complained in my heart because many pleasures of human experience have been withheld from me, but when I recollect the treasure of friendship that has been bestowed upon me I withdraw all charges against life. If much has been denied me, much, very much has been given me. So long as the memory of certain beloved friends lives in my heart I shall say that life is good.

The affluence of Mr. Clemens's mind impressed me vividly. His felicitous words gushed from it with the abundance of the Shasta Falls. Humour was on the surface, but in the centre of his nature was a passion for truth, harmony, beauty.

Once he remarked in his pensive, cynical way, "There is so little in life that is not pretence."

"There is beauty, Mr. Clemens."

"Yes, there is beauty, and beauty is the seed of spirit from which we grow the flowers that shall endure."

I did not realize until I began this sketch how extremely difficult it would be to recapture Mr. Clemens's happy phrases from my memory. I am afraid I should not have succeeded at all if I had not made a few notes after my conversation with him. But I believe I have never falsified a word or an emphasis of the spirit of his utterances.

Time passed at Stormfield as it passes everywhere else, and the day came when we had to say good-bye. The kindly white figure stood on the verandah waving us farewell, as he had waved his welcome when we arrived. Silently we watched the stately villa on the white hilltop fading into the purple distance. We said to each other sadly, "Shall we ever see him again?" And we never did. But we three knew that we had a picture of him in our hearts which would remain there forever. In my fingertips was graven the image of his dear face with its halo of shining white hair, and in my memory his drawling, marvellous voice will always vibrate.

I have visited Stormfield since Mark Twain's death. The flowers still bloom; the breezes still whisper and sough in the cedars, which have grown statelier year by year; the birds still sing, they tell me. But for me the place is bereft of its lover. The last time I was there, the house was in ruins. Only the great chimney was standing, a charred pile of bricks in the bright autumn landscape.

As I sat on the step where he had stood with me one day, my hand warm in his, thoughts of him, like shadowy presences, came and went, sweet with memory and with regret. Then I fancied I felt someone approaching me; I reached out, and a red geranium blossom met my touch! The leaves of the plant were covered with ashes, and even the sturdy stalk had been partly broken off by a chip of falling plaster. But there was the bright flower smiling at me out of the ashes. I thought it said to me, "Please don't grieve." I brought the plant home and set it in a sunny corner of my garden, where always it seems to say the same thing to me, "Please don't grieve." But I grieve, nevertheless.

Chapter V

LEADING THE BLIND

I HAVE been writing about the play days in Wrentham. I have not dwelt upon the perplexities I went through trying to find my special niche in life. Even while I was in college I had asked myself how I could use the education I was receiving. I felt that there must be some particular task for me, but what was it?

My friends had all manner of plans. While I was still at Radcliffe one of them conceived the idea that I was wasting precious time on books and study which would do nobody good. She said I was becoming self-centred and egotistical and that I could accomplish more for humanity if I devoted myself to the education of children afflicted like myself. She told me that God had laid this work upon me and that it was my duty to hearken to His voice. She said it would not be necessary for us to do anything about financing the project, that she would attend to it herself. We begged her to wait until I finished my education, but she said that procrastination was the greatest of sins. She spent the night with us in Cambridge, arguing, and as hour after hour passed my

teacher and I became more and more exhausted. Our
friend was still charging our defences. She took our
feeble counterattack for surrender, and before we
were up the next morning she was off for New York
and Washington to acquaint my friends with the mission I had undertaken. She called on Dr. Alexander
Graham Bell, Mrs. Lawrence Hutton, Mr. Harsen
Rhoades, and many others, and told them how strongly
I felt that I must pass on the blessings I had enjoyed
to other deaf-blind children. Mrs. Hutton asked me
to come to New York and tell them how I felt in
the matter. I had written her that the project was
giving me infinite trouble, and seriously interfering
with my college work. We met in Mr. Rhoades's
private office in the Greenwich Savings Bank. Mr.
H. H. Rogers, who was financing my college course,
could not be present, and so he sent Mark Twain as
his representative. The matter was thoroughly
threshed out. When Mr. Clemens rose to speak he
said that, unlike the lady who was sponsoring the
scheme, he did not know what the Lord wanted him
to say, but that he did know what H. H. Rogers
wanted him to say. "Mr. Rogers wishes it to be understood," he said, "that he does not intend to finance
any of the Lord's projects on the recommendation
of Mrs. So and So. She seems thoroughly familiar
with the Lord's intentions. She made it clear in her
conversation that her plan for a school for afflicted

children embodied His idea exactly. I couldn't help wondering how she got every detail of the divine idea right when there were no written instructions. Perhaps the Lord appointed her His deputy with power to act for Him. There is no other possible explanation of how, out of the countless good ideas for this institution, she was able to pick the one which had the Deity's sanction every time."

All through my life people who imagine themselves more competent than my teacher and I have wanted to organize my affairs. No doubt it would have been to our advantage if some of these ideas had been carried out. On the other hand, it is hard to see how all their excellent suggestions could have been followed; for they had opposite aims. We were strangers when we met. Usually we were friends for a space of time, but when we parted, the bonds of our friendship creaked considerably, and on several occasions they snapped. These friends pointed out our incompetence, and assured us that if we followed their plan, we should win fame and fortune, and incidentally benefit some good cause. They talked, they wrote, they brought their friends to help them, and went away, and the next day others came. Sometimes it was necessary, as in the case of the plan about which I have just written, to call upon my staunch friends Mr. Rogers, Mrs. Hutton, and Mrs. William Thaw, to get me out of their toils.

Some of these entanglements had memorable and unfortunate consequences for me.

There was an effort on the part of Mr. Anagnos, the successor of Dr. Howe as director of the Perkins Institution for the Blind when I was a little girl to keep my teacher and me at the Institution. Miss Sullivan thought that it would be detrimental to my development to remain in an institution. She has always believed that handicapped people should not be herded together when it is possible to keep them in a normal environment. There were many reasons why it would have been delightful for me to live at the Institution. Nearly everyone there could spell to me, and I was happy with the blind children. Moreover, I loved Mr. Anagnos like a father. He was exceedingly kind to me, and I owe him some of the brightest memories of my childhood; best of all, it was he who sent my teacher to me. When we left the Institution and went on our wayward quest of education Mr. Anagnos bitterly resented what he was pleased to call Miss Sullivan's ingratitude, and shut us out from his heart. I like to think that if he lived, he would have come to see that she chose the wiser course.

Some of the would-be directors of my life have staged the little dramas in which I was to play the leading rôle with such delicate art, they almost seemed like my own conceptions, and their failure to materialize gloriously has hurt my pride not a little. The beautiful Queen of Roumania, who used to write to me under her nom de plume, Carmen Sylva, had a plan for gathering all the blind of her kingdom into one place and giving them pleasant homes and employment. This city was to be called "Vatra Luminosa"—"Luminous Hearth." She wanted me to help her finance it. The idea had its origin in a generous heart; but it was not in accordance with modern methods of helping the sightless to help themselves. I wrote Queen Elizabeth that I did not feel that I could coöperate with her. She was deeply hurt. She thought I was selfish and had not the true happiness of the blind at heart. Our pleasant correspondence was broken off, and I never heard direct from her again.

But I cannot leave this subject without a word of appreciation of the friends who have not tried to manage me. Curiously enough, they are the ones who have contributed most to my usefulness and joy. If those who believe in us, and give money to enable us to realize our ambitions, have a right to a say in the shaping of our lives, certainly my teacher, my mother, Mr. Rogers, Mr. Carnegie, Mrs. Thaw, and Dr. Bell had that right; but they never exercised it in word or deed. And since they left me free to choose my own work (within my limitations) I looked about to see what there was that I could do.

I resolved that whatever rôle I did play in life it would not be a passive one.

Before I left Radcliffe I had heard the call of the sightless. In 1903, while I was a junior, I received a visit from an enthusiastic young man, Mr. Charles F. F. Campbell, whom I had met while he was still a student at the Massachusetts Institute of Technology. I knew about his famous father, Sir Francis Campbell, an American blind man, educated at the Perkins Institution, who founded the Royal Normal College and Academy of Music for the Blind in England and was knighted by the King for his services to the sightless. Young Mr. Campbell wished me to join an association which had just been formed by the Women's Educational and Industrial Union in Boston to promote the welfare of the adult blind. I did so, and soon after I appeared before the legislature with the new association to urge the necessity of employment for the blind and to ask for the appointment of a State Commission that would make them their special care. The commission was appointed, and although I did not know it at the time, the curtain rose on my life work.

The association established an experimental station under Mr. Campbell's direction for the purpose of testing out industries that seemed practicable. The blind were taught trades in their homes and a sales room was opened in Boston for the disposal of their wares. The new Commission opened a series of shops in different parts of the state, and a great movement was launched in which Mr. Campbell was the leader until 1922. No one in our day has done more to put the blind on an equal footing with the seeing. I have never ceased to lament that he is no longer connected with the work and I hope the day is not distant when he will again join our crusade against darkness.

It was not until the autumn of 1904, after we had moved to Wrentham, that I seriously began to study blindness and the problems it creates. I found that one of the greatest needs was a central clearing house. Much time and money were wasted in unorganized effort. Scarcely anyone in Massachusetts knew what was being done in other parts of the United States. There was "a separation in space and spirit" between the various schools and societies which rendered it very difficult to collect and distribute information. There was no accurate census of the blind in America. Nor was there a national survey of occupations. There was no central group to go out into new territory and start the work for the blind. There was no bureau of research or information. The apparatus used by the blind was primitive. Books were expensive and there was no unified system of embossed printing.

The first printing ever done in relief was in an embossed Roman letter. It was never satisfactory.

The classroom instruction in literature and music remained chiefly oral. Tangible writing was impossible. But with the introduction of Braille's alphabet of raised dots that could easily be felt by the finger and arranged in combinations to represent letters, the era of educating the blind, as we understand it to-day, began. Every pupil could learn to read it and to write it. It was of universal application: to any language, longhand or shorthand, to mathematics and to music. As a system it was and is adequate to all purposes. More than any other single lever it has served to lift the educational status of blind people.

Its inventor, Louis Braille, blinded by accident at the age of three years, became first a pupil and then a teacher at the National Institution for the Blind in Paris, which was the parent of all such schools. At the age of sixteen he had worked out his alphabetical system, boldly addressing it to the finger only, not at all to the eye; and he had supplied a slate to write it on. The whole world of educated blind people uses it to-day, practically as he left it. Next to Valentin Haüy himself, the founder of the first school for the blind, we consider Louis Braille our greatest benefactor.

Unfortunately, Dr. Howe, the director of the Massachusetts School for the Blind, whose word carried more weight than that of anyone else in America, rejected this invention and continued to print books in the Roman letter, and other schools in America followed the example of Massachusetts. But the greater part of the blind could not read the Roman letter. Naturally, they wanted something they could read, and so a number of dot systems sprang up all over the United States. The confusion of prints went from bad to worse. Each party clung tenaciously to its own theory, and the blind themselves had no voice in the matter. It was so expensive to make books in the different systems that the number remained extremely limited, and furthermore the multiplicity of prints resulted in duplication. Even our magazines were printed in several different types, thus multiplying the expense of their production. I learned five different prints—New York point, American braille, European braille, Moon, and Line type—in order to avail myself of all that had been printed for the blind. The Bible and other books universally demanded were printed in all five systems.

The condition of the adult blind was almost hopeless. Many of them were idle and in want, and not a few of them were in almshouses. Many had lost their sight when it was too late to go to school. They were without occupation or diversion or resources of any kind. The cruelest part of their fate then as now was not blindness but the feeling that they were a burden to their families or the community.

I was surprised to find when I talked to seeing persons well informed about other matters, a medi-æval ignorance concerning the sightless. They assured me that the blind can tell colours by touch and that the senses they have are more delicate and acute than those of other people. Nature herself, they told me, seeks to atone to the blind by giving them a singular sensitiveness and a sweet patience of spirit. It seemed not to occur to them that if this were true it would be an advantage to lose one's sight.

The most important phase of all the work, namely, the prevention of blindness in new-born children, could not even be discussed. The medical profession had known since 1881 that at least two thirds of the children admitted to the schools had been blinded as a result of a germ which attacked the eyes in the process of birth, and that the disease caused by this infection, *ophthalmia neonatorum,* was easily pre-ventable. But because it was associated with venereal disease, though not always caused by it, very few had the courage to bring the matter to the attention of the public. By 1900 a number of physicians had done this, among them Dr. F. Park Lewis of Buffalo, Dr. A. Morrow of New York, and Dr. North of Boston. It was this group that began urging the association and commission I had joined to take up the work of prevention, and a lay campaign was started which resulted in the formation of a National

Committee for the Prevention of Blindness, which is still active.

A few years later when I visited Kansas City, the physicians in charge of the eye clinic there asked me to see if I could persuade Colonel Nelson, editor of the Kansas City *Star,* to allow blindness in the new born to be discussed in his paper. At first he refused but when he saw how disappointed I was, he said "Well, write what you have to say, and I'll see what I can do." I wrote out the facts for him, and he printed the article on the front page of the *Star.* Thus another barrier was broken down before the march of progress.

The year 1907 was a banner year for the blind. Mr. Edward Bok threw open the pages of the *Ladies Home Journal* for a frank discussion of the causes of blindness and I wrote a series of articles for him. Other periodicals of more or less prominence followed suit, and a great barrier went down before the march of progress. It was in 1907 that the *Matilda Ziegler Magazine for the Blind* was established. It was financed by Mrs. William Ziegler of New York whose generosity has created more real happiness for the sightless than that of any other living person. For twenty years the magazine has been edited by Mr Walter Holmes, who has won for himself a warm chimney corner in the hearts of all the blind. This same year Mr. Campbell began issuing *The Outlook for the Blind,* the first magazine in America to bring together all matters of interest concerning the sightless. He carried it through sixteen years without any financial return to himself and during all that period succeeded in holding the good will of those who were battling over the types.

It was in 1907 or 1908, I think, that I was asked to prepare a paper on the blind for an *Encyclopedia of Education.* This rather took my breath away, for it was before I was familiar with the history of their education, and the only book available on the subject was in German, Alexander Mell's *Blindenwesen.* It was not in raised letters, and so Mr. Macy read it to me after his day's work. As I penetrated more deeply into the problems of the blind he also read me Diderot's rich, suggestive essay on blindness, and a French story, *Sous les Trembles,* which invested blind people with a stirring human interest.

The more I did the more the requests multiplied. Over and over I was asked to write articles and attend meetings and speak to legislatures. Repeatedly I was invited to go abroad and visit the schools of France, Germany, England, and Italy, to interest people in the deaf or the blind.

Dr. Bell and Dr. James Kerr Love of Scotland were urging me to bring the problems of the deaf before the public, and although I was as deeply interested in the cause of the deaf as I was in that of the blind and had always thought deafness before the acquisition of language a greater affliction than blindness, I found that it was not humanly possible to work for both the blind and the deaf at the same time.

I did everything I could and several times made addresses, although my voice could be understood only in a small auditorium, and I had had no training in public speaking. An occasion I especially remember was when I went to the St. Louis Exposition in the hope of creating a wider interest in children who were deaf and blind.

I was to speak one morning before a gathering of educators. The crowd was so great that it was obvious that I could not be heard. Mr. David Rowland Francis, President of the Exposition, who had a fine speaking voice, offered to read my address, but I had not brought a copy with me. "Well," he said, "I understand you perfectly. I will repeat what you say." In fear and trembling I began. He kept his hand on my arm to signal me when to stop and when to go on. After half a dozen sentences I was satisfied that all was going well. When he finished we both received an ovation.

In the meanwhile the crowd around the building had become so dense that it was impossible for us to get through it. Mrs. Macy and I were separated from our escort, our clothing was torn, and the flowers were snatched off my hat for souvenirs. Mr. Francis called out the guards to disperse the crowd and we were given six stalwart soldiers to conduct us through the grounds.

In spite of this warm-hearted reception, nothing constructive was done for the deaf-blind of America. And now, after more than twenty years, I still grieve that so few of these little unhappy ones have been led out of their imprisonment. No moments in my life are sadder than those in which I have felt their groping hands in mine, mutely appealing for help I could not give. But it is useless to repine. I mention my young dream of their deliverance only because it is sweet to remember.

Life was very strenuous. Often we would leave home with all the housework undone, hasten to a meeting, go through with its inevitable tiresome social functions, and return to Wrentham to find fresh tasks added to our already heavy burden. It is not strange that we both broke down several times after a series of public appearances. The requests and must-be-written letters continued to multiply—they would have kept a whole staff of assistants busy if we could have afforded it.

We were hemmed in on all sides by unromantic obstacles. I had hoped to translate Maurice de la Sizeranne's *Psychologie des Femmes Aveugles* because it contained much valuable information about

the education of the blind in France. There was
nothing in this country comparable with it except
possibly Dr. Howe's reports of his work at the
Massachusetts School, and these, unfortunately, were
not generally available and naturally were not as
up-to-date as the French book. Someone in Germany
sent me a small volume of poems by Lorm, who lost
both his sight and his hearing in adult life and who
wrote many lines of courage and beauty about "The
inner Sun I create in my Soul." But there were no
adequate dictionaries of foreign languages in braille,
and it was impossible for Mr. and Mrs. Macy to
read me all the books I should have liked to put into
English. We could not have paid a special reader
even if the right kind had been forthcoming.

During many years we had no servant. I learned to
do all I could without sight to help my teacher. Mr.
Macy went to Boston every morning, and Mrs. Macy
drove him to the train and attended to the marketing.
I cleared the table, washed the dishes, and tidied up
the rooms. Letters might come in multitudes, articles
and books might clamour to be written, but home
was home, and somebody had to make the beds, pick
the flowers, start the windmill and stop it when the
tank was filled, and be mindful of the little almost
unnoticed things which constitute the happiness of
family life. Of course I could not take the helm of

the ship in hand, but I found tasks sufficient to keep me on my feet most of the day, and everyone who loves knows how gratifying it is to be able really to help others through a hard day's routine.

We were pursued by misunderstandings. Not long after we had started our Wrentham home life an incident occurred which explains how such misunderstandings began. Madame Elizabeth Nordin, a Swedish educator, called on us one day and talked with us for hours. She said she was in charge of a school for deaf-blind children in Sweden, and was visiting America for the purpose of studying the best methods to educate her pupils. We gladly gave her what information we could. She asked me to speak in French and German, and seemed surprised that I could pronounce the words as well as I did. She was full of pleasant compliments, and embraced me cordially when she departed. Afterwards we learned that she was indignant because we had not offered to entertain her as our guest for three weeks while she was studying American schools for the sightless! She had told me with amusement the myths she had read about me—that I could paint pictures and play the piano, and that I had a great gift for sculpture. Yet when she returned to Sweden she disseminated myths quite as absurd as these. She wrote an article full of misinformation in which she said I had received every honour at Radcliffe, and that Boston had presented me with a house and a park! It was she who gave the educators of the blind in Europe exaggerated accounts of my good fortune and liberal friends, and unparalleled opportunities to help all the deaf-blind to be taught and placed in homes where they would be well cared for! While professing the utmost devotion to "the poor, unhappy, doubly afflicted ones whose fate I shared," she placed me in a trying position from which I have never been able to extricate myself. It was she who brought upon my dear ones and me all the remonstrances and disappointed expostulations of people who believed I could help them. If any of my European friends happen to read this record, I hope they will understand that my refusals were not because I was indifferent.

We tried to change our mode of living into something like what we had hoped for when we moved to Wrentham, but we never succeeded. Now and then we resolutely withdrew from the world, to use the mediæval phrase, and applied ourselves each to his or her own task. We barricaded ourselves with the sacrosanct privacy to which tradition and the necessities of concentrated thinking entitle writers and artists. But in spite of our attempted hermit life, we were imperatively called out to new duties.

It was in the summer of 1906 that my teacher and I assumed the additional responsibility of attending the sessions of the Massachusetts Commission for the Blind, of which the Governor appointed me a member. Mrs. Macy sat beside me hour after hour, as she had done in college, and spelled to me everything that was said. We had found it a tax upon our faculties to keep up with the lecture of one professor talking steadily for a whole hour; but at these meetings we were breathless with the effort to keep up with comments, criticisms, questions and replies exchanged rapidly by four or five different persons, and the endless minutiæ which characterize the sessions of a state board. From the beginning I was full of misgivings as to my qualifications for serving on the board. The more I listened to the discussions the less competent I felt to take part in them. It is never a simple matter to assist the blind. There are no rules which can be applied in all cases, because the circumstances and needs of each blind person differ from those of every other. It is, therefore, necessary to decide individually what method is best. The other commissioners had advantages which I did not. They could go from place to place visiting the blind, obtaining first hand information about their needs, and giving them expert advice as to the best means of overcoming their handicap. Besides, I was hampered by the slowness of my speech and never spoke up as I should when my turn came. In college the professor talked on the same subject connectedly, and indicated any change of thought; but when several people are talking the viewpoint shifts constantly, and the felicitous remark which is on the tip of one's tongue never gets uttered. Of course this is true of most conversation, but I was chagrined at my useless figure in a group of earnest servants of the public seeking to promote a cause which truly appealed to me. After some months I resigned from the Commission, and I resolved sternly that never again would I allow myself to be dragged into undertakings for which I was not intended by fate.

I knew now that my work was to be for the blind, and I had begun to realize that I could not do for them what I wanted unless I could present their problems for discussion before legislatures, medical associations, and conventions, more competently than I had done before. To do that I must improve my speech.

I had tried a number of teachers and had always been disappointed. But during the Christmas holidays in 1909 when we were at Woodstock, Vermont, we met Mr. Charles A. White, a well-known teacher of singing at the Boston Conservatory of Music. At that time he had been very much interested in my speech and expressed a wish to see what he could do with it. A year later we arranged to have him come out to Wrentham every Saturday and stay over Sunday that he might give me lessons. The old longing to speak like other people came back stronger than ever. I felt the tide of opportunity rising and longed for a voice that would be equal to the surge that was sweeping me out into the world.

Chapter VI

PER ARDUA PROXIME AD ASTRA

THE acquirement of speech is not easy for those who cannot hear. The difficulties are doubled if they are blind also. But the educational importance of speech to the deaf cannot be exaggerated. Without a language of some sort one is not a human being; without speech one is not a complete human being. Even when the speech is not beautiful there is a fountain of joy in uttering words. It is an emotional experience quite different from that which comes from spelled words.

When Miss Sullivan took me for my first lessons in articulation to Miss Sarah Fuller, principal of the Horace Mann School for the Deaf, and one of the pioneer teachers of speech in this country, I was nearly ten years of age. The only sounds I uttered were meaningless noises, usually harsh because of the great effort I made to produce them. Miss Fuller put my hand on her face, so that I could feel the vibrations of her voice, and slowly and very distinctly made the sound "ahm," while Miss Sullivan spelled into my hand the word arm. I imitated the sound as well as I could, and succeeded after several attempts in articulating it to Miss Fuller's satisfaction.

I learned to speak several words that day in breathy, hollow tones. After eleven lessons I was able to say, word by word, "I-am-not-dumb-now." Miss Fuller tried to make me understand that I must speak softly, and not stiffen my throat or jerk my tongue, but I could not help straining and mouthing every word. I know now that my lessons should have been conducted differently. My vocal organs should have been developed first, and articulation afterwards.

This would have approached the normal method of learning speech. The normal baby hears sounds from the moment he is born into the world. He listens more or less passively. Then he cries and coos, and in countless ways exercises the delicate organs of speech before he attempts a word. Speech descends upon his lips like dew upon a flower. Without effort or conscious thought he utters spontaneous melodious sounds.

How different is the situation of the little deaf child! He hears no sound. No voice enters the silent cloister of his ear. Even if he has heard for a little while, as I did for nineteen months, he soon forgets. In his still world words once heard fly like swallows in the autumn, leaving no memory of their music. He does not use his vocal organs, because he feels no desire to speak. He goes to school and learns slowly, painfully, to substitute his eyes for his ears. Intently he watches his teacher's mouth as she makes a sound, and patiently he tries to form his lips and move his tongue in imitation. Every step is won at the cost of painful effort.

Four years after I went to Miss Fuller I entered the Wright-Humason Oral School in New York, where for two years I received lessons in speech and lip reading. From that time until I began to study with Mr. White, Miss Sullivan helped me as well as she could to improve my articulation. I was happy because my family could understand me, also those who met me frequently enough to become accustomed to my speech. I found out that to speak at all intelligibly meant the incessant mastery of difficulties that had been mastered a thousand times. For years I put my hand on Miss Sullivan's face, observed the motions of her lips, put my fingers in her mouth to feel the position of her tongue, and repeated over and over the sounds she uttered, sometimes imitating them perfectly, then losing them again. Yet I never wavered in my determination to learn to talk, nor did she waver in her determination to help me.

It is to her that I owe most of the progress I made in this, as in everything else. Her work with me has been based on instinctive good sense rather than on technical knowledge of vocal problems. By persistent effort she improved my diction and kept my voice as pleasant as was possible under the circumstances. She has tried to cultivate softness, but this very process tended to make the vocal organs deficient in resonance. Moreover, the enormous amount of work required for my education rendered it difficult to give my speech sufficient attention. This was unfortunate, because in those formative years much more could have been done for my voice, and more easily than now. I say this to emphasize the need of early and continuous training throughout the growing years of the deaf child.

At first Mr. White and I regarded my speech lessons as experimental. But he became so interested in the problems that presented themselves at each lesson that he continued to teach me for three years. He spent the greater part of two summers in Wrentham. He would not take money for these lessons, declaring that he would be amply repaid if he succeeded in helping me. His delightful personality, his patience and perseverance and his quick sympathy endeared him to us all. I have a memory picture of his kind, expressive face which I cherish, and of his dear hand spelling out instructions without end. My heart warms as I recall the tireless encouragement with which he braced me when I failed and failed.

I can give only a brief account of Mr. White's work with me here. He learned the manual alphabet so he could work with me just as he would with any other pupil. First, he directed my attention to position and breathing, and proceeded to get the lower ribs and diaphragm to participate more freely in the act of respiration. I then practised to open the resonating cavities through inhalation, and maintain this position through control of breath. His idea was to get the cavities of resonance under the control of the will before using the larynx. I therefore practised exercises without tone. The failure of my vocal cords to come together was the chief defect, and I still have much trouble in getting proper glottic closure. After securing this, I experimented in different degrees of resistance in order to vary the tension of the cords.

Having obtained some control of these three factors of voice—motor, vibrator, and resonator—I studied vowels and consonants separately and in combination. Mr. White classified them according to a plan which he had thought out and used in his work with his pupils in the Conservatory.

After this drill, I was ready to practise actual speech. But when Mr. White tried to give me accents and rhythm. he found that although I could recognize the changes of accent and rhythm he gave me, I could not project rhythms myself. Therefore it was necessary for him to train this sense. After repeated trials I got two units of equal duration, which opened the way for further development. Mr. White did this by patting my hand, first taking double, then triple and quadruple, measure, in simple and compound forms, and in syncopation. After this preparatory work, Mr. White was surprised that I could not coördinate the spoken word with the motion of the hand. This difficulty was soon overcome, however, and rhythm and accent could be utilized.

Finally came the matter of pitch and quality. At first I showed no ability to raise or lower the pitch at will, and had to experiment with it. By this time I had become somewhat expert in detecting the changes which took place in the throat by lightly placing my fingers on Mr. White's throat and my own, and when he started a tone in a low pitch and suddenly raised it, say, an octave, I soon caught the idea. To Mr. White's amazement, after following this method for some time, he found that I could approximate definite pitches. He would ask me to sing an octave on "sol," and I did it from my own sense of pitch. Then he asked for an octave one note higher, "La, la." When I sounded the note, Mr. White struck a tuning fork against the desk. My tone corresponded with that of the fork, and I also sounded the intervals of a third and a fifth.

It was a long time before he could build my voice up so that I could practise anything for the platform. Then the voice we had laboured for so hopefully became quite unmanageable. It would dive down so low or jump up so high that we were all disconcerted. A little rain or wind or dust, a wave of excitement, was enough to send it on a rampage, and I still marvel at the forbearance of the family who had to hear me morning, afternoon, and evening. A hearing person speaks a language learned he knows not how, and can foreshape his words without conscious thought. I had not this boon of nature. What I said at night in one way I would say the next morning very differently, the sensations varied so disturbingly from day to day. A multitude of little vibrations that I had not noticed before bewildered me. I would practise, practise, and perhaps capture a firm, clear tone, only to have it escape me mysteriously. If I let fall a natural utterance without thinking, and tried to repeat it, it eluded me.

It was three years before we felt I might try a public appearance. Then it was arranged that my teacher and I should give a demonstration of her work and my speech in Montclair, New Jersey. It was in February, 1913.

I wonder if anyone has ever made his first appearance upon the platform with keener anguish. Terror invaded my flesh, my mind froze, my heart stopped beating. I kept repeating, "What shall I do? What shall I do to calm this tumult within me?" Desperately I prayed, as the moment approached to go out before the audience, "O God, let me pour out my voice freely." I know I felt much as General Wolfe's men must have felt when in broad daylight they measured with their eyes the Heights of Abraham they had scaled in the dark—walls bristling with cannon!

Oh, that first appearance in Montclair, New Jersey! Until my dying day I shall think of that stage as a pillory where I stood cold, riveted, trembling, voiceless. Words thronged to my lips, but no syllable could I utter. At last I forced a sound. It felt to me like a cannon going off, but they told me afterwards it was a mere whisper.

I tried to remember everything Mr. White had told me to do, but alas! Not a rule came to my assistance. Mustering all the will power and obstinacy of my nature I went on to the end of the speech. I was constantly between Charybdis and Scylla; sometimes I felt my voice soaring and I knew that meant falsetto; frantically I dragged it down till my words fell about me like loose bricks. Oh, if that kindly custom of Athens, that of accompanying an orator with a flute, could have prevailed, or if only an orchestra could have drowned my faltering speech, it would not have been so terrible. At last the ordeal was over. Everyone was kind and sympathetic, but I knew I had failed. All the eloquence which was to bring light to the blind lay crumpled at my feet. I came off the stage in despair, my face deluged with tears, my breast heaving with sobs, my whole body crying out, "Oh, it is too difficult, too difficult, I cannot do the impossible." But in a little while faith and hope and love came back and I returned to my practising.

I have not succeeded completely in realizing the desire of my childhood to "talk like other people." I know now how vain that wish was, and how extravagant my expectations were when I began my speech lessons. It is not humanly possible, I believe, for one who has been deaf from early infancy to do more than approximate natural speech.

Since my tenth year I have laboured unceasingly to speak so that others can understand me without concentrated attention. I have had excellent instructors and the constant assistance of my teacher. Yet I have only partially conquered the hostile silence. I have a voice that ministers to my work and my happiness. It is not a pleasant voice, I am afraid, but I have clothed its broken wings in the unfading hues of my dreams and my struggle for it has strengthened every fibre of my being and deepened my understanding of all human strivings and disappointed ambitions.

Chapter VII

WANDERINGS

WE LECTURED only occasionally at first, as we were feeling our way towards a programme which would be acceptable to our audiences. All kinds of people came to hear us—the poor, the young, the blind, the deaf, and others handicapped in the race of life, and naturally their interest in me made me want to give them special messages of cheer or encouragement.

We were warmly received wherever we went, and encouraged to go on with our work. Mrs. Macy had a natural gift of public speaking, and I was frequently told by strangers with what pleasure the audience listened to her story of how she taught me. She lectured a whole hour, while I sat quietly in the anteroom, reading to pass the time. When my turn came, my mother, or anyone who happened to accompany us, brought me to the platform. I placed my fingers on Mrs. Macy's mouth, and we showed the audience how I could read the lips. The people asked questions, and I answered them as well as I could. Thus they became more accustomed to my imperfect speech. Afterwards I talked about happiness, or the value of the senses when well trained, or the intimate dependence of all human beings one upon another in the emergencies of life. I never attained ease of delivery or pleasantness of voice. There were times, I am sure, when the audience could not follow me at all. Either my voice would rise into a queer falsetto, or it would dive down in the depths. It shunned the *via media*. I swallowed the very words I especially wanted my listeners to hear. I pushed and strained, I pounded. I defeated myself with too much effort. I committed every sin against the dignity and grace of speech. The slightest noise I felt in the hall was disconcerting, as I could not tell if I was heard or not, and I almost collapsed when a chair was moved, or a street car rattled past the doors. But the audience was always patient. Whether they understood me or not, they showered me with good wishes and flowers and encouragement, as the Lord loads us with benefits despite our imperfections. Little by little they began to get more of what I said. One of my happiest moments was when I spoke to a large number of children at a school on the East Side in New York, and they were able to understand me when I repeated "Mary had a little lamb." Always I was compensated for my crippled speech by the interest and enthusiasm with which my teacher's lecture on my education was received. I was told by those who heard her more than once that it always seemed as if she were giving her story for the first time, she put such freshness and imagination and love into it. Sometimes the audience was so silent that we were rather disturbed, thinking that we had bored them; but afterwards I found out that they were so interested in my teacher's story, they forgot to applaud, and we felt it the highest compliment they could have paid us.

At first we lectured only occasionally in New England, New York, New Jersey, and other states near by, but little by little we began to go farther afield.

We spoke at the opening of the New York Lighthouse for the Blind by Henry Holt's beautiful daughter who is now Mrs. Mather. On that occasion we met President Taft who had a second time left his arduous duties in Washington to lift up his voice for the cause of the sightless. I shall always picture him, big, kind, benevolent, as he exhorted the audience, "Let us bring about as nearly as possible equal opportunity for the seeing and those who are denied the blessings of sight."

The Lighthouse grew out of one of the happiest thoughts of our generation. One day Mrs. Mather and her sister saw some blind boys enjoying a concert in Italy. Others had seen blind persons enjoy music, but had not acted upon the suggestions it offered. When these two young ladies came back to New York they formed a committee for the distribution among the blind of unsold tickets to concerts. Thus they came into contact with the needs of the blind, and it was not long before they were asking themselves and others why the blind should not be employed. They were told that in the world of machinery, specialized industry, and keen competition, the blind man could not expect to find profitable occupation. They were even told that it would be cruel to add the burden of labour to the burden of infirmity. As if to be without work were not the heaviest burden mortal could be called upon to endure!

They organized the New York Association for the Blind and opened the first Lighthouse. The work has grown strong and prospered these many years under the direction of Mrs. Mather. She tells the public, "We do not ask for charity but for justice—for an opportunity for your blind brother and sister to have a fair chance. Won't you help to give it to them, and won't you give yourself the rare opportunity of investing in a gift of light? Help us by your generosity to approach successfully our ideals of service. As that great friend of our organization in its early days, Carl Schurz, said: 'Ideals are like stars—you cannot touch them with your fingers, but like the mariner on the desert of waters, you can follow them, and following come to port.'"

In 1913 I spoke in Washington. I went down

shortly before the inauguration of Woodow Wilson
to attend a woman suffrage demonstration and
stayed through the inauguration because the United
Press asked me to report the event for its papers. I
remember that it was a mild, gray day. I felt no sun,
but a slight breeze. It was good marching weather
for the troops, and I noticed a delightful smell of
spring in the air. We waited about two hours before
the parade began. The crowd was already considerable. It kept increasing, and I felt the masses of
humanity as they moved up the steps, causing the
stand to vibrate. It was a clean, good-natured crowd,
and I enjoyed being in a multitude of men, women,
and children who were having a good time. I liked
best of all the rich and far-rolling music of the bands
and the descriptions my teacher and Mr. Macy gave
me of the handsome troops. The parade was ornate,
elaborate, and expensive, but it was very jolly, and
as regiment after regiment passed I could not help
wishing that our soldiers never had to do anything
but look handsome and salute the President.

I should have been more deeply stirred if I could
have felt that the great ceremony ushered in a new
day. For Mr. Wilson himself I had the highest respect, but I felt, even then, that the forces arrayed
against him were stronger than he could combat.

I had met him some years before at Mr. Lawrence
Hutton's on the occasion of which I have already

spoken when Mark Twain denounced the murder of noncombatants in the Philippines by American soldiers. During the whole of Mr. Clemens's speech while the rest of us were listening breathlessly Mr. Wilson sat at a window looking out into the night. When Mr. Hutton asked him what he thought of it he replied something like this: "Much heroism does not always keep military men from committing follies." He asked me why I had chosen Radcliffe College rather than Wellesley, Smith, or Bryn Mawr. I said, "Because they didn't want me at Radcliffe, and as I was stubborn by nature, I chose to override their objections." He asked if I thought a personal triumph was worth the expenditure it entailed. Mr. Wilson was exceedingly reserved, but I did not think he was cold. Far from it. He seemed like a smouldering fire that might blaze up at any moment. I gathered from the conversation round Mr. Hutton's table that most of the men thought him shrewd, and that his wisdom surpassed that of most scholars of the day.

There is no way of measuring what President Wilson might have accomplished for his country if the War had not upset the world. History must judge the men who are entrusted with power by the blessings they confer on mankind. It seems like bitter irony to ask whether President Wilson did all that was possible under the circumstances which surrounded him. If we judge him by the rule of his associates at Versailles, his conduct was not more reprehensible than theirs; but if we judge him by the standard of his intentions, his failure was colossal. Commander-in-chief of a vast and splendidly equipped army with inexhaustible resources, and head of a country that was the provider and creditor of all Europe, it seems as if he might have stood steadfast, especially as the good will of the common people of all countries was with him. Even if the bankers of the world had ultimately forced an unrighteous peace upon the belligerents President Wilson would have kept his prestige and the moral leadership of the people, and he would have gone down in history as one of the noblest champions of humanity. As it was, he made compromise with his own soul. He lost his health, he lost popular favour, and he lost his self-confidence. No one can tell how many centuries his failure set back the progress of the world; but only those blinded by hate can doubt the nobility of his aims.

He did not live to see the victory of his cause, but he thought and wrote things that no head of a country before him had thought and written. The humblest and the mightiest of the earth listened to his words, which seemed to announce in golden accents a fairer morality among nations. The better day which he prophesied will come because it must come. Great ideals do not attain the summit of our vision in a day. Great ideals must be tempered to human understanding, as the wind to the shorn lamb.

Kipling tells an ancient legend which seems to me to apply to President Wilson. A man who wrought a most notable deed wished to explain to his tribe what he had done. As soon as he began to speak, however, he was smitten with dumbness, and sat down. Then there arose a man who had taken no part in the action, and who had no special virtues, but who was gifted with the magic of words. He described the merits of the notable deed in such a fashion that the words became alive, and walked up and down in the hearts of all his hearers. Thereupon the tribe, seeing that the words were certainly alive, and fearing lest the man with the words would hand down untrue tales about them to their children, took and killed him. But later they saw that the magic was in the words, not in the man. Future generations will discover that the power of President Wilson was in his words, not in him.

Chapter *VIII*

MY OLDEST FRIEND

I DO not remember whether I lectured before or after the Inauguration, but I do remember that I was introduced by Dr. Alexander Graham Bell. It was a very happy occasion. This was not the first time I had appeared on the platform with him. When I was a little girl, just learning to talk, my teacher and I used to go with him to conventions to further the teaching of speech to the deaf.

Someone has said that a beautiful memory is the most precious wealth one can possess. I am indeed rich in happy memories of Dr. Bell. Most people know him as the inventor of the telephone; those who are familiar with his work for the deaf, believe that what he did for them was as important as his great invention. I admired him for both, but I remember him not so much as a great inventor or as a great benefactor, but as an affectionate and understanding friend.

I could almost call him my oldest friend. Even before my teacher came he held out a warm hand to me in the dark; indeed, it was through him that Mr. Anagnos sent her to me, but little did he dream, or

I, that he was to be the medium of God's best gift to me.

From the beginning he enthusiastically approved Miss Sullivan's methods in teaching me. In a letter to Mr. Macy shortly after *The Story of My Life* was published he says of some letters of hers which are printed there in which she tells how she taught me:

They reveal the fact that has long been suspected, that Helen's remarkable achievements are as much due to the genius of her teacher, as to her own brilliant mind. . . . They also prove that Miss Sullivan was wrong when she gave us the impression that she acted without method in the instruction of Helen—groping her way along and acting only on the spur of the moment. They show that she was guided all along by principles of the greatest importance in the education of the deaf—that she did have a method, and the results have shown that her method was a true one.

In a letter to Mrs. Macy about the same time, he says:

They are of the greatest value and importance. These letters . . . will become a standard, the principles that guided you in the early education of Helen are of the greatest importance to all teachers.

Dr. Bell's interest in the deaf did not begin with his own life. The science of speech had long been studied in the Bell family. Dr. Bell's grandfather was the inventor of a device to overcome stammering, and his father, Mr. Melville Bell, whom I used often to see when I visited the Bells in Washington, perfected a system of visible speech as a means of teaching the deaf which Dr. Bell considered more important than his invention of the telephone, though, as Mr. Melville Bell is reported to have said, "There was not so much money in it." To learn speech by means of it demands more patience than our western countries have, but it has been found serviceable in the Orient, and his classification of speech sounds is the basis of the pronunciation system in the Oxford Dictionary which has just been completed.

The devotion of Dr. Bell to his father was beautiful. How like they were, and how different! Melville Bell was the more reposeful and domestic. His tastes were simple, and did not change when wealth came to his son. He continued to live in the same little house in the same contented and frugal manner. His breakfast, though he had been many years away from Scotland, still consisted of oatmeal porridge, which he ate in Scotch fashion, dipping the spoon of hot porridge into the bowl of cold milk.

If anything kept Dr. Bell from visiting his father for a day or two, he would say, "Come, I must see my father. A chat with him is just the tonic I need."

In Professor Bell's charming little cottage at Colonial Beach at the point where the Potomac meets the sea I used often to see these two noble men sitting on the porch for hours without speaking a word, smoking peacefully and watching the steamers and boats pass along the river on their errands of service. Sometimes an unusual bird note would attract their attention, and the son would ask, "How would you record that, father?" Then the resources of the visible speech system would be tested out, and the two men would become absorbed in phonetics, unmindful of everything about them. Every note was analyzed and visibly recorded. Occasionally a twitter presented difficulties which took hours to solve.

Both men had an intense desire to remedy every defect of enunciation, and I have been told that it was a joy to listen to their speech. My teacher often spoke of it, and Mr. Watson, Dr. Bell's assistant in the invention of the telephone, says, in his book, *Exploring Life,* "His clear, crisp articulation delighted me, and made other men's speech seem uncouth." Both had at various periods been teachers of elocution, and both loved to recite.

Dr. Bell was exceedingly tender to his mother, who was quite deaf when I knew her. I recall a spring afternoon when Dr. Bell took Miss Sullivan and me for a drive in the country. We gathered quantities of honeysuckle, pink and white dogwood, and wild azaleas. On our way back we stopped to give them to Mrs. Melville Bell. Dr. Bell said, "Let us go in by the porch door and surprise them." On the steps he paused and spelled into my hand, "Hush! They are both asleep." We tiptoed about, arranging the flowers. It was a picture never to be forgotten —those two dear people seated in armchairs, Mrs. Bell's white head bowed on her breast, Mr. Bell's head thrown back on the chair, his beard and curly hair framing his ruddy face like a statue of Zeus. We left them undisturbed with the flowers and their dreams.

I was always glad to visit Dr. Bell's family in Washington or at their summer home in Cape Breton. I admired Mrs. Bell for the courage and perseverance with which she conquered her handicap of deafness. She was a wonderful lip reader, and certainly she needed patience, skill, and humour to read the lips of the countless visitors who came to the house. She never spelled on her fingers because she believed that this system of communication isolated the deaf from normal people. She loved beautiful lace and used to hold a filmy web in her hands and show me how to trace the woven flowers and leaves, the saucy Cupids, the silken winding streams, and the lacy criss-cross of fairy paths bordered with aërial boughs. The two small daughters, Elsie and Daisy, were always ready to play with me, and Daisy tried to put all the bright things she heard into my hand so I could laugh with her.

There were often distinguished gatherings when I was introduced to learned scientists—Professor Langley, Professor Newcomb, Major Powell, and others. Dr. Bell used to spell what they said to me. He always assumed that anyone could understand anything. He would explain to me the laws of physics or some principle of magnetism; but no matter how abstruse his discourse might be, or how little of it I understood, I loved to listen to him.

He was one of those exceptional mortals who can never be in a room two minutes before the whole talk converges in their direction. People chose to listen to him instead of talking. He had an extraordinary gift of presenting difficult problems in a simple and vivid manner, a gift which, in my experience, is one of the rarest possessed by human beings. Professor Langley did not have it in the slightest degree.

Dr. Bell was never dogmatic in his conversation. He was, I think, the only person I ever knew who could look at a subject from a point of view entirely different from his own with genuine interest and enthusiasm. When it was presented to him he would say, "Perhaps you are right. Let us see."

His gifts as an orator are not known to the public in general because he chose to exercise them in behalf of an obscure group, living in silence, in whom the public interest is not what it should be. But I know what eloquent speech is. I have stood beside Dr. Bell on the platform and felt speech coming from his lips, and eloquence in his voice, his attitude, his gestures all at once. Never have I longed more intensely for natural speech than on these occasions. After he had talked awhile he would touch my arm, I would rise and place my hand on his lips to show the audience how I could read what he was saying. I wish words could portray him as I saw him in those exalted moods—the majesty of his presence, the noble and spirited poise and action of his head, the strong features partly masked by a beautiful beard that rippled and curled beneath my fingers, the inspired expression which came into his face when he was deeply moved. His splendid head is lifted, his nostrils dilate, and his gestures are large, harmonious movements of the body, like his thoughts. No one can resist so much energy, such power.

All his life Dr. Bell earnestly advocated the oral method of instruction for the deaf. Eloquently he pointed out the folly of developing a deaf variety of the human race, and showed the economic, moral, and social advantages that would result from teaching them in the public schools with normal children. He regarded the sign system as a barrier to the acquisition of language and insistently urged its abolition. He deplored the segregation and intermarriage of deaf mutes, and felt that so long as their only way of communication was through signs and the manual alphabet, they would be isolated from society and very few of them would ever rise to the position of the average intelligent man or woman.

Yet the manual alphabet and the sign system have zealous defenders. They are both easier to acquire, but the ultimate results are not comparable to those of the oral system by means of which the pupil is taught to read the lips and answer in his own voice. In my case there was no choice: my additional handicap of blindness made the use of the manual alphabet essential. Later I learned to read the lips, but I think my education would have been greatly retarded if I had begun with the lip reading in the first place.

Every teacher of the deaf, no matter what system he advocates, has been influenced by Dr. Bell. He broadcast his ideas in the truest scientific spirit, with no ambitious aim. For a number of years he maintained at his own expense an experimental school in Washington where practical work could be carried on in finding better ways of teaching very young deaf children. He helped Dr. Fay, of Gallaudet College, collect statistics concerning the deaf, and it was at his suggestion that the American Association for Promoting the Teaching of Speech to the Deaf was organized in 1890. He contributed twenty-five thousand dollars towards its work and was tireless in devoting his energy to placing its cause before the public. With the money which was given him as the

Volta prize for his invention of the telephone he established the Volta bureau in Washington for the dissemination of information regarding the deaf. He strove unceasingly to make it possible for every child without hearing to acquire speech.

You who see and hear may not realize that the teaching of speech to the deaf is one of the divinest miracles of the Nineteenth Century. Perhaps it is impossible for one who sees and hears to realize what it means to be both deaf and dumb. Ours is not the stillness which soothes the weary senses; it is an inhuman silence which severs and estranges. It is a silence not to be broken by a word of greeting, or the song of birds, or the sigh of a breeze. It is a silence which isolates cruelly, completely. Two hundred years ago there was not a ray of hope for us. In an indifferent world not one voice was lifted in our behalf. Yet hearing is the deepest, most humanizing, philosophical sense man possesses and lonely ones all over the world, because of Dr. Bell's efforts, have been brought into the pleasant social ways of mankind.

Dr. Bell was a young son of an old country, a self-reliant Scot, but so long did he live among us he seems our own. His life was singularly free from harassments both of temperament and circumstances. No allowance was ever needed for the eccentricity or waywardness of genius. His nature was too fine to breed rivalries or tolerate animosities. I have never met anyone who knew Dr. Bell personally who did not feel that he had made a lasting impression upon his or her life; indeed, his nature was so rich in sympathy that it is difficult to speak of him in terms which will not seem exaggerated.

"Life is extraordinarily interesting!" he used to say, especially when we spoke of the telephone. "Things happen, but they are not the things we thought would happen. We can see clearly enough to the turn of the road, but beyond that we do not know what surprises may be in store for us." He told us how Mrs. Bell, who was not at that time his wife but his pupil, persuaded him to go to the Centennial Exposition in Philadelphia to exhibit the telephone. The time was set for a Sunday afternoon, but when the hour arrived, it was hot, the judges were tired, and it looked as if there would be no demonstration. "But"—Dr. Bell would smile his refulgent smile— "but the unexpected may happen at Philadelphia as anywhere else. It happened just as I had made up my mind to leave the Exposition. At that moment Dom Pedro, the Emperor of Brazil, appeared, and recognizing me as the man he had talked to in Boston about methods of teaching the deaf (he was interested in establishing schools for the deaf in Brazil and was investigating the various methods of teaching them in the United States), he came towards me, holding out his hand. Observing my apparatus, he asked me what it was. I told him about it, and that I had expected to give an exhibition of it that afternoon. 'Well, why not!' the Emperor exclaimed, 'I should like to hear it.' " A wire was strung across the room. Dr. Bell took the transmitter and told Dom Pedro to hold the receiver close to his ear. "My God, it talks!" he cried. Then Lord Kelvin took the receiver. "Yes, it speaks," he said. The judges took turns in listening, and the exhibition lasted until ten o'clock that night. The instrument was the centre of interest during the remainder of the Exposition. The commercial development of the telephone dated from that day.

It was in 1892 when the invention was being contested in the courts of Boston that I first became aware of the telephone. We saw a great deal of Dr. Bell in those days. We were staying at Chelsea with a friend of ours, Mrs. Pratt, who had assisted him in some of his investigations relating to the deaf. When the session at court was over he would come for us or we would go to the Bellevue Hotel and wait for him. It was a strenuous time for him, and we felt it incumbent upon us to get him to relax as much as possible. He was very fond of the theatre and of music, and it was never difficult to persuade him to take us to a play or a concert.

We took many drives in and around Boston, which

is one of the most delightfully situated of cities, in the heart of a beautiful, accessible country. Often we went to the shore, and if we could find an old sailor to take us out in his boat, Dr. Bell was the happiest man alive.

Naturally, our talk turned frequently to scientific matters. In his youth, Dr. Bell was profoundly interested in the laying of the Atlantic cable. He told me vividly how it was laid after many failures and discouragements, and how many lives were lost before it was finally completed, in 1866. I was twelve years old, and that story of heroism and the wonder of the human imagination, as told by Dr. Bell, thrilled me as a fairy tale thrills other children. I still have an impression of words fluttering along wires far, far down under the ocean, East and West, annihilating time.

It was Dr. Bell who first spelled into my hand the name Charles Darwin. "What did he do?" I asked. "He wrought the miracle of the Nineteenth Century," replied Dr. Bell.

Then he told me about *The Origin of Species,* and how it had widened the horizon of human vision and understanding. That achievement also became an integral part of my mental equipment.

He showed us the building where the telephone was born and spoke appreciatively of his assistant, Mr. Thomas A. Watson, without whom, he said, he doubted if the invention would ever have been carried through. It was on March 10, 1876, that Mr. Watson, who was working in another room, was startled to hear Dr. Bell's voice say, "Mr. Watson, come here, I want you." That was the first audible telephone talk. It was as casual and commonplace as any of the millions of conversations that go on every day over the telephone. I said I wished the first sentence transmitted had had more significance. Dr. Bell answered, "Helen, time has shown that the chief use of the telephone is the repetition of that original message. The transmission of the words, 'Come here, I want you,' to the millions of workaday Watsons is the highest service the telephone renders a busy world."

"Had you been hopeful of the success of the instrument before that day?" I asked.

"Oh, yes," said Dr. Bell, "There had been words spoken prior to that message. Nevertheless, I was filled with astonishment when I learned that Mr. Watson had heard my voice."

Dr. Bell had no telephone in his own study, and he used to say somewhat ruefully, "What should be done to the man who has destroyed the privacy of the home?" And I have heard him say, when people spoke admiringly of the invention, "Yes, but I doubt if it will ever carry human speech as far as Shakespeare and Homer have carried it."

One evening when we were waiting for a street car beside a telephone pole, Dr. Bell placed my hand on the weather-smoothed wood and said, "Feel. What do the vibrations mean to you—anything?" I had never put my hand on a pole before.

"Does it hum like that all the time?"

"Yes, all night. That even singing never stops; for it is singing the story of life, and life never stops." He then described how the wires were strung and insulated, and explained many other details that I suppose everyone except a blind girl would know about, and he said, "Those copper wires up there are carrying the news of birth and death, war and finance, failure and success from station to station around the world. Listen! I fancy I hear laughter, tears, love's vows broken and mended."

This reminds me of another time when we were walking in the rain and he asked me if I had ever felt a tree when it was raining. He put my hand on the trunk of a small oak, and I was astonished to feel a delicate murmur—a silvery whisper, as if the leaves were telling each other a lot of little things. I have often touched trees since when raindrops were descending in little pearly columns from every twig and leaf. They feel like elves laughing.

On these walks and drives Dr. Bell's mind spread out restfully. Snatches of poetry, anecdotes, reminiscences of Scotland, descriptions of Japan, which he had visited some years earlier, flowed through his skillful fingers into my hand. He loved Portia's speech on the quality of mercy, and he once told me that his favourite quotation was Dryden's paraphrase of Horace:

Happy the man, and happy he alone,
  He, who can call to-day his own;
  He who, secure within, can say,
To-morrow, do thy worst, for I have lived to-day;
  Be fair or foul or rain or shine,
The joys I have possessed, in spite of Fate, are mine
  Not heaven itself upon the past has power,
But what has been, has been, and I have had my hour.

The period of litigation lasted a number of years— eight, I believe. The case was finally decided in Dr. Bell's favour by the Supreme Court of the United States. When Dr. Bell died it was estimated that there were twelve million telephones in use in the world, and it has been said that the basic patent which he received on his twenty-ninth birthday was the most valuable patent ever issued.

I saw Dr. Bell soon after the New York to San Francisco telephone line was opened. Telephone lines had by that time connected nearly all parts of the country. Mr. Watson was in San Francisco and Dr. Bell was in New York. The same sentence was repeated:

"Mr. Watson, come here, I want you."

"He heard me," said Dr. Bell, "but he did not come immediately. It is not long now, however, before men will be able to appear from across the continent within a few hours after they are summoned." He said that the transatlantic flight would some time be made in one day. I thought of him when Lindbergh flew across in thirty-three and a half hours.

Of course Dr. Bell experienced the annoyance as well as the happiness of having done something that his fellow creatures appreciated. Wherever he went he was approached by people who wished to shake hands with the man who made the telephone. Once he spelled to me, "One would think I had never done anything worth while but the telephone. That is because it is a money-making invention. It is a pity so many people make money the criterion of success. I wish my experiments had resulted in enabling the deaf to speak with less difficulty. That would have made me truly happy."

Dr. Bell was interested in many other inventions besides the telephone—the gramophone, the photophone, and an induction balance. He invented a telephone probe which was used to locate the bullet that killed President Garfield.

When he wished to work on one of his theories or inventions he would retire to Beinn Breagh, Cape Breton, or to his retreat near Washington, or to a cocoanut grove in Florida—the home of his daughter, Mrs. Fairchild. "I must have perfect quiet," he would say, "but that is no easy thing to secure in this busy world." Once he remarked, "The telephone is the man Friday's footprint on the sands of life. Wherever we go, it reminds us that no man can live wholly alone."

When our paths lay in different courses I used to write to him now and then. Knowing how absorbed he was in his work I never expected an answer, but I never wrote without receiving one. I did not expect him to read my books, but he always did, and wrote to me about them in such a way that I knew he considered me a capable human being and not some sort of pitiable human ghost groping its way through the world.

"You must not," he wrote after he had read *The World I Live In,* "put me among those who think that nothing you have to say about affairs of the universe would be interesting. I must confess I should like to know what you think of the tariff, the conservation of our natural resources, or the conflicts which revolve about the name of Dreyfus. I would also like to know how you would propose to reform the educational system of the world. I want to see you come out of yourself and write of the great things outside. The glimpse you give us into your own world is so fascinating and interesting that I would like to hear what you have to say of things outside." He afterwards greeted my *Song of the Stone Wall* with delight because "it is another achievement demonstrating that you are not exiled from our world of beauty and music." Is it any wonder that I loved him?

It was a part of his joyous nature that he loved to give and receive surprises. I remember a letter I had one morning shortly before my teacher was married. On the outside was written "A Secret for Helen Keller" and under that, "I don't want Miss Sullivan or Mr. Macy to read this note. Let someone else read it to Helen." I took the letter to Lenore, who was staying with us at the time, and she read me that Dr. Bell had sent a check for me to get my teacher a wedding present. "The trouble is," he said, "I don't know what would please her and I want someone to help me. Why not you? I enclose a check payable to your order and would be very much pleased if you could spend the money for me on a wedding present for Miss Sullivan and not tell her anything about it until you give her the present for me."

We went off to Boston that very day and examined the beautiful things gathered into the shops from all over the world. Finally we selected a clock which struck the hours with a soft chime. I had not spent all the money. So we went back the next day, and I chose a silver coffee urn. Dr. Bell was much amused when I wrote him about the two gifts. He said he could see that I had some of the "canny Scot" in me.

It is strange what things crowd into the mind as one writes about a beloved friend. Little incidents that I have not thought of in years come back to me now as if they had been written on the pages of my mind in secret ink. I remember that first visit of ours to Washington on our way to the Perkins Institution, after my teacher had been with me a year, but curiously enough it is not so much Dr. Bell who stands out in my mind as it is President Cleveland. I was a demonstrative, affectionate child, and my first thought was to kiss the President. Not understanding my intentions, or perhaps understanding them only too well, he pushed me away. I am ashamed to confess that I was never able to see much good in Cleveland's administration after that.

Dr. Bell was very fond of animals and we used to go to visit the "zoo" together, not only in Washington but in other cities where we were attending meetings for the advancement of the deaf. Once when I was a little girl—I think it was on my fourteenth birthday—he gave me a cockatoo which I called Jonquil because of his glorious yellow crest. Jonquil was a beauty, but he was a menace armoured in lovely white and gold feathers. He used to perch on my foot as I read, rocking back and forth as I turned the pages. Every now and then he would hop to my shoulder and rub his head against my ear and face, sometimes putting his long, sharp, hooked bill in my mouth, sending ripples of terror down my spine. Then he would dart off, screeching fiendishly, to alight on the back of a dog or the head of a person. After a while my father tried to give him away, but his fame had spread so far that no one would take him. Finally, the owner of a saloon in Tuscumbia gave him shelter. I don't know what happened to him after the passage of the eighteenth amendment.

Dr. Bell was always eager for adventure—night or day, no matter what the weather was like. "Hoy, Ahoy!" was his call for his friends and associates, and one they were always delighted to answer.

I remember an evening in Pittsburgh when we drove along the embankment of the river to see the spectacular display of fireworks when the furnaces made their periodic runs. I shall never forget how excited Dr. Bell was when the show began. We were chatting about the enormous industries which make Pittsburgh one of the great cities of the world when Dr. Bell jumped up exclaiming, "The river is on fire!" Indeed, the whole world appeared to be on fire. Out of the big, red, gaping mouths of the furnaces leaped immense streams of flame which seemed to fan the very clouds into billows of fire. Around the huge shaft-necks of the furnaces they flung rosy arms. As the columns ascended, the stars blushed as if a god had kissed them. The shoulder of the moon turned pink as she threw a scarlet scarf over her head. More and more curtains of scarlet, crimson, and red gold unroll, cloud mixes with cloud, fold tangles in fold, until the sky is an undulating sea of flame. Miss Sullivan and Dr. Bell spell into my hands, again and again erasing their words, searching their memories for phrases and similes to describe the scene. "A cataract of pink steam!" one would say, "it bubbles and drips through the air." "There goes a crimson geyser licking up the night!" said the other. "A molten rod of hot iron ducks into a black hole like a rabbit." "There are silvery grottoes and caves of ebony and abysses of blackness beyond the river bank." "The belching furnace must be part of the central fires of earth." Every few seconds there was a flare of fiery cinders resembling "Greek Fire." Between the red flames and the black wall of the furnace moved the shadowy forms of men, the slaves of the insatiable beast which roared into darkness and spread flamingo wings upon the night.

When my teacher and I visited the Bells at their Beinn Breagh home near Baddeck the summer after my first year at Radcliffe Dr. Bell's leading scientific interest was aëronautics. He had built a huge tetra-bedral kite with which he hoped to establish some new principles in the art of flying. The kite never achieved the success he thought it would; but we had no end of fun with it. He appointed me his chief adviser, and would never loose a kite until I had examined the cables and imparted the information that they could stand the strain. Once, while I was holding the cable, someone released the kite from its moorings, and I was nearly carried out to sea hanging to it. Dr. Bell insisted that I should wear a helmet and a waterproof bathing suit, just as he did, so that we might be ready for any emergency. "You can never know what perverse idea a kite may get into its head," he would spell to me seriously. "We must always be ready to outwit it." Once in a while he would pause to report, "We are getting on swimmingly." This was not infrequently true; for a recalcitrant breeze would catch us, and we would find ourselves swimming, not in the air, but in the "Bras d'Or." I do not think I ever saw Dr. Bell discouraged. He was always ready to jest about his experimental misfortunes.

It was about this time that Professor Langley visited Beinn Breagh. Our talk was chiefly about aviation. My teacher and I would accompany them in an observation boat, and hour after hour either Miss Sullivan or Dr. Bell spelled to me what they were talking about. I was interested because they were though I did not understand much of what they discussed. They were terribly scientific and mathematical. But I have had occasion to observe that men who are doing important things like to talk about their problems to a sympathetic listener even though he is quite ignorant of the subject.

One of the playthings at Beinn Breagh was an old houseboat, permanently anchored on a strip of shore about a mile from Dr. Bell's house. It had one foot in the "Bras d'Or," on the starboard side, and on the port side it looked into a fresh pond. There were some beds and plenty of blankets in the cabin, and food was kept in the locker, so that anyone who wished to could sleep there.

One time there were a number of guests staying at the house, and from their talk one might have thought they were holding a scientific congress. Miss Sullivan, Daisy, Elsie, and I decided to spend the night on the boat. It was a gloriously clear summer evening, and we were as eager for adventure as young dogs for the chase. We started early, hurrying down the path that led along the shore to the boat, so that we could eat our supper on deck at sunset while the "Bras d'Or" lay in golden splendour. What an experience it was to be part of such an enchanting scene with two beautiful girls, who thoroughly enjoyed the fun. Daisy kept spelling to me the exquisite tints of sky and water until it was dark, and a profound silence descended upon us—a silence only broken by the lapping of the waves, which gave a tongue to solitude.

When the moon rose, trembling with excitement, we got down into the lake by means of a rope ladder. There we were, we four alone with ourselves and perfection of water and moonlight! The air was quite cold; but the water was deliciously warm, and our joy knew no bounds. Then what a scramble we had up the ladder to see who could get to her blankets first! We were up at dawn. As we came out on the deck a storm of gulls burst from the island, veering and wheeling above the lake, in whose golden arms day, like a mermaid, was combing out the bright strands of her hair. At that hour there were great flocks of gulls shaking the sleep out of their wings before diving into the water for their breakfast. It was a magnificent picture—worth lying awake to see, and we had slept lightly, so as not to miss anything. Many years have passed since, but that happy night in the old houseboat is as bright in my remembrance as the stars which filled the sky.

Another time when we were at the houseboat, Dr. Bell and Professor Newcomb, the astronomer, came down and sat with us on deck. It was one of those magical evenings of the north when the moon weaves a bright chain of light across the waters, and the "queen of propitious stars" appears amid falling dew. The bosom of the lake rose and fell softly, like the breast of a sleeping infant, and the winds wandered to us with fragrant sighs from mountain and meadow. All the world seemed to be left to the stars and to us.

It was one of the evenings that smile upon fancy, friendship, and science, and high hopes. Professor Newcomb talked about eclipses and comets, the Leonidas meteor showers which I believe occur only once in a century, and astronomical calculations, while Dr. Bell interpreted all he said to me. Once he paused and said, "Helen, do you know that when a star is shattered in the heavens, its light travels a million years or so before it reaches our earth?" I had never had the sense of being utterly lost in the vastitudes of the universe which I experienced that night as I listened to the mysteries of sidereal phenomena. I thought of Blanco White's lines,

Who could have thought such darkness lay concealed
Within thy beams, O sun? Or who could find
That while leaf and fly and insect stood revealed,
To such countless orbs thou madest us blind?

It has ever been thus with me—that the wonderfulness of life and creation grows with each day I live.

The last evening of my visit at Beinn Breagh, Dr. Bell and I were together on the piazza, while Mrs. Bell was showing some pictures of Cape Breton to Miss Sullivan in the library. Dr. Bell was in a dreamy mood, and spelled his thoughts into my hand, half poetry, half philosophy. He was weary after a long day of experiments; but his mind would not rest, or rather, it found sweet rest in the poets he had read as a young man. He recited favourite passages from "In Memoriam," "The Tempest," and "Julius Cæsar," and I remember with what earnestness he repeated, "There is a tide in the affairs of men," and ended by saying, "Helen, I do not know if, as those lines teach, we are masters of our fate. I doubt it. The more I look at the world, the more it puzzles me. We are forever moving towards the unexpected."

"When I was a young man," he continued, "I loved music passionately, and I wanted to become a musician. But fate willed otherwise. Ill health brought me to America. Then I became absorbed in experiments with an instrument that developed into the telephone, and now here I am giving my days and nights to aëronautics. And all the time you know that my chief interest is the education of the deaf. No, Helen, I have not been master of my fate—not in the sense of choosing my work." He paused and went on, "Your limitations have placed you before the world in an unusual way. You have learned to speak, and I believe you are meant to break down the barriers which separate the deaf from mankind.

There are unique tasks waiting for you, a unique woman."

I told him my teacher and I intended to live in some retreat "from public haunt exempt" when I graduated from college, and then I hoped to write.

"It is not you, but circumstances, that will determine your work," he said. "We are only instruments of the powers that control the universe. Remember, Helen, do not confine yourself to any particular kind of self-expression. Write, speak, study, do whatever you possibly can. The more you accomplish, the more you will help the deaf everywhere."

After a long pause he said, "It seems to me, Helen, a day must come when love, which is more than friendship, will knock at the door of your heart and demand to be let in."

"What made you think of that?" I asked.

"Oh, I often think of your future. To me you are a sweet, desirable young girl, and it is natural to think about love and happiness when we are young."

"I do think of love sometimes," I admitted; "but it is like a beautiful flower which I may not touch, but whose fragrance makes the garden a place of delight just the same."

He sat silent for a minute or two, thought-troubled, I fancied. Then his dear fingers touched my hand again like a tender breath, and he said, "Do not think that because you cannot see or hear, you are debarred from the supreme happiness of woman. Heredity is not involved in your case, as it is in so many others."

"Oh, but I am happy, very happy!" I told him. "I have my teacher and my mother and you, and all kinds of interesting things to do. I really don't care a bit about being married."

"I know," he answered, "but life does strange things to us. You may not always have your mother, and in the nature of things Miss Sullivan will marry, and there may be a barren stretch in your life when you will be very lonely."

"I can't imagine a man wanting to marry me," I said. "I should think it would seem like marrying a statue."

"You are very young," he replied, patting my hand tenderly, "and it's natural that you shouldn't take what I have said seriously now: but I have long wanted to tell you how I felt about your marrying, should you ever wish to. If a good man should desire to make you his wife, don't let anyone persuade you to forego that happiness because of your peculiar handicap."

I was glad when Mrs. Bell and Miss Sullivan joined us, and the talk became less personal.

Years later Dr. Bell referred to that conversation. Miss Sullivan and I had gone to Washington to tell him of her intention to marry John Macy. He said playfully, "I told you, Helen, she would marry. Are you going to take my advice now and build your own nest?"

"No," I answered, "I feel less inclined than ever to embark upon the great adventure. I have fully made up my mind that a man and a woman must be equally equipped to weather successfully the vicissitudes of life. It would be a severe handicap to any man to saddle upon him the dead weight of my infirmities. I know I have nothing to give a man that would make up for such an unnatural burden." And I repeated Elizabeth Barrett Browning's sonnet:

> What can I give thee back, O liberal
> And princely giver, who hast brought the gold
> And purple of thine heart, unstained, untold,
> And laid them on the outside of the wall
> For such as I to take or leave withal,
> In unexpected largess? Am I cold,
> Ungrateful, that for these most manifold
> High gifts, I render nothing back at all?
> Not so; not cold—but very poor instead.

"You will change you mind some day, young woman, if the right man comes a-wooing." And I almost did—but that is another story.

The last time I saw Dr. Bell he had just returned

from a visit to Edinburgh. For the first time he seemed melancholy. This was in, I think, 1920. He said he had found himself a stranger in a strange land, and that it seemed good to get back to America. The War had left its cruel scar upon his spirit. I felt the lines of sorrow graven upon his noble features; but I thought a smile had fallen asleep in them. He told us he was going to work on hydroplanes the remainder of his life. He prophesied that in less than ten years there would be an air service between New York and London. He said there would be hangars on the tops of tall buildings, and people would use their own planes as they do automobiles now. He thought freight could be carried by air cheaper than by rail or steamships. He also predicted that the next war would be fought in the air, and that submarines would be more important than battleships or cruisers.

Dr. Bell also foresaw a day when methods would be discovered by engineers to cool off the tropics and bring the heated air into cold lands which need it. He told me that beneath the warm surface of the tropic seas flow currents of icy cold water from the Arctic and Antarctic regions, and he said that in some way these streams would be brought up to the surface, thus changing the climate of hot countries and rendering them pleasanter to live and work in. His wonderful prophecies set my heart beating faster; but little did I dream that in six years I should read of French engineers laying plans to capture the ocean as an ally against climates inimical to man!

We felt very sad when we said good-bye to him. I had a presentiment that I should not see him again in this life.

He died at his summer home on August 3, 1922. He was buried at sunset on the crest of Cape Beinn Breagh Mountain, a spot chosen by himself. Once he had pointed out that spot to me, and quoted Browning's verse:

"Here is the place, Helen, where I shall sleep the last sleep"—

> Where meteors shoot, clouds form,
> Lightnings are loosened,
> Stars come and go!

Sunset was chosen as the time for burial because at that moment the sun enfolds the lakes in its arms of gold, which is what the name "Bras d'Or" means.

If there were no life beyond this earth-life, some people I have known would gain immortality by the nobility of our memory of them. With every friend I love who has been taken into the brown bosom of the earth a part of me has been buried there; but their contribution of happiness, strength, and understanding to my being remains to sustain me in an altered world. Although life has never seemed the same since we read in the paper that Alexander Graham Bell was dead, yet the mist of tears is resplendent with the part of himself that lives on in me.

Chapter IX

I CAPITULATE

AFTER the lecture in Washington at which Dr. Bell introduced me I spoke in a few other places, including Richmond, Virginia, before I returned to Wrentham. My teacher and I were tired and discouraged, and very uncertain about the future.

Our financial difficulties increased. At the time of my teacher's marriage, Mr. Rogers had cut his annuity in half. I had thought that I would be able to make enough with my pen to supply the deficiency, but there were too many interruptions and I was annoyed at having always to write about myself. The editors of the magazines said, "Do not meddle with those matters not related to your personal experience." I found myself utterly confined to one subject—myself, and it was not long before I had exhausted it.

Financial difficulties have seemed nearly always an integral part of our lives, and from time to time many people have tried to help us extricate ourselves from them. I do not know just when Mr. Carnegie began to take an interest in my affairs, but late in 1910, when he learned through our friend,

Lucy Derby Fuller, of our difficulties, he came to my aid with characteristic promptness and generosity. A few days after she talked with him he wrote her that he had arranged an annuity for me.

It had been done without my knowledge or consent, and I declined as gracefully as I could. I was young and proud, and still felt that I could succeed alone. Mr. Carnegie suggested that I give the matter further consideration, and assured me that the annuity was mine whenever I wanted it. "Mrs. Carnegie and I gladly go on probation," he said. So the matter rested for about two years.

In the spring of 1913, when my teacher and I were in New York, we called on the Carnegies at their invitation. I shall never forget how kind they were. They made me feel that they wanted to help me. Mrs. Carnegie was very sweet, and I liked Mr. Carnegie. Their daughter, Margaret, a lovely young girl of sixteen, came into the library while we were talking. "Margaret is the philanthropist here," Mr. Carnegie said, as she put her hand in mine. "She is the good fairy that whispers in my ear that I must make somebody happy."

Over a cup of tea we conversed on many subjects. Mr. Carnegie asked me if I still refused his annuity. I said, "Yes, I haven't been beaten yet." He said he understood my attitude and sympathized with it. But he called my attention to the fact that fate had added my burden to that of those who were living with me, and that I must think of them as well as of myself. It had weighed heavily upon my heart, but no one with great power of giving had ever reminded me that I was responsible for the welfare of those I loved. He told me again that the annuity was mine whenever I would take it, and asked me if it was true that I had become a Socialist.

When I admitted that it was true he found many disparaging things to say about Socialists, and even threatened to take me across his knees and spank me if I did not come to my senses.

"But a great man like you should be consistent," I urged. "You believe in the brotherhood of man, in peace among nations, in education for everybody. All those are Socialist beliefs." I promised to send him my book, *Out of the Dark,* in which I tell how I became a Socialist.

He asked me what I lectured about. I said happiness. "A good subject," was his comment. "There's plenty of happiness in the world, if people would only look for it." He then asked me how much the people who engaged me sold the tickets for. I told him a dollar and a dollar and a half. "Too much, far too much," he said, "you would make more money if you charged fifty cents—not more than seventy-five cents as a limit."

Mr. Carnegie asked why I didn't write more. I

told him I did not find writing easy, that I was very slow, and there were few subjects editors thought me capable of writing about. He said he didn't think writing was easy for anyone, except in rare moments of inspiration. "Labour must go into anything that's worth while. Burns is said to have dashed off 'A man's a man for a' that' in a jiffy, but I don't believe it. Anyhow, years of thinking on injustice preceded the miracle. I tell you, Burns's life is in that poem."

He showed us a portrait of Gladstone, whom he admired tremendously. "You know, the great English statesman was a Scot." I said I did not know it. Mr. Carnegie seemed surprised that I knew so little about Gladstone. I said he was the sort of a man that bored me, and that I couldn't be enthusiastic about him, even when he acted nobly. "Perhaps his being a Scot has something to do with your admiration," I remarked. "May be," he said. "Blood is thicker than water, and it's much thicker in Scotland than anywhere else. I tell thee, Scoffer, he was one of the greatest men of our age. He was seventy when I saw him, and Milton's lines came into my mind:

> "With grave
> Aspect he rose, and in his rising seemed
> A pillar of state; deep on his front engraven
> Deliberation sat, and public care;
> And princely counsel in his face yet shone,
> Majestic, though in ruin."

Mr. Carnegie was also a great admirer of Queen Victoria. I told him that if he had said to her all the flattering things he was saying about her, she would have given him two garters—Disraeli's and her own. He gave a very animated description of a birthday party at Windsor when Victoria was seventy-something. The Queen was presented with a silver ornament encrusted with birds and flowers. I cannot remember whether it was Mr. Carnegie's gift, or not. Anyway, Her Majesty surprised everyone at the table by rising and thanking her friends very charmingly.

Mr. Carnegie was fond of Gray's "Elegy," and told me he had visited Gray's tomb. He quoted the inscription on the grave of the poet's mother:

DOROTHY GRAY,
the careful, tender mother of many children, one of whom alone had the misfortune to survive her.

He asked me if I knew the words that Carlyle had graven on his wife's tomb. I did not; but I read them from Mr. Carnegie's lips, "And he feels that the light of his life has gone out." Mr. Carnegie was a walking anthology of verse. He constantly quoted Browning, Shakespeare, Burns, Wordsworth, and Walter Scott. One of his favourite quotations, and one which he recited with fine feeling, was Portia's speech beginning "The Quality of mercy is not strained." These lines were often on Dr. Bell's lips also.

Mr. Carnegie was quite an actor, too. With fire in his eye he would declaim,

> Know this, the man who injured Warwick
> Never passed uninjured yet.

On one occasion—I think it was the first afternoon I was with him—he led me around his library and study, and showed me the innumerable jewel boxes containing the thanks of towns and cities which had accepted his gift of a library. He called my attention to the exquisite workmanship of these boxes; one of them, I remember, had his name set in jewels. A letter he was especially proud of was from King Edward, expressing appreciation of something Mr. Carnegie had given, I cannot recall what it was.

He told me about walking through southern England when he was a boy with a knapsack on his back. He enjoyed the trip so much that he promised himself that if his ship ever came in he would drive a party of his friends from Brighton to Inverness. The idea took possession of him. It became his castle in Spain, and in the eighties he was able to attain it.

He said his idea of wealth when he was a young man was fifteen hundred dollars a year—enough to live on and keep his parents comfortable in their old age. "But fate gave me thousands more than that.

The fickle goddess does that sometimes, and laughs in her sleeve."

I said, "Fate has been very good to you, Mr. Carnegie, in that your dream came true when you were young and full of the joy of life."

"That's it," he replied eagerly, "I'm the happiest mortal alive, only sometimes I can't believe it's true. You see, I never thought in my wildest flights of fancy that the dream would assume the princely proportions it has."

He said, "I spend a good deal of time in the garden. Out there I feel as if 'the air had blossomed into joy.' Can you tell me who said that?"

"It sounds like Shelley," I said.

"Wrong!" he triumphed. "It was Robert Ingersoll. He said when he saw the American flag in a foreign land, 'I felt the air had blossomed into joy.' Who told the southern Confederacy, 'There is not air enough upon the American continent to float two flags?' "

"Ingersoll," I shot back, without having the faintest idea who said it. Mr. Carnegie patted me saying, "You've got a head on your shoulders, I see."

Mr. Andrew Carnegie was an optimist. I thought I was one dyed-in-the-wool until I met him. "A pessimist has a poisoned tongue," he declared. "I would banish every one of them to Siberia if I had the power. Good cheer is worth money."

"Not very much," I teased him. "You told me my lecture on happiness was worth only fifty cents."

Some callers happened in while we were there. He introduced to me one gentleman as "one of the twelve men I have made millionaires," and then added, "Life is much more interesting and worth while since I left money-making to these fellows. I wouldn't have had any time for you in the old days, Helen. I have changed my views about many things since I have had time to think."

After our call on the Carnegies my teacher and I continued our lectures. Mrs. Macy was far from well. She was still convalescing from a major operation which she had undergone in the autumn. But we hoped we could keep things going by our own efforts, especially if I could write a few articles during the summer.

We both appreciated Mr. Carnegie's desire to assist me, and still more the insight and sympathy with which he understood our motives in declining his offer. Mrs. Carnegie was as tender as he, and I remember a letter which I had from her in December after our visit in which she says that she hopes I will let them prove their friendship for me.

The first of April brought me face to face with the necessity of surrender. We were in Maine filling a lecture engagement. When we reached Bath, the weather turned suddenly cold. The next morning my teacher awoke very ill. We were alone in a strange place. My helplessness terrified me. With the assistance of the manager of the hotel we got on the train and went home. A week later I wrote Mr. Carnegie telling him what had happened, and confessing my folly in not letting him assist me. The return mail brought a warm-hearted letter from him, enclosing a check which I was to get semi-annually. I will quote part of it here:

The fates are kind to us indeed—I thought that text of mine would reach your brain and penetrate your heart. "There are a few great souls who can rise to the height of allowing others to do for them what they would like to do for others." And so you have risen. I am happy indeed—one likes to have his words of wisdom appreciated. Remember Mrs. Carnegie and I are the two to be thankful, for it is beyond question more blessed to give than receive.

I cannot pretend that it was not humiliating to surrender, even to such a kind and gracious friend. Like Jude, I can say, "It was my poverty and not my will that consented to be beaten."

For some time the lack of money had been only a small part of our worry. Mr. Macy was considering leaving us. He had wearied of the struggle. He had many reasons for wishing to go. I can write about that tense period of suffering only in large terms. There is nothing more difficult, I think, than to reconstruct situations which have moved us deeply.

Time invariably disintegrates the substance of most experiences and reduces them to intellectual abstractions. Many of the poignant details elude any attempt to restate them. It is not merely the difficulty of recapturing emotions, it is almost equally difficult to define attitudes, or to describe their effects upon others. They are, as it were, in solution, or if they do crystallize, they appear different to the persons concerned. It seems to me, it is impossible to analyze honestly the subtle motives of those who have influenced our lives, because we cannot complete the creative process with the freshness of the situation clinging to it. Analysis is as destructive of emotion as of the flower which the botanist pulls to pieces. As I recall the Wrentham years, they appear to my imagination surrounded by an aura of feeling. Words, incidents, acts, stir in my memory, awakening complicated emotions, and many strings vibrate with joy and pain. I shall not try to resolve those experiences into their elements.

Chapter X

ON "THE OPEN ROAD"

DURING the autumn of 1913 we were for the first time constantly on the road. It was pleasant to find myself generally known, and people glad to come to hear me, but it was hard to accustom myself to the strangeness of public life. At home I had always been where I could breathe the woodland air. My life had been as it were "between the budding and the falling leaf," and I had felt along my veins the thrill of vine and blossom. Winter and spring had brought me wind-blown messages across marsh, brook, and stone-walled field. I had felt

> God's great freedom all around,
> And free life's song the only sound.

All such peaceful, expansive sensations cannot be enjoyed in the throbbing whirl of a train, the rattle of lurching taxis, or the confinement of hotels and lecture halls.

I have never been able to accustom myself to hotel life. The conventional atmosphere wearies me, and there is no garden where I can run out alone and sense the wings of glorious days passing by. At such times I am painfully aware of the lack of personal liberty which, next to idleness, is the hardest part of being blind.

When one sees and hears, one can watch the pageant of life from the city building or the rushing train. The features and colours of one landscape blend with those of another, so that there is a continuity of things visible and audible. A succession of faces, voices, noises, changes in the sky, carry on the story of life, and lessen the effect of loneliness and fatigue. But when I go from one place to another, I leave suddenly the surroundings that have become familiar to me through touch and daily association and I cannot readily orientate myself in a strange locality. I am conscious of the same kind of remoteness one senses out at sea, far from all signs of land; and on my first tours this feeling was quite oppressive. I missed the charm of the roads I had walked over—the ripples of the earth and billows of grass underfoot, the paths trod by men and horses and the ruts made by wheels, the dust from automobiles and other tangible signs of life. But after a while I learned to enjoy the rhythmic vibration of the train as it sped over long distances. In the swift, steady motion my body found rest, and my mind kept pace with the stretch of the horizon and the ever shifting clouds. I could not tell which interested me most, the excitement of departure from a city, or the rush over great plains and undulating country, or the arrival at the next lecture with hope of accomplishment in my heart. Everyone seemed eager to show us attention, and all along the road we were shown appreciation in ways which touched and pleased us, but we could not take part in the social functions that were arranged for us or even meet many of the people who called. It would have been too great a tax upon human strength.

Social functions have always been trying for me. I confess I never feel quite at ease at them. I know that nearly everybody has heard of me, and that people want to see me, just as we all want to see places and persons and objects we have heard a great deal about. I have been meeting and talking to strangers ever since I was eight years old, but even now I can seldom think of anything to say. The difficulty of presenting people to me through the medium of hand-spelling sometimes causes me embarrassment and confusion. But I feel certain that these functions must have a useful purpose which I cannot understand. Otherwise we should not tolerate the absurdity of shaking hands with hundreds of curious human creatures whom we have never seen, and shall in all probability never see again.

I do not know a more disturbing sensation than that of being ceremoniously ushered into the presence of a company of strangers who are also celebrities, especially if you have physical limitations which make you different. As a rule, when I am introduced to such people, they are excessively conscious of my limitations. When they try to talk to me, and find that their words have to be spelled into my hand, their tongues cleave to the roofs of their mouths and they become speechless. And I am quite as uncomfortable as they are. I know that I should have clever things to say which would tide over the embarrassing moment, but I cannot remember the bright casual remarks with which I intended to grace the occasion.

After several of these mortifying occasions, I decided to commit to memory every sprightly repartee I could find. But alas! my proud intentions were frustrated by the perversity of my memory. The brilliant remarks I thought of were never suited to the occasion. I realized that to be of any use my *bons mots* would have to be mentally card catalogued, and even if I went to this trouble, I wondered if I could get the right one quickly enough. No, there certainly would be horrible blank intervals when people would stare and wait for an answer that could not be found! I decided to cultivate the art of silence, a subterfuge by which the dull may achieve the semblance of wisdom.

Even now where people are gathered, I say little,

beyond explaining patiently that I am not Annette Kellermann, that I do not play the piano, and have not learned to sing. I assure them that I know day is not night and that it is no more necessary to have raised letters on the keys of my typewriter than for them to have the keys of their pianos lettered. I have become quite expert in simulating interest in absurdities that are told me about other blind people. Putting on my Job-like expression, I tell them blind people are like other people in the dark, that fire burns them, and cold chills them, and they like food when they are hungry, and drink when they are thirsty, that some of them like one lump of sugar in their tea, and others more.

We were always amused at the newspaper accounts of our appearance in a place. I was hailed as a princess and a prima donna and a priestess of light. I learned for the first time that I was born blind, deaf, and dumb, that I had educated myself, that I could distinguish colours, hear telephone messages, predict when it was going to rain, that I was never sad, never discouraged, never pessimistic, that I applied myself with celestial energy to being happy, that I could do anything that anybody with all his faculties could do. They said this was miraculous— and no wonder. We supplied the particulars when we were asked for them; but we never knew what became of the facts.

Our travels were a queer jumble of dull and exciting days.

I recall an amusing ride we had in the state of Washington on a sort of interurban car, which we called the "Galloping Goose" on account of its peculiar motion. It resembled a goose in other ways, too. It stopped when there was no reason for stopping; but we did not mind, as it was a lovely day in spring, and we got out and picked flowers by the side of the track.

Another time, when we were criss-crossing northern New York, it was necessary for us, in order to fill our engagement, to take an early morning train that collected milk. It was a pleasant experience. We literally stopped at every barn on the way. The milk was always waiting for us in tall, bright cans, and cheerful young farmers called out greetings to the trainmen. The morning was beautiful. It was a joy to have the country described to me. The spring foliage was exquisite, and I could picture the cows standing knee-deep in the luscious young grass which I could smell. They said the apple trees in bloom were a vision of loveliness.

Once we happened to be on the last train going through the flooded districts of Texas and Louisiana. I could feel the water beating against the coaches, and every now and then there was a jolt when we hit a floating log or a dead cow or horse. We caught an uprooted tree on the iron nose of our locomotive and carried it for quite a distance, which reminded me of the lines is "Macbeth":

> Macbeth shall never vanquish'd be, until
> Great Birnam wood to high Dunsinane hill
> Shall come against him.

and I wondered if it was a good or a bad omen. It must have been a good one; for we arrived at our destination many hours late, but safe and very thankful.

Whenever it was at all possible, I visited a school for the blind or the deaf in the city where I was speaking; but our schedule was strenuous to begin with, and I was not equal to such additional effort. Several times I was treated most discourteously because I did not rush out of the hotel, just after arriving, and shake hands with a whole school. In one city, at a time when I could scarcely speak because of a cold, the superintendent of the school for the blind asked me to visit his institution and was exceedingly hurt when both my teacher and my mother told him I was not able. It grieved me that I could not always make these visits, not only because of the disappointment of those who invited me, but also because I was greatly interested in what was being done for the blind and deaf all over the country.

Frequently when I am speaking in a city I receive letters from invalids who tell me they have read my books, and wish to see me, but are unable to come to my lecture because they are shut in—or shut out from the normal activities of life. Whenever it is at all possible, I go to see them before or after the lecture. Their brave patience stirs the depths of my soul, and I bow my head in shame when I think how often I forget my own blessings and grow impatient with thwarting circumstances. I carry away with me sharp emotional pictures of thin, tremulous hands and suffering deeply graven in delicate lineaments, the cruel refinements of the sick room, of gentle pride in dainty things made in the intervals of anguish—bead necklaces, crocheted lace, paper flowers, sketches, and kewpie dolls, happy exclamations mingled with moans of pain, the smell of medicines and dreadful pauses of adjustment when the attendant tries to make some part of the maimed body more comfortable.

New ideas kept crowding into my mind, and my attitude changed as different aspects of civilization were presented to me. I had once believed that we were all masters of our fate—that we could mould our lives into any form we pleased. I was sure that if we wished strongly enough for anything, we could not fail to win it. I had overcome deafness and blindness sufficiently to be happy, and I supposed that anyone could come out victorious if he threw himself valiantly into life's struggle. But as I went more and more about the country I learned that I had spoken with assurance on a subject I knew little about. I forgot that I owed my success partly to the advantages of my birth and environment, and largely to the helpfulness of others. I forgot that whatever character I possessed was developed in an atmosphere suitable to it. I was like the princess who lived in a palace all composed of mirrors, and who beheld only the reflection of her own beauty. So I saw only the reflection of my good fortune. Now, however, I learned that the power to rise in the world is not within the reach of everyone, and that opportunity comes with education, family connections, and the influence of friends. I began to realize that although in fifty years man had acquired more tools than he had made during the thousands of years that had gone before, he had lost sight of his own happiness and personal development. It was terrible to realize that the very forces which were meant to lift him above hopeless drudgery were taking possession of him.

This realization came most poignantly when we visited mining and manufacturing towns where people were working in an unwholesome atmosphere to create comfort and beauty in which they could never have a part. I learned that to be a worker, poor and undefended, is

To suffer woes which hope thinks infinite;
To forgive wrongs darker than death or night;
To defy power, which seems omnipotent;
To love and bear; to hope till hope creates
From its own wreck the thing it contemplates.

But as time went on my thoughtless optimism was transmuted into that deeper faith which weighs the ugly facts of the world, yet hopes for better things and keeps on working for them even in the face of defeat.

It was in January, 1914, that we started on our first tour across the continent, and my mother accompanied us, which was a great happiness to me. She had always wanted to travel, and now I could make it possible for her to see our wonderful country from coast to coast! The first place we spoke in was Ottawa, Canada. From there we went to Toronto and London, Ontario, where we were received with the beautiful courtesy and friendliness characteristic of the Canadian people. Then we crossed the border into Michigan. We spoke in Minnesota and Iowa and in other parts of the Middle West and we had many amusing, exciting, and exasperating experiences.

When we left Salt Lake City, it was bitter cold. We wore fur coats, fur-lined gloves, and overshoes, and still felt the cold keenly. In the middle of the night our train jumped the track, and our car got stuck fast in the roadbed. The violence of the motion

nearly threw us out of our berths. We were obliged
to dress as quickly as we could in the darkness and
change to an immigrant car with straw seats. We did
not get to sleep again.

About daylight we dropped into Riverside, the
heat became oppressive, and I began to catch whiffs
of ravishing fragrance. My mother and my teacher
spelled into my hands as the train sped past orange
and eucalyptus groves, through the soft sage-scented
brown hills, with snow-capped mountains in the distance. We raced through the misty maze of pepper
trees and the blue, gold, and scarlet of millions of
flowers until we came at last to Los Angeles.

No sooner had we stepped out on the platform
than we were greeted by a great gathering of friends,
reporters, and photographers.

We had looked forward to this arrival and wanted
to make a pleasant impression, but, weighted down
with our furs and desperately in need of rest, we
knew that we could not do it. We tried to escape
to the hotel and remove the stains of travel, but our
friends assured us that they had special cars waiting
for us.

All the ladies present were daintily dressed in
summer gowns with flowers on their hats and gay
sunshades over their heads. We were so embarrassed
by our appearance that we declined the special automobiles, jumped into a taxi, and told the driver to

take us as fast as he could to the Alexandria Hotel. But as we turned the corner, something went wrong with the car, and he had to stop for a few minutes until it was fixed. Instantly reporters sprang upon the running board and demanded an interview, and the photographers caught up with us and pointed their cameras at us! Every effort was made to delay us, but we insisted on going on to our hotel. Our friends' feelings were hurt, the newspaper people were indignant, our manager was in a rage. Our rooms were full of exquisite flowers, beautiful fruits, and everything to add to our comfort and pleasure; but we were too exasperated and weary to enjoy them. Indeed, it was several days before we could feel like human beings, and not like wild creatures in a gilded cage.

My mother used to say that the years she travelled with us were the happiest, as well as the most arduous, she had ever known. She said she lived a lifetime in her first trip with us across the continent. Going to California was an experience she had never dared hope for. Her greatest delight was crossing and recrossing San Francisco Bay, especially at night. She described to me the splendour of the sky and the encircling hills. She amused herself by feeding the gulls which followed the ferry boat and sometimes alighted on the rail. Her poet's soul sparkled in her words when she told me how the sun sent its shafts through the Golden Gate as it journeyed westward, and how Mt. Tamalpais stood, silent and majestic, keeping eternal vigil with the sky, the ocean, and mortality. My mother simply worshipped the redwoods—"nature's monarchs," she called them, and she declared that they were more impressive even than the mountains, "because human faculties can compass them. They are earth's noblest aristocrats." This was a bond between them. For she had the Adams pride in family, which had been greatly augmented by Southern traditions.

We went often to the Muir Woods on that first trip, and I have visited them many times since. How shall I describe my sensations upon entering that Temple of the Lord! Every time I touch the redwoods I feel as if the unrest and strife of earth were lulled. I cease to long and grieve—I am in the midst of a Sabbath of repose, resting from human futilities. I am in a holy place, quiet as a heart full of prayer. God seems to walk invisible through the long, dim aisles.

I never met Mr. William Kent, the noble gentleman who bought this grove of mighty redwoods to save them from destruction, but some years later when I was lecturing in California in behalf of the blind I spoke at his home. I had already learned how he had given the trees to the United States as a park and how when Roosevelt wished to name the park Kent's Woods he replied, "I suggest that as a tribute to our great naturalist, John Muir, the park be named Muir Woods. I am not unappreciative of your kindness, and I thank you; but I have five stalwart sons, and if they cannot keep the name of Kent alive, I am willing that it should be forgotten." I have never ceased to regret that he was not at home that day.

There is something attractive, individual, memorable, in nearly every city; but their charms, like those of women, are varied, and appeal to different temperaments. San Francisco bewitches me. She sits upon her glorious bay, a queen in many aspects, a royal child when she plays with the gray-winged gulls which circle round her like bubbles rising from the dark water. The God who moulded the Canadian Rockies was an Old Testament Jehovah—a mighty God! The God who moulded the hills around San Francisco had a gentle hand. Their outlines are as tender as those of a reclining woman.

In the distance is Mt. Tamalpais, like an old Indian chief asleep in the doorway of his wigwam at close of day, beneath him the bay and the Golden Gate opening to the Pacific Ocean. At the left of the Gate is an old Spanish fort. Yonder is Alcatraz Island with guns pointing west. When "rosy-fingered dawn" touches the eyes of the Indian chief, and they open to behold his beloved, he will see ships sailing through the portals of the Golden Gate to the breast of their mistress, the Pacific, "strong as youth, and as uncontrolled."

Happy memories, like homing birds, flutter round me as I write—breakfast at the Cliff House, and huge rocks sprawling in the blue waters, where the sea lions play all day long, warm sand dunes where blue and yellow lupins grow, groves of eucalyptus whose pungent, red-tinted leaves I loved to crush in my hand. Standing on the Twin Peaks, my mother said, drawing me close to her, "This is a reparation for all the sorrow I have ever known." We could see the city far below, and Market Street stretching from the Peaks to the Bay, and at the foot of Market Street the clock tower, and ferry boats leaving every few minutes, steep Telegraph Hill—more like a ladder than a street, about which many stories are told by sailors and searchers for gold, and the Mission Dolores, founded by Father Junipero Serra, whom the Golden State honours for his heroism, the Church of St. Ignatius, whose bells ring at seven every morning, the great cross on Lone Mountain, which reminds us to make the most of life, since our days on earth are few.

Sometimes the city surrounds herself with clouds or wraps herself in gray vapours, as if to be alone. Sometimes the Twin Peaks shake off their ghostly garments and gaze at the starlit sky, while the moon turns her luminous face in such a way as to make herself visible from every side. At sunset the Twin Peaks wear a many-coloured crown. We have climbed them at dawn when pillars of light, shaped like a Japanese fan, throw a bridge of flame between their summits. Even as we gaze, awe-stilled, they pull up great mantles of cloud from the sea and cover their faces. The next moment city, mountains, ocean, are blotted out—we look into white darkness! I have often puzzled my brain to discover the difference between black and white darkness. To my physical perception there is no difference, yet the words "white darkness" bring to my mind an image of something diaphanous which extinguishes the glare of day, but is not gloom, like black darkness. It suggests the sweet shadows which white pines cast upon me when I sit under them.

I usually know what part of the city I am in by the odours. There are as many smells as there are philosophies. I have never had time to gather and classify my olfactory impressions of different cities, but it would be an interesting subject. I find it quite natural to think of places by their characteristic smells.

Fifth Avenue, for example, has a different odour from any other part of New York or elsewhere. Indeed, it is a very odorous street. It may sound like a oke to say that it has an aristocratic smell; but it has, nevertheless. As I walk along its even pavements, I recognize expensive perfumes, powders, creams, choice flowers, and pleasant exhalations from the houses. In the residential section I smell delicate ood, silken draperies, and rich tapestries. Sometimes, when a door opens as I pass, I know what kind of cosmetics the occupants of the house use. I know if there is an open fire, if they burn wood or soft coal, if they roast their coffee, if they use candles, if the house has been shut up for a long time, if it has been painted or newly decorated, and if the cleaners are at work in it. I suggest that if the police really wish to know where stills and "speakeasies" are located, they take me with them. It would not be a bad idea for the United States Government to establish a bureau of aromatic specialists.

I know when I pass a church and whether it is Protestant or Catholic. I know when I am in the Italian quarter of a city by the smells of salami, garlic, and spaghetti. I know when we are near oil wells. I used to be able to smell Duluth and St. Louis miles off by their breweries, and the fumes of the whiskey stills of Peoria, Illinois, used to wake me up at night if we passed within smelling distance of it.

In small country towns I smell grocery stores, rancid butter, potatoes, and onions. The houses often have a musty, damp aura. I can easily distinguish

Southern towns by the odours of fried chicken, grits, yams and cornbread, while in Northern towns the predominating odours are of doughnuts, corn beef hash, fishballs, and baked beans. I think I could write a book about the rich, warm, varied aromas of California; but I shall not start on that subject. It would take too long.

The first tour was typical of all our subsequent ones. In the years that followed we journeyed up and down the immensity of America from the storms of the Atlantic to the calms of the Pacific, from the Pine Tree State to the Gulf States, along the banks of muddy creeks or following the Mississippi until it seemed to me as if we were tearing our way through life just like that tameless river. On we went through desolate morasses and swamps ghostly with mossy trees, over endless leagues of red clay, past wretched cabins of whites and negroes, then suddenly the glory of Southern spring burst upon us with the songs of mocking birds, the masses of dogwood blossoms and wild azaleas, and the lonely vastnesses of Texas. Then back home for a few months' rest, and another long tour from the settled East through Sandburg's "stormy, brawny, shouting city," across the sun-soaked prairies of Nebraska, through the immense gulches of Colorado, up the mountains of Utah, sparkling in the winter sunshine, across the

limitless plains of the Dakotas and past the thousand
sparkling lakes of Minnesota. I lost all sense of
permanence, and even now I never feel really as
if I were living at home. Unconsciously I am always
expecting to be borne again over the vast distances
which so powerfully fascinate me. I am like a young
spruce tree which is transplanted often, and keeps
its root in a ball, so that it can adapt itself to any
new place whither it may be carried.

Those tours are a symbol to me of the ceaseless
travelling of my soul through the uplands of thought.
My body is tethered, it is true, as I follow the dark
trail from city to city and climate to climate; but the
very act of going satisfies me with the feeling that
my mind and body go together. It is a never-ending
wonder for me how my days lead to

. . . the start of superior journeys,
To see nothing anywhere but what you may reach it and pass it,
To conceive no time however distant, but what you may reach
     it and pass it,
To look up and down no road but it stretches
And waits for you, however long but it stretches and waits for
     you,
To gather the minds of men out of their brains as you encounter
     them, to gather the love out of their hearts,

and

to know the world itself as a road, as many roads to hope, as
roads for travelling souls.

That is why Walt Whitman's "The Open Road" is one of my favourite long poems, it holds up to me so faithfully a mirror of my own inner experience. However dreary or tiresome I may find some of these roads, there is *"la seduction éternelle du chemin."* I look forward to other journeys on a celestial highway, where all limitations shall disappear, and my voice, perfect with immortality, shall ring earthwards with sweet might to bless; and looking forward is another mode of happiness.

Chapter XI

IN THE WHIRLPOOL

ON OUR second trip across the continent Miss Polly Thomson, who became my secretary in October, 1914, accompanied us in place of my mother. Her position was, and has been ever since, nominally that of secretary, but as the years passed she has taken upon herself the burden of house management as well. She has never known the luxury of the usual secretary's hours or well-defined duties. A new day for her frequently begins an hour or two after the previous day ends. She has to account for all our engagements, lightning changes and caprices, our sins, commissions, and omissions. Yes, Polly Thomson manages it all. She is our friend, kind and true, full of good nature, often tired, but always with time to do something more. Had it not been for her devotion, adaptability, and willingness to give up every individual pleasure we should long ago have found it necessary to withdraw into complete isolation. For in spite of our income from Mr. Carnegie and the money we made ourselves our expenses were always a ravenous wolf devouring our finances.

After the outbreak of the World War it was impossible for me to enjoy the lecture tours as I had before. Not a cheerful message could I give without a sense of tragic contradiction. Not a thought could I sing in the joy of old days! Even the deepest slumber could not render me quite unconscious of the rising world calamity. I used to wake suddenly from a frightful dream of sweat and blood and multitudes shot, killed, and crazed, and go to sleep only to dream of it again. I was often asked why I did not write something new. How could I write with the thunder of machine guns and the clamour of hate-filled armies deafening my soul, and the conflagration of cities blinding my thoughts? The world seemed one vast Gethsemane, and day unto day and night unto night brought bitter knowledge which must needs become a part of myself. I was in a state of spiritual destitution such as I had not before experienced. Works are the breath and life of happiness, and what works could I show when cry upon cry of destruction floated to me over sea and land? Nothing was sadder to me during those years of disaster than the thousands of letters I received from Europe imploring me for help which I could not give while my teacher and I were with difficulty working our way back and forth across the continent to earn our daily bread. If I did not reply to them it was because I was utterly helpless.

It was extremely hard for me to keep my faith as I

read how the mass of patriotic hatred swelled with ever wider and more barbaric violence. Explanations without end filled the pages under my scornful fingers, and they all amounted to the same frightful admission—the collapse of civilization and the betrayal of the most beautiful religion ever preached upon earth.

I clung to the hope that my country would prove itself a generous, friendly power amid the welter of hostility and misery. I believed that President Wilson possessed the nobility and steadfastness required to maintain his policy of neutrality and "Christian gentleness." I determined to do and say my utmost to protest against militarism in the United States. My teacher and I were both worn out; but we felt that we must at least try to carry a message of good will to a stricken world.

Accordingly, during the summer of 1916 we undertook an anti-preparedness Chautauqua tour. We were booked for many towns in Nebraska and Kansas and a few in Michigan. This tour was far from successful. Most of our audiences were indifferent to the question of peace and war. Fortunately, the weather was unusually cool, and we took advantage of the early morning hours to motor to the next place where we had an engagement. It was a restful experience to ride past hamlets and towns buried in fields of corn and wheat, or over immense prairies bright with sunflowers which were as large as little trees, with big, rough leaves and heavy-headed blossoms. When one saw them at a distance they must have seemed like yellow necklaces winding in and out the bright grass of the prairies. I loved the odour of great harvests which followed us mile after mile through the stillness. But it was not always sunshine and calm. I remember terrific storms with metallic peals of thunder, warm splashes of rain and seas of mud through which our little Ford carried us triumphantly to our destination.

We spoke sometimes in halls or in big, noisy tents full of country folk, or at a camp on the edge of a lake. Occasionally our audience evinced genuine enthusiasm; but I felt more than ever that I was not fitted to address large crowds on subjects which called for a quick cross-play of questions, answers, debate, and repartee.

The attitude of the press was maddening. It seems to me difficult to imagine anything more fatuous and stupid than their comments on anything I say touching public affairs. So long as I confine my activities to social service and the blind, they compliment me extravagantly, calling me the "archpriestess of the sightless," "wonder woman," and "modern miracle," but when it comes to a discussion of a burning social or political issue, especially if I happen to be, as I so often am, on the unpopular side, the tone changes completely. They are grieved because they imagine I am in the hands of unscrupulous persons who take advantage of my afflictions to make me a mouthpiece for their own ideas. It has always been natural for me to speak my mind, and the pent-up feelings which kept beating against my heart at that time demanded an outlet. I like frank debate, and I do not object to harsh criticism so long as I am treated like a human being with a mind of her own.

The group of which I was a part was doing all it could to keep America out of the war. At the same time another group, equally earnest, was doing all it could to precipitate America into the war. In this group, the one who at the time seemed most important, was ex-President Roosevelt.

I had met President Roosevelt in 1903 during a visit to my foster father, Mr. Hitz. He sent me a great basket of flowers and expressed the wish that I might find it agreeable to call upon him at the White House. The President was very cordial. He asked Miss Sullivan many questions about my education. Then he turned to me and asked me if there was any way in which he could talk to me himself. I told him he could learn the manual alphabet in a few minutes, and at his request showed him the letters. He made a few of them with his own hand.

"F" bothered him, and he said impatiently, "I'm too clumsy." Then Miss Sullivan showed him how he could communicate with me by lip-reading.

He asked me if I thought he should let young Theodore play football. I was embarrassed because I could not tell whether he was joking or seriously asking my opinion. I told him, with straight face, that at Radcliffe we did not play football, but that I had heard that learned Harvard professors were objecting to it because it took so much of the boys' time away from their studies. Then he asked me if I had heard of Pliny and when I told him I had he asked if I had read his letter to Trajan in which he says that if the Greeks are permitted to keep up their athletics their minds will be so occupied with them that they will not be dangerous to Rome. We talked about Miss Holt's work for the blind in New York and what I had been doing in Massachusetts and he urged me to keep on prodding people about their responsibilities to the blind. "There's nothing better we can do in the world than to serve a good purpose."

My impression of him then was of an alert man, poised as if to spring, and besides alertness there was a kind of eagerness to act first. During those years preceding America's entrance into the war it seemed to me, as it has seemed ever since, that he was more precipitate than wise. It was the speed at which he moved that gave us the impression that he was ac-

complishing mighty things. Only in aggressiveness
was he strong.

What the group I represented desired was fair
discussion and open debate. I wanted to have the
whole matter put before the people so they could
decide whether they wanted to go into the conflict
or stay out. As it was, they had no choice in the
matter.

I do not pretend that I know the whole solution of
the world's problems, but I am burdened with a
Puritanical sense of obligation to set the world to
rights. I feel responsible for many enterprises that
are not really my business at all, but many times I
have kept silence on issues that interested me deeply
through the fear that others would be blamed for my
opinions. I have never been willing to believe that
human nature cannot be changed; but even if it cannot, I am sure it can be curbed and led into channels
of usefulness. I believe that life, not wealth, is the
aim of existence—life including all its attributes of
love, happiness, and joyful labour. I believe war is
the inevitable fruit of our economic system, but even
if I am wrong I believe that truth can lose nothing
by agitation but may gain all.

I tried to make my audiences see what I saw, but
the people who crowded the great tents were disappointed or indifferent. They had come to hear me talk
about happiness, and perhaps recite "Nearer, My

God, to Thee, Nearer to Thee," or "My Country, 'Tis of Thee, Sweet Land of Liberty," and they did not care to have their peace of mind disturbed by talk about war, especially as the majority of them believed then that we would not be drawn into the European maelstrom.

No words can express the frustration of those days. And, indeed, what are words but "painted fire" before realities that lift the spirit or cast it down? No real communication of profound experiences can ever pass from one to another by words. Only those who are sensitive to spiritual vibrations can hear in them the fluttering of the soul, as a disturbed bird flutters in the depths of a thicket. One's life-story cannot be told with complete veracity. A true autobiography would have to be written in states of mind, emotions, heartbeats, smiles, and tears, not in months and years, or physical events. Life is marked off on the soul-chart by feelings, not by dates. Mere facts cannot present to the reader an experience of the heart in all its evanescent hues and fluctuations.

I am now going to dig an episode out of my memory which has contradictory aspects. For that reason I would rather keep it locked up in my own heart. But when one writes an autobiography, one seems, tacitly at least, to promise the reader that one will not conceal anything just because it is unpleasant, and awakens regrets of the past. I would not have anyone think that I have told in this book only such things as seemed to me likely to win the approbation of the reader. I want whoever is interested to know that I am a mere mortal, with a human being's frailties and inconsistencies.

On the second Chautauqua tour I was accompanied by Mrs. Macy and a young man who interpreted for me. Miss Thomson was on a vacation at her home in Scotland. The young man was very much in earnest, and eager to have the people get my message. He returned to Wrentham with us in the autumn of 1916 after our disappointing and exhausting summer. Our homecoming was far from happy. Mr. Macy was not there to greet us. Dear Ian had done everything he could to make the house attractive and the garden beautiful with flowers; but there was no cheerfulness in our hearts, and the flowers seemed to add to the gloom. I telegraphed my mother to come to Wrentham, and in a few days her presence sweetened our loneliness.

But we were scarcely settled when Mrs. Macy fell ill. She had succumbed to fatigue and anxiety. She developed pleurisy and a tenacious cough, and her physician advised her to go to Lake Placid for the winter. That meant that our home would be broken up. We should have to let Ian go, since we could no longer afford to keep him. This hurt us more than anything. For we all loved Ian. Mrs. Macy had taken him from the fields—a Lithuanian peasant who could not speak three words of English—and trained him to be a cook and butler and houseman. He was devoted to us, and we felt when he went that the heart of the Wrentham place would stop beating.

I could not work, I could not think calmly. For the first time in my life it seemed folly to be alive. I had often been asked what I should do if anything happened to my teacher. I was now asking myself the same question. I saw more clearly than ever before how inseparably our lives were bound together. How lonely and bleak the world would be without her. What could I do? I could not imagine myself going on with my work alone. To do anything in my situation, it was essential to have about me friends who cared deeply for the things I did. My experience of the summer had brought home to me the fact that few people were interested in my aims and aspirations. Once more I was overwhelmed by a sense of my isolation.

Such was the background of the adventure I shall relate. I was sitting alone in my study one evening, utterly despondent. The young man who was still acting as my secretary in the absence of Miss Thomson, came in and sat down beside me. For a long time he held my hand in silence, then he began talking to me tenderly. I was surprised that he cared so much about me. There was sweet comfort in his loving words. I listened all a-tremble. He was full of plans for my happiness. He said if I would marry him, he would always be near to help me in the difficulties of life. He would be there to read to me, look up material for my books and do as much as he could of the work my teacher had done for me.

His love was a bright sun that shone upon my helplessness and isolation. The sweetness of being loved enchanted me, and I yielded to an imperious longing to be a part of a man's life. For a brief space I danced in and out of the gates of Heaven, wrapped up in a web of bright imaginings. Naturally, I wanted to tell my mother and my teacher about the wonderful thing that had happened to me; but the young man said, "Better wait a bit, we must tell them together. We must try to realize what their feelings will be. Certainly, they will disapprove at first. Your mother does not like me, but I shall win her approval by my devotion to you. Let us keep our love secret a little while. Your teacher is too ill to be excited just now, and we must tell her first." I had happy hours with him. We walked in the autumn splendour of the woods, and he read to me a great deal. But the secrecy which circumstances appeared to impose upon us made me suffer. The thought of not sharing my happiness with my mother and her who had been all things to me for thirty years seemed abject, and little by little it destroyed the joy of being loved.

As we parted one night, I told him I had made up my mind definitely to tell my teacher everything the next morning. But the next morning Fate took matters into her own hands and tangled the web, as is her wont. I was dressing, full of the excitement of what I was going to communicate to my loved ones, when my mother entered my room in great distress. With a shaking hand she demanded, "What have you been doing with that creature? The papers are full of a dreadful story about you and him. What does it mean? Tell me!" I sensed such hostility towards my lover in her manner and words that in a panic I pretended not to know what she was talking about. "Are you engaged to him? Did you apply for a marriage license?" Terribly frightened, and not knowing just what had happened, but anxious to shield my lover, I denied everything. I even lied to Mrs. Macy, fearing the consequences that would result from the revelation coming to her in this shocking way. My mother ordered the young man out of the house that very day. She would not even let him speak to me, but he wrote me a note in braille, telling where he would be, and begging me to keep him informed. I kept on denying that I knew anything about the story in the papers until Mrs. Macy went to Lake Placid with Miss Thomson, who had returned from Scotland, and my mother took me home to Montgomery.

In time she found out how I had deceived her and everyone else. The memory of her sorrow burns me to the soul. She begged me not to write Mrs. Macy anything about it until we knew that she was stronger. "The shock would kill her, I am sure," she said. It was months later when my teacher learned the truth.

I cannot account for my behaviour. As I look back and try to understand, I am completely bewildered. I seem to have acted exactly opposite to my nature. It can be explained only in the old way—that love makes us blind and leaves the mind confused and deprives it of the use of judgment. I corresponded with the young man for several months; but my love-dream was shattered. It had flowered under an inauspicious star. The unhappiness I had caused my dear ones produced a state of mind unfavourable to the continuance of my relations with the young man. The love which had come unseen and unexpected departed with tempest on its wings.

As time went on, the young man and I became involved in a net of falsehood and misunderstanding. I am sure that if Mrs. Macy had been there, she would have understood, and sympathized with us both. The most cruel sorrows in life are not its losses and misfortunes, but its frustrations and betrayals.

The brief love will remain in my life, a little island of joy surrounded by dark waters. I am glad that I have had the experience of being loved and desired. The fault was not in the loving, but in the circumstances. A lovely thing tried to express itself; but conditions were not right or adequate, and it never blossomed. Yet the failure, perhaps, only serves to set off the beauty of the intention. I see it all now with a heart that has grown sad in growing wiser.

All that winter was a time of anxiety and suffering. My teacher's health did not improve and she was very unhappy in the bleak climate of Lake Placid. Finally, about the beginning of December, she sailed for Porto Rico, accompanied by Polly Thomson. She remained there until the following April, and almost every week brought me a letter written with her own hand in braille, full of delight over the wonderful climate of Porto Rico. She described "the loveliest sky in the world," the palms and cocoanuts, tree-like ferns, lilies, poinsettias, and many beautiful flowers she had never seen before. She declared that if she got well anywhere, it would be on that enchanted island. But she did not really recover until the fall after she returned to Wrentham; she could not lecture again for more than a year.

I had often been urged to write a book about the blind, and I was eager to do it now, not only because I thought it might help their cause but because I wanted something to take my mind away from war questions. I might have done it that winter, but I could not collect material for such a book without my teacher's help and I could not afford expert assistance. I dwell so much on the inadequacy of my income, not because I see in it a reason for complaint, but because many people have criticized my teacher and me for the things we have left undone. If they only knew how many of our years have been sacrificed to practical and impractical ways of earning a living!

In various ways our small fortune had become so depleted that we were obliged to sell our home in Wrentham. We had been one with the house, one with the sweetness of the town. Our joys and affections had peopled the rooms and many objects had woven themselves by long companionship into my daily life there. There was a friendly sense about the long, handsome oak table where I wrote and spread out my papers with comfort, the spacious bookcases, the big study windows where my plants had welcomed me with blossoms and the sofa where I had sat by a cheery fire. How many of those fires had shone upon faces I loved, had warmed hands whose clasp I shall feel no more, and gladdened hearts that are now still! The very sorrows we had endured there had endeared that home all the more to us.

The house seemed to have a personality, and to

mourn our going away. Each room spoke to us in unheard but tender accents. I do not think of a house merely as wood, stone, and cement, but as a spirit which shelters or casts out, blesses or condemns. It was a sweet old farmhouse that had enfolded me, and which had stored away in its soul the laughter of children and the singing of birds. It was a home where rural peace had smiled upon my work. There I watched the ploughing and harrowing of the fields, and the sowing of seed, waited for new flowers and vegetables in the garden. When we left the sun was shining, and the magic of June was everywhere, except in our hearts. My feet almost refused to move as we stepped out of a house where I had thrilled to the beauty of so many golden seasons! Oh, those Mays with dainty marsh-marigolds and a sea of violets, pink and white drifts of apple blossoms! Oh, the Junes with the riot of ramblers up the walls, the red clover and white Queen Anne's lace, purple ironweed, and all about the divine aroma of pine needles! Oh, the breezes with the coolness of deep woods and rippling streams! All my tree-friends were there, too—the slender white pines by my study, the big, hospitable apple trees, one with a seat where I had sat wrapped in bright dreams, the noble elms casting shadows far over the fields and the spruces nodding to me. Nowhere was there a suggestion of world wars, falling empires, and bitter disillusionment, but a sense of permanence and charm which I have not experienced so fully since. Thirteen years we had lived there. It was not a long period measured by years and much of the time we had perforce been away, yet it was a lifetime measured in seasons of the heart.

The one thought which cheered us as we drove away that sad morning was that the house we had loved so well would be good to others. It is now a rest home for the girls working at Jordan Marsh department store, Boston; but it is so endeared to me by all intimate joys and sorrows that no matter who lives in it and no matter where I go I shall always think of it as home.

Chapter XII

I MAKE BELIEVE I AM AN ACTRESS

AFTER wandering about the country for a time we decided to make our home in Forest Hills, a pretty suburb of New York City. We bought a small, odd-looking house which has so many peaks and angles that we call it our Castle on the Marsh. "We" were Mrs. Macy, Polly Thomson, myself and Sieglinde.

We were glad to be out of the noise and rush and confusion of public life. We planted trees and vines in the garden. I had a little study upstairs open to the four winds of heaven. I began the study of Italian because I wanted to read Dante and Petrarch in their own tongue, and we hoped to live quietly with our books and our dreams. But we had hardly settled down before we had a letter from Dr. Francis Trevelyan Miller proposing that a motion picture be made of the story of my life. The idea pleased me very much because I thought that through the film we might show the public in a forceful manner how I had been saved from a cruel fate, and how the distracted, war-tortured world we were then living in could be saved from strife and social injustice—

spiritual deafness and blindness. That is why the picture was called "Deliverance."

It seems strange to me now that I ever had the conceit to go the long, long way to Hollywood, review my life on the screen, and expect the public not to fall asleep over it. I was not an exciting subject for a motion picture. I was awkward and big, while most of the actresses I met were graceful and sylph-like. I could not, like Ariel, "do my spiriting gently." I could not glide like a nymph in cloudlike robes. I had no magic wand to conjure up tears and laughter. But I enjoyed being in Hollywood, and my only regret now is that the picture proved a financial loss to all who were interested in it and that my shadow-self is still an elephant upon the shoulders of the producer.

Life in the vicinity of Hollywood is very exciting. You never know what you may see when you venture beyond your doorsill. Threading your way between the geraniums which grow on the curb, and spread out under your feet like a Persian rug, you behold a charge of cavalry or an ice wagon overturned in the middle of a street, or a shack in flames on the hillside, or an automobile plunging down a cliff. When everything was new to us, we motored out to the desert. There was nothing to see but glare and sand mounds, with here and there a cactus or a greasewood bush. At a bend in the road someone exclaimed, "Look! there's an Indian—a real wild Indian." We got out of the car and reconnoitred. The Indian seemed to be the only moving object in the universe. The men in the party approached him with the idea of asking him to let me touch his headdress, which was a gorgeous affair of painted eagle feathers. When we got near enough, we began to gesticulate to tell him in pantomime what we wanted. In perfectly good English the Indian said, "Sure, the lady can feel me as much as she likes." He was a motion picture actor waiting for his camera men.

Every morning at sunrise Miss Thomson and I went for a ride through the dewy stillness. Nothing refreshed me as did the cool breeze, scented with sage, thyme, and eucalyptus. Some of the happiest hours of my life were spent on the trails of Beverly Hills. I loved Peggy, the horse I rode, and I think he liked me; for she seldom lost her temper, although I know she must have found my riding very clumsy indeed. I am sure things fell out very much to her liking one day when a girth broke, and she slipped the saddle and galloped away into the hills for a holiday, leaving me in the middle of a strawberry patch. I should not have minded if the farmer had not already finished picking all the ripe strawberries.

We set out to make a simple picture with *The Story of My Life* as a background. We worked at the Brunton studio under the direction of Mr. George Foster Platt, who was most patient with me. He devised a signal system of taps that I could follow and allowed plenty of time for Polly Thomson to interpret his direction to me. After general directions had been spelled into my hand, I was supposed to go through the action with the help of signal taps. "Tap, tap, tap"—walk toward the window on your right. "Tap, tap, tap"—hold up your hands to the sun (a blaze of heat from the big lamps). "Tap, tap, tap"—discover the bird's cage; (I had already discovered the cage five times). "Tap, tap, tap"—express surprise, feel for the bird, express pleasure. "Tap, tap, tap"—be natural. In my hand impatiently: "There's nothing to be afraid of; it isn't a lion in the cage—it's a canary. Repeat."

I was never quite at my ease when I posed. It was hard to be natural before the camera, and not to see it at that! I had little skill to throw myself into the spirit of the scene. There I sat or stood for a picture, growing hotter and hotter, my hands more and more moist as the light poured upon me. My embarrassment caused my brow and nose to shine inartistically. Instead of putting on a winning smile, I often discharged all life and intelligence from my countenance, and gazed stiffly into vacancy. When I became too absorbed in a difficult detail, like writing in large letters suited to the screen, I unconsciously frowned, and I believe that only the good nature of those about me saved my reputation for amiability. Besides, we had to go to the studio twice a day, and that meant "making up" and "unmaking" each time.

At first when I was told what effect they were trying for in a scene, I used to ask myself how I should do it if I were alone in my room, or with friends in a familiar place; but the signal "Be natural" came emphatically after one of my best efforts. I learned that thinking was of no use in a motion picture—at least not my thinking. After a while, if I caught myself thinking about what I was doing, I would pull myself up sharp, and concentrate on the signals that came to me from the director.

Of course I could not act in the early scenes. A child named Florence Roberts, whose stage name now is Sylvia Dawn, impersonated me as a little girl. With perfect eyes and ears she acted this part astonishingly well, and besides the affection I felt for her, I had a certain tenderness for the small me that she presented so realistically. There was also Ann Mason, the sweet, laughter-loving, daintily dressed young girl who was myself in the college scenes of the picture. I was amused whenever she tried to shut her eyes so as to look blind, and they would pop open, so interested was she in the scene. I also loved the way she dreamed my dreams of beauty, and the delightful picture she made side by side with Ulysses and the Greek divinities I had read about in my books.

Another difficulty arose when it came to presenting my friends. I was anxious to have as many of them as possible appear in the picture, but many of them had died—Henry Rogers, Mark Twain, Phillips Brooks, Oliver Wendell Holmes, Edward Everett Hale—and those who were living, had, like myself, grown older.

I wrote Dr. Bell, who was then in Nova Scotia. He sent me a beautiful letter which runs in part as follows:

Your letter has touched me deeply. It brings back recollections of the little girl I met in Washington so long ago, and you are still that little girl to me. I can only say that anything you want me to do I will do for your sake, but I can't go down to the States before you go to California, and we will have to wait until you come back.

You must remember that when I met you first I wasn't seventy-one years old and didn't have white hair, and you were only a little girl of seven, so it is obvious that any historical picture will have to be made with substitutes for both of us. You will have to find someone with dark hair to impersonate the Alexander Graham Bell of your childhood, and then perhaps your appearance with me in a later scene when we both are as we are now may be interesting by contrast.

It occurred to me it might be attractive to present my friends in a somewhat symbolic way. In Gibbon's *Autobiography* there is a memorable passage in which he speaks of a walk he took under the acacias outside his study at Lausanne when he had completed his twenty years' work on *The Decline and Fall*. It seemed to me that the acacia walk would be an effective symbol for my picture. What could be more appropriate than a berceau of acacias to suggest my life-journey through shadow and silence? What could be more dramatic than to meet my friends and have them walk with me in that secluded path, with glimpses of lake, mountain, and river beyond? The idea was never carried out. This was a deep disappointment to me because I had desired to make my picture a grateful testimony to the gracious deeds and the understanding sympathy which had made the story of my life.

But each one of us, and I assure you there was an army of us, had his own idea of the way the picture should be made. The substitute for the acacia walk struck me as most grotesque and ludicrous. It was a great banquet bristling with formality where all my friends, both living and dead, were assembled. There was my dear father who had been on the Heaven side of the Great River for twenty years. There were Dr. Hale, Bishop Brooks, Dr. Oliver Wendell Holmes, Dr. Bell, Mrs. William Thaw, Henry Rogers; and Joseph Jefferson looking much more alive than when he came down the mountain from his twenty years sleep.

I felt as if I had died without knowing it, and passed on to the other world, and here were my friends who had gone before coming to greet me. But when I grasped their hands, they seemed more substantial than I had imagined spirit-hands would be. Moreover, they did not resemble the hands of the friends they were impersonating, and the conversation of these resurrected friends did not have the flavour of the talk to which I had been accustomed. It gave me a little shock every time one of them interjected a remark into the conversation, and when Mark Twain made a witty or complimentary speech, I did not know whether to laugh or cry. The climax of incongruities came when, after all the music, banqueting, and talk, the scenario required that I say words to this effect: "Eighty thousand blind people are unhappy and unhelped, and in the present state of society it is impossible to give them the opportunities they should have. . . . Millions of human beings live and die without knowing the joy of living. . . . Let us resolve now and here to build a saner, kindlier world for everybody."

In another scene I danced for the camera, I poured tea for the callers and after the last guest was sped, there came the "tap, tap, tap" from the director: "Lift up your hands and let them fall, express relief that the last bore has left." There was a bedroom scene in which I was directed to show the curious public that I could dress and undress myself alone and that I closed my eyes when I went to sleep. Charlie Chaplin proposed to break in and wake the "sleeping beauty," and I wish now that we had let him do it.

Our visits with Charlie Chaplin were among the most delightful experiences we had in California. He invited me to his studio to see "A Dog's Life," and "Shoulder Arms," and when I said I would come he seemed as pleased as if I were doing him a favour. His manner was shy, almost timid, and his lovely modesty lent a touch of romance to an occasion that might otherwise have seemed quite ordinary. Before he reeled off the pictures he let me touch his clothes and shoes and moustache that I might have a clearer idea of him on the screen. He sat beside me and asked me again and again if I was really interested— if I liked him and the little dog in the picture.

This was ten years ago. Twice since then he has been overpowered by the tragedy of life and the fleeting show of the world he lives in. When I knew him in 1918, he was a sincere, thoughtful young man, deeply interested in his art and his violin. His mind seemed to me sensitive and fine. Apropos of somebody's remark about the power of mere words to amuse and enchant, the Prince of Jesters quoted from Omar Khayyám:

> We are no other than a moving row
> Of magic Shadow-shapes that come and go
> Round with the Sun-illumined Lantern held
> In Midnight by the Master of the Show.

But I must get back to my own picture. We had not been long at work before we began to realize that there was very little drama in the story of my life. The chorus that surrounded Mr. Platt suggested that a mystical unfoldment of my story would be more interesting than a matter-of-fact narrative. When he said that it would be impossible to film they chanted that nothing was impossible to those who tried.

"Can't you see," they wailed, "that there has been no romance in Helen Keller's life—no lover, no adventures of the heart? Let her imagine a lover and follow him in fancy. The picture will be a dismal failure without excitement."

One of our experiments in getting excitement was to introduce a fight in which Knowledge and Ignorance contended fiercely for my mind at the entrance of the Cave of Father Time. The whole company went out to find a suitable location for the battle, and a spot that seemed fairly appropriate was chosen about forty miles away among the hills. It was more exciting than a real prize fight because one of the combatants was a woman. Ignorance, a hideous giant, and Knowledge, white and panting, wrestled on the hillside for the spirit of the infant Helen.

I held my breath when Ignorance hurled Knowledge over the cliff, wondering what insurance we should pay her if she was dead. Ignorance, laughing a bloodthirsty laugh, stretched his mighty limbs on the hill, while wild surmises ran from tongue to tongue. After what seemed an eternity, Knowledge's pale brow appeared above the edge of the rocks. Apparently she was only a little breathless from her precipitous descent and laborious climb back to the battlefield. The fight recommenced fiercer than ever. Finally, Knowledge got Ignorance at a disadvantage, her floating garments having entangled him and thrown him to the ground. She held him down until he gave a pledge of submission. The evil genie then departed with a madman's glare of hate into the shadows of the earth, while Knowledge covered the infant with her mantle of conscious light.

The mystic vapours of this performance distilled into an overflowing cup of optimism. It was now clear to the dullest of us that there was no limit to what might be wrought into the Helen Keller picture. Why waste time on a historic picture when the realm of imagination was ours for the taking?

While Dr. Edwin Liebfreed (the man who paid the bills) raged, everyone else imagined vain things and set the cameras to work on them. Suggestions came thicker than flies in summer, confusing the director and depriving him of his judgment, raising such a dust of ideas that it was hard to see anything clearly. We believed we were to contrive a great masterpiece. I am sure that the other picture people must have stood by and marvelled at our tremendous doings.

It was in connection with one of these symbolic episodes that we had our most distressing experience in Hollywood. The scene represented a dream my teacher had when she was feeling discouraged because I did not yet understand the meaning of language. She fell asleep, and lo! there was Christ saying, "Suffer the little children to come unto Me." She was filled with new courage. To "make" this picture, we all went out into the arid waste-lands near Hollywood.

The cars and buses debouched a hundred or more little children upon the scorched and glaring solitude of a vacant hillside. This very rough spot had been selected because it resembled Jerusalem. Hurriedly and with great trepidation the director tried to marshal his unhappy little army into position; but no sooner had they started to climb the hill than they set up howls of pain. The ground was thick with sharp burrs. The grown-ups tried to carry the children in their arms and on their backs; but there were so many of them, and the climb was so steep, it took a long time to get them all up. We worked in the blazing sun, and the little ones grew very thirsty. Then it was discovered that the milk for the children had been forgotten! They cried pitifully, and the mothers whose fault it was had much to say about the cruelty of directors. Messengers were dispatched to town, but we had an hour or more of wretched discomfort before they returned.

I hope that sometime a director will write a book about his experiences on location. His opinion of the members of the human species who sell their children to producers for three dollars a day would be enlightening.

Before I went to Hollywood, I used to imagine that artists must have a peculiarly kind feeling toward the models who embody their creations in films or in marble or on canvas. This I found to be a delusion. It appears that, for the most part, the workers in human material despise the portion of mankind who help them to realize their ideal. I suppose Mark Twain had this in mind when he said, "Let us be thankful for the fools. But for them the rest of us could not succeed."

We planned a group of scenes to show how real the adventures of Ulysses were to me. Since I had no lover Ulysses could be mine. I remember how excited and troubled I was over the scene in which he and his crew were shipwrecked. The "stars" went away to Balboa, where the waves are terribly rough and the coast is full of treacherous rocks. The realism of the details that were spelled to me made me tremble—the shattering of the boat against the rocks, the frantic struggling of the men amid the billows, the sudden disappearance of those who were supposed to be drowned, the final emergence of Ulysses and a few strong sailors on the beautiful but baleful Isle of Circe. There was, I declare, nothing shadowy about this dangerous acting!

The pilot told me afterwards that I myself was in danger for a few minutes in what was to me the most thrilling event connected with the picture—my ride in an aëroplane. It was only material for more film-shadows; but to me it was a mighty reality, and I completely forgot my picture self. At first Mrs. Macy, my mother, and my brother, who had lately come out to California for the last part of the picture, would not hear of my being taken up; but I insisted. There was only room for the pilot and me. Was I afraid? How could fear hold back my spirit, long accustomed to soar? Up, up, up the machine bore me until I lost the odours of the flying dust, the ripening vineyards and the pungent eucalyptus! Up, up, up, I climbed the aërial mountains until I felt rain-clouds spilling their pearls upon me. With lightning speed we shot over the tallest buildings of Los Angeles and returned to the field after half an hour's race with a high wind. Then the machine went through a series of amazing dips! I felt in them, as it were, organ music and the sweep of ocean, winds from off mountains and illimitable plains. As the machine rose and fell, my brain throbbed with ecstatic thoughts that whirled on tiptoe, and I seemed to sense the Dance of the Gods. I had never had such a satisfying sense of physical liberty.

Another thrilling day came when we went down to the shipyards at San Pedro. The idea was to show that I had caught spiritual vibrations from the unrest and suffering of toiling mankind—that I had felt the gigantic throbs of labour's thousand hammers welding the instruments with which fire, water, and the winds are yoked to the service of man. At the shipyards I found myself actually in the midst of the most tremendous industrial activity. I felt the rhythmic thunder of the triple hammers in the forge and the searching flame and the sharp, quick blows of the men driving in rivets, the vibrations of huge cranes lifting and lowering burdens.

The men stopped work to watch me. There was a babel of voices. The bosses shouted, ordering the men back to their jobs; but they were too interested watching a blind woman on the monster crane. We were told that our visit had cost Uncle Sam thousands of dollars by slowing up the work for three hours.

Afterwards we went on board a ship that had just been finished and was about to be launched, and I christened it by breaking a bottle of champagne against the bow. I was too hot and thirsty to be duly impressed by the solemn ceremony, and, as I hurled the bottle, I let escape a profound sigh at the waste of so precious a liquid. At twelve o'clock the men shared their lunch with me and brought me a glass of cold water and showed the kindest interest in me. When finally we got into the automobile and turned hotelward I could scarcely move or think, so over-weighted was I with a world of emotions and new impressions.

But our days of exaltation were followed by days of discouragement. Pessimists said, "The picture will be a hodge-podge. There are too many points of view in it." What particular point of view any particular person held it was difficult to find out, and no wonder, for it shifted with events and with the coming and going of different personalities.

We could not stifle our yearnings for the bright vistas of an immaterial sphere. Our thoughts turned from the heat of the studio to ethereal locations. Mr. Platt protested, but when someone suggested that it was foolish to be making the picture of a mortal woman when we might as well be depicting a mys- tical Mother of Sorrows wandering lonely, and grieving for the blind, the wounded, and the fallen of humanity, he was completely overruled. Here was inspiration and no mistake.

The average person comforts himself with the reflection that he did not make human beings, and is not responsible for their defects. But such a philosophy had no comfort for the "Mother of Sorrows." There was no satisfaction in such muddle-headed serenity.

The day this part of the picture was to be filmed we found within the gates of our studio a great crowd of strange creatures—men and women of all races, colours, ages, and degrees of deformity. As we waited in line to be disinfected (the influenza was in full swing, and everyone who entered the studio had to have his nostrils and throat sprayed) we asked the uniformed attendants if all that mob had been disinfected before us. His answer made us believe we were reasonably safe, and we hurried on.

Several men minus one or more arms and legs were performing acrobatic stunts on the mounds of earth beside a ditch where water pipes were being laid. One shard with two sticks for legs and a bent piece of steel in place of an arm swung himself back and forth across the ditch on his crutches, much to the delight of the spectators. A blind man tapped his way along the walk. Some Chinese squatted on the hot sand playing fan-tan. An old man with a thick white beard and bushy white hair sat on a canvas stool playing a concertina. Women chattered in a medley of tongues.

Miss Thomson asked a man who might have been Jack-the-giant-killer what picture they were making. "Keeler's," he said. "Who's that?" she inquired. "Ask me something easy," he grinned.

In the studio our people were very busy. Yes, we were going out on location that day. The "Mother of Sorrows" would appear to the afflicted of the world bearing a torch of hope. To our amazement the crowd through which we had just passed clambered into our location buses, the director, camera men and principal actors got into waiting automobiles, and the procession started. On the way we learned some of the details of what was going to happen.

The police had given us permission to use a notorious alley which had recently been closed. It was a short, narrow street with two entrances, one from the main street and the other from a higher level reached by a long flight of rough steps.

The alley was deserted when we arrived, but when the buses unloaded their cargo it became a veritable Bedlam. It was as if invisible hands had emptied a nondescript Noah's ark there. Dogs, resembling their human partners, appeared from nowhere. Soon the booths were filled with merchandise. The pawn shops

and second hand clothing shops displayed their wares
from poles outside the door. There were tobacco
stands, shoe repair booths, saloons, and there were
scissors grinders, peddlers, and fruit venders walking
up and down shouting and singing. The noise was
demoniacal, and the smells were nauseating. But
even more irritating than noise and odours was the
mad jostling of the crowd. I had an almost irresistible impulse to strike out—to clutch some support
amid the swaying confusion.

I was relieved when Mr. Platt's boy, Guy, came
for me. He took me out of the crowd on the main
street, so that the people should not see me before I
made my appearance at the upper entrance to the
alley. The "Mother of Sorrows" robe was draped
over my head and arms in long, flowing folds of
heavy material. I was given instructions to descend
the steps very slowly, and when I reached the pavement, I was to walk to the middle of the alley and
stand with upraised face and arms. Afterwards I
was told that when I first started down the steps,
nobody noticed me. Then one of the women, lean-
ing out of a window, caught sight of me and
screamed. There was a wild scramble. Every face
was turned towards the steps. As I came on down
the mass seemed to become one body. No directing
was necessary. They behaved as their instincts of
superstition and fear dictated. The swaying, uncer-

tain motion of my body, due to lack of balance, seemed to hypnotize them. They sensed something strange in my bearing and my unseeing eyes. When my feet touched the pavement, those near me fell on their knees, and before I reached the middle of the alley, everyone was kneeling without a signal from the director! I stood as motionless as a statue for a few terrifying seconds, not knowing exactly what to do. I sensed the hushed and unnatural stillness—the palpitating wall of fear that encircled me. I reached out my hands and touched the bowed heads of those who were nearest me. The contact smote my soul, and the tears rolled down my cheeks and fell upon my hands and the heads they rested upon. The people around me began to sob aloud, and draw closer. I felt them touching my robe and my feet. All the love and pity which until that moment I had been trying to simulate suddenly rushed over me like a tide. I thought my heart would burst, so overcharged was it with longing to lift the weary load of misery beneath my hands. Scarcely knowing what I said, I prayed as I had never prayed in my life before.

"Pity us, O God! Pity our helplessness, our broken lives and desecrated bodies! Pity our children who wither like flowers in our hands! Pity all the maimed and the marred! We beseech Thee, give us a sign that Thou seest our blindness and hearest our dumbness. Deliver us out of the alleys and gutters of the world! Deliver us from the poverty that is blindness and the denial that is deafness! With our groping hands we pray Thee, break the yoke that is heavy upon us. Come, O come to our hearts choked with weeds, to our sin-fettered souls, to Thy people without a refuge! Come to the children whose paradise we have betrayed! Come to the hungry whom no one feeds, to the sick whom no one visits, to the criminals whom no one pities! Forgive us our weak excuses and the sins we have committed one against another in Thy Name."

The scene that capped the climax for absurdity was one in which I was supposed to go to France during the conference at which the Big Four were deciding the fate of the world, and urge them to bring the war to a finish. I was to stuff my mouth with golden opinions and placatory speeches to the councillors and generals against whose wicked stupidities I had never missed a chance to vent my indignation. To this day I am glad of the opportunity they gave me to tell those spinners of human destiny all that I thought of them! Full of "pomp and circumstance" without, and a volcano within, I walked stiffly to the council board, escorted by Mr. Lloyd George, and I remember I touched only the finger tips of Monsieur Clemenceau's gloved hand. Fortunately, we realized before we left Hollywood that this was too ridiculous, and it was not incorporated in the picture, nor were many of our other flights of fancy.

The memory of the last scenes always causes me to smile, they were such a curious fantasy. I was supposed to be a sort of Joan of Arc fighting for the freedom of the workers of the world, and a vast procession was gathered for the march upon the bulwarks of the enemy. I was placed at the front on a white horse. I might have managed Peggy, for I was accustomed to her gait, but alas! Peggy was dark, and we must needs have a big white horse for that grand occasion. The powerful creature I rode was named Sligo, which is Irish, and his temperament was like his name. I really believe that he was in his element in that wild charge of the imagination. Of course it was a motley swarm of people dressed in all sorts of queer costumes to represent all the peoples of the earth, and there was a dreadful confusion of horses, shouts, waving banners, and trumpets blown loud and long. Naturally, Sligo became restive and charged as he should; but the violence of his movements was disconcerting to me, especially as I held the reins in one hand and a trumpet in the other, which I was directed to blow every now and then. Out there in the fierce California sun I grew hotter, redder, and more embarrassed every second. The perspiration rolled down my face, and the trumpet tasted nasty. When without warning Sligo decided to stand up on his hind legs, one of the camera men, at the risk of his life, ran under him and pulled on an invisible rein to bring him down to earth again. I was glad when it was all over, and my quaint fancy of leading the people of the world to victory has never been so ardent since.

Chapter XIII

THE PLAY WORLD

THE picture was not a financial success. My sense of pride mutinies against my confession; but we are the kind of people who come out of an enterprise poorer than we went into it, and I am sorry to say, this condition is not always confined to ourselves.

We returned to our home in Forest Hills and for two years lived quietly. But we were faced with the necessity of earning more money. The funds my friends had provided for my support would cease with my death, and if I died before my teacher, she would be left almost destitute. The income I had I could live on, but I could not save anything.

In the winter of 1920 we went into vaudeville and remained until the spring of 1924. That does not mean that we worked continually during all four years. We appeared for short periods in and around New York, in New England, and in Canada. In 1921 and 1922 we went from coast to coast on the Orpheum Circuit.

It had always been said that we went into public life only to attract attention, and I had letters from friends in Europe remonstrating with me about "the deplorable theatrical exhibition" into which I had allowed myself to be dragged. Now the truth is, I went of my own free will and persuaded my teacher to go with me. Vaudeville offered us better pay than either literary work or lecturing. Besides, the work was easier in an essential respect—we usually stayed in one place a week, instead of having to travel constantly from town to town and speak so soon after our arrival that we had no time for rest or preparation. We were on the stage only twenty minutes in the afternoon and evening, and the rules of the theatre usually protected us against the friendly invasion of the crowds who used to swarm around to shake hands with us at the lectures.

My teacher was not happy in vaudeville. She could never get used to the rush, glare, and noise of the theatre; but I enjoyed it keenly. At first it seemed odd to find ourselves on the same "bill" with acrobats, monkeys, horses, dogs, and parrots; but our little act was dignified and people seemed to like it.

I found the world of vaudeville much more amusing than the world I had always lived in, and I liked it. I liked to feel the warm tide of human life pulsing round and round me. I liked to weep at its sorrows, to be annoyed at its foibles, to laugh at its absurdities, to be set athrill by its flashes of unexpected goodness and courage. I enjoyed watching the actors in the workshop of faces and costumes. If I should relate "the strength and riches of their state"—the powder, the patches and masks, the ribbons, jewels, and livery; and if I should describe the charming bits of acts which were performed for me off stage I should be more voluminous than *Who's Who in America*. I must be content to say I was often admitted to the dressing room of the other actors, and that many of them let me feel their costumes and even went through their acts for me. The thought often occurred to me that the parts the actors played was their real life, and all the rest was make-believe. I still think so, and hope it is true, for the sake of many to whom fate is unkind in the real world.

I can conceive that in time the spectacle might have grown stale. I might have come to hear the personal confessions of my fellow actors without emotion, and to regard the details of wild parties and excursions with impatience. But I shall always be glad I went into vaudeville, not only for the excitement of it, but also for the opportunities it gave me to study life.

In the nature of things a lecture tour exposes one to many unpleasant experiences. Our lecture contract required that we collect the money before we went on the platform, but that was seldom possible and we disliked to imply distrust by demanding payment. In Seattle we gave two lectures to appreciative audiences, one in the afternoon and the other in the evening. The local manager told us he would not be able to pay us our share, which was a thousand dollars, until after the evening performance. He did not appear in the theatre after the evening lecture, and we had no way of getting our money from him. Our manager was not interested in a lawsuit so far away, and we were obliged to pay him a percentage whether we were paid or not; so he suffered no loss on our account.

This happened many times—in Dunkirk, New York; Meadville, Pennsylvania; Ashtabula, Ohio; and San Diego and Santa Rosa, California. In no case was the town responsible; it was the fault of the local manager. Once when we did demand payment and refused to appear when it was not made, the audience became indignant, and the next morning the newspapers came out with a great headline, "Helen Keller refused to speak unless she held the money in her hand." We decided never to put ourselves in that position again. Once when we spoke at Allerton, Iowa, a crowd came to hear us, and our share of the proceeds—we were to go fifty-fifty with the manager—was over seven hundred dollars. It was amusing to see how reluctant the men in charge were to pay it. In Vancouver we had so much larger audience than the local manager expected that he paid us twice as much as the contract called for.

Some of the theatres where we went were beautiful, and most of them comfortable. Mr. Albee, who is at the head of the organization, is a man of singular ability and kindness of heart, and he concerns himself earnestly with everything that promotes the welfare of the actors and the efficiency of their work. Very few of them are permitted to come into his presence, but his good will radiates through his staff from one end of the system to the other. We found most of our managers courteous, and some of them were beloved. I shall always be grateful to my personal manager, Mr. Harry Weber, who never failed us in service and loyalty. Mr. Albee is interested not only in the functioning of his mammoth machine, but also in the human cogs and wheels that make it go. Not one of these small ceaselessly moving parts gets out of order but he knows it, and makes every effort to repair it, whatever the cause or the cost. He has kept individuals in shows who are blind or deaf or crippled, but whose handicap is cleverly concealed from the public. An important branch of his humanitarian work is the National Vaudeville Association, which has ten thousand members. Each membership carries with it a paid-up insurance policy of a thousand dollars, and in cases of illness, idleness, or other misfortune, everyone is sure to receive financial aid, no matter in what part of the world he may be. The Association maintains a sanitarium for tubercular members, and there are health camps in California, Arizona, Colorado, and other places.

The audiences always made us feel their interest and friendliness. Sometimes many of them were foreigners, and could not understand what we said, but their applause and sympathy were gratifying. After my teacher had explained how I was taught, I made my entrance and gave a brief talk, at the end of which the audience was allowed to ask questions. Some of them were very funny. Can you tell the time of day without a watch? Have you ever thought of getting married? Have you ever used a ouija board? Do you think business is looking up? Am I going on a trip? Why has a cow two stomachs? How much is too many? Do you believe in ghosts? Do you think it is a blessing to be poor? Do you dream? There were hundreds of them.

I am always intensely conscious of my audience. Before I say a word I feel its breath as it comes in little pulsations to my face. I sense its appreciation or indifference. I found vaudeville audiences especially easy to speak before. They were much more demonstrative than most others, and showed instantly when they were pleased. One of the queerest experiences I ever had was the first time I spoke from a pulpit. The audience seemed so quiet and the reading desk was so high I felt as if I were speaking to them over a wall. A similar experience came when I spoke over the radio. I felt as if I were speaking to ghosts. There were no life vibrations—no shuffling feet, no sound of applause, no odour of tobacco or cosmetics, only a blankness into which my words floated. I never had that bewildered feeling before a vaudeville audience.

Chapter XIV

MY MOTHER

IT WAS while I was in vaudeville that the first bereavement came which struck at the very roots of my life. My mother died while we were appearing in Los Angeles. My father's death, which occurred while I was a young girl sixteen years old, never seemed so real to me. But I had had my mother all those years and fine ligaments of love and sympathy had knit us together.

I have no vivid recollections of her before my education began. I have a dim sensation of arms about me, and hands that wiped away my tears; but such memories are too vague to bring before me a picture of her.

She used to tell me how happy she was when I was born. She dwelt on her memories of the eighteen months when I could see and hear. She told me how, as soon as I could walk, I chased sunbeams and butterflies, how I held out my little hands to pet every creature I saw and was never afraid. "And what wonderful eyes you had!" she would say, "you were always picking up needles and buttons which no one else could find." She had a pretty workbasket

which stood on three slender legs, quite high above
the floor. It had holes all round near the top. She
loved to tell how I would come to her knees and lisp
something which she interpreted to mean, "I wonder
when I shall be tall enough to look through those
holes and see what is in the basket." She also remembered my delight in the open wood fire, and told
how I insisted upon sitting up late watching the
sparks and laughing as they danced up the chimney.
"Yes, life was good to us both for a few brief
months," she would say wistfully. Then when she was
twenty-three came the illness which left me deaf and
blind, and after that life was never the same to her.
It was as if a white winter had swept over the June
of her youth; I know, although she never said it,
that she suffered more through me than through her
other children. Her nature was not expansive or
happy. She made few close friends, and wherever she
sojourned, the sorrow and loneliness of her spirit
persisted. The larger opportunities for enjoyment
and intellectual enrichment which she gained on her
journeys with us or her visits in our home at Wrentham did not erase from her heart the sense of tragedy
and denial which my limitations kept always before
her. That her suffering was crushed into silence did
not lessen its intensity. But there was nothing selfish
in her sorrow. What she had suffered broadened and
deepened her sympathy for others.

She never talked about herself. She was sensitive even to the point of pain, and shy of revealing herself even to her children. But, veiled as her personality was, she was always an intimate part of our lives. It was inexpressibly sweet the way she said to me that her last thought at night and her first thought in the morning was of me. She suffered much from rheumatism in her hands, and she found it most difficult to write in braille, which disappointed her keenly because she never liked to have anyone read her letters to me.

It is a comfort to me to believe that all she hoped and prayed for was fulfilled in her second child, my lovely sister Mildred. Five years after her birth came my brother Phillips, who bears the name of one of my earliest and dearest friends, Phillips Brooks. When my father died, my mother devoted herself to the bringing up of her two younger children. (I was away from home most of the time, in New York and Boston.) Then Mildred married Warren L. Tyson of Montgomery, Alabama, and my mother spent the later years of her life partly with them and partly with me.

By temperament my mother was not domestic; but after she married my father, she had a large Southern household to manage. She carried the whole burden of housekeeping, supervision of negro workers, gardening, looking after the poultry, preparing hams and lard, sewing for the children, and entertaining the guests whom my father brought home to dinner almost every day. She was an expert in the science of poultry-raising. Her hams were praised all the country round; her jellies and preserves were the envy of our neighbours. She went about these homely tasks silent, unutterably sad, with me clinging to her skirts. Tall and stately as Juno, she stood beside the great iron kettles, directing the negroes in all the processes of making lard. My teacher often wondered how such a sensitive, high-strung woman could endure this sort of work; but my mother never complained. She threw herself into these tasks as if she had no other interest in life. Whatever the problem, whether in the house, the chicken yard or out on the farm, for the time being she gave her whole mind to it. She said to Miss Sullivan once, "Of course lard-making hasn't the charm of sculpture or architecture or poetry; but I suppose it has its importance in the universal scheme of things."

She was passionately devoted to her gardening and to her flowers. Nothing delighted her more than to nurse a plant weakling into strength and bloom. The wealth of her heart had to spend itself even upon the most unworthy of nature's children. One early spring morning she went out to look at some young rose bushes which she had set out some time before, thinking that the warm days were surely coming. She found that a heavy frost had killed them, and she wrote me that very morning that "like David when his son died, she lifted up her voice and wept."

Her love of birds was equal to her love of flowers. She would spend hours in the little wood near our house in Wrentham watching their pretty antics when they made love, or built their nests, or fed the young birds and taught them to fly. The mocking bird and the thrush were the darlings of her heart.

My mother talked intelligently, brilliantly, about current events, and she had a Southerner's interest in politics. But after my mind took a radical turn she could never get over the feeling that we had drifted apart. It grieves me that I should have added to the sadness that weighed upon her, but I have the consolation of remembering that no differences could take away from us the delight of talking together.

She was an omnivorous reader. She welcomed all books new or old, in the English of Chaucer or the English of Ruskin. She had a horror of mediocrity and hypocrisy. I remember the scorn in her words as she quoted some bromide that was pronounced by a dull celebrity. In keenness of wit she resembled Mrs. Carlyle, whose letters she read with pleasure. Mr. Macy introduced her to Sydney Smith, and she used to say that his sayings were a silent accompaniment to her thoughts. Boswell's *Johnson* also gave her many bright moments. Bernard Shaw irritated her,

not because he was radical or sarcastic, but because he
was a chronic iconoclast. She had no patience with
Lawrence's books. She would exclaim, "He seems
incapable of conceiving purity and innocence in a
woman. To him love is indecent. No modest violets
grow in the fields of life for him."

But in the presence of true genius her humility
was complete. Walt Whitman did not shock her. She
knew several of Balzac's books almost by heart. She
read Rabelais, Montesquieu, and Montaigne. When
she read Lanier she said "his 'gray and sober dove,'
with the eye of faith and the wing of love, nestled in
her bosom."

One memorable summer we rented a cottage on
Lake St. Catherine, in Vermont. How we all enjoyed
the lovely lake, the pine-covered hills, and the winding green alleys they call roads in Vermont! I have
a mental picture of her which I treasure, seated on
the little porch which overlooked the lake, in the evening, her dear hands idle for a few minutes, while
she watched the children and young people in boats
and canoes, with a tender, wistful expression on her
beautiful face as the sun disappeared behind the
green hills.

When the World War burst upon us she refused
to talk about it, and when she saw the thousands of
young men who were encamped round about Montgomery, her heart yearned to shield them from the

horrors which awaited them. When Russia offered her splendid peace terms to the Allies, my mother said she wanted to stretch her arms across the ocean and embrace the one country which had the courage and the generosity to call war a crime against humanity.

Her death came as she had always prayed it would, swiftly, before she was old and dependent. She had dreaded illness and the slow parting scenes that usually precede death, and she desired that she might die in her sleep, or suddenly. So it was according to her wish that the end came. She was with her dear ones in Montgomery, but no one saw her die.

I received the telegram telling of her death two hours before I had to go on the stage. I had not even known she was ill. Every fibre of my being cried out at the thought of facing the audience, but it had to be done. Fortunately, they did not know what I was suffering, and that made it a little easier for my teacher and me. One of the questions asked me that day was, "How old are you?" How old, indeed! I felt as old as time, and I answered, "How old do I look?" The people laughed, pleased that I had evaded telling my age, which they supposed would have been embarrassing to me. Another question was, "Are you happy?" I swallowed hard and answered: "Yes, because I have confidence in God." Then it was over, and for a little while I could sit alone with my sorrow. I had absolute faith that we should meet again in the Land of Eternal Beauty; but oh, the dreary blank her going left in my life! I missed her everywhere I went over the road she had travelled with me. I missed her braille letters, and she seemed to have died a second time when I visited my sister in Montgomery the following April. The only thought that upheld me was that in the Great Beyond where all truth shines revealed she would find in my limitations a satisfying sense of God's purpose of good which runs like a thread of gold through all things.

Chapter XV

LUX IN TENEBRIS

IT WAS in 1921 that the central clearing house which had for so many years been recognized as the chief need of the blind came into being. It was conceived by a blind man, Mr. H. Randolph Latimer, Superintendent of the Western Pennsylvania Institution for the Blind, and launched at the annual meeting of the American Association of Workers for the Blind, in Vinton, Iowa.

Its first president was Mr. M. C. Migel of New York. It is because of his constant helpfulness that the American Foundation for the Blind has achieved the degree of usefulness which it has to-day. With the coöperation of his friends he financed it until 1924 when an appeal was made to the public for a permanent endowment and Mrs. Macy and I were asked to lecture in its behalf.

It is not pleasant to go begging even for the best of causes, but in our present civilization most philanthropic and educational institutions are supported by public donations and gifts from wealthy citizens. This is a wretched way, but we have not yet learned a better one, and until we do, individuals like myself will continue to travel up and down the land, and up and down in the elevators of great office buildings, to solicit funds from rich men. We will stand at doors and street corners, hat in hand, begging pennies from every passer-by, we will climb on to the running board of automobiles held in traffic to plead with some wealthy person to take our precious cause under his golden wing.

During all the years of lecturing, picture-making, and vaudeville I had never ceased to dream of a happier world for the sightless, but no practical way of realizing this dream had presented itself until now. Throughout my journeys all over the country I had realized that in spite of all that had been done for the blind, in spite of all that had been written about them, people still considered them a group apart.

Dear reader, let me ask you to stop for a moment and try to visualize your blind neighbour. You have met him often in the street, in sunshine and in rain, cautiously threading his way among his unseen fellows, his cane tapping the pavement, his body tense, his ears straining to hear sounds that will guide him in the invisible maze. You have glanced at him pityingly, and gone your way thinking how strange his thoughts must be, his feelings how different from your own. My friend, have done with this cruel illusion and try to learn the truth. Hearts are hearts and pain is pain, and joy, ambition, and love are in the blind man even as in you. He wants the same things that you do. Like you he dreams of love and success and happiness. You would still be yourself if an accident blinded you to-morrow; your desires would be the same.

You have perhaps thought that his greatest loss is that he is not able to enjoy the colours of the sunset, the contours of the hills, the moon and the stars, but he could tell you that he would not mind very much that the blue sky is blotted out if he could shake off the thousand petty restraints that encompass him. The hardest thing we have to bear is that we cannot go about the simplest matters of life alone. With all our hearts we desire to be strong, free, and useful.

In most countries and most ages, the blind have been considered, with a few outstanding exceptions, as objects of charity, of pity, of contempt, even of cruelty. The affliction has frequently been looked upon as a Divine visitation, and the rôle of the blind man has been that of the beggar by the wayside, and his dwelling place has been the almshouse. Yet even under these hard conditions there have emerged from this realm of never-ending darkness many heroic figures. As Milton proudly said, "It is not so wretched to be blind as it is not to be capable of enduring blindness."

We do not ask to be coddled. It is the last thing

the blind need. It is not helpful but in the long run harmful to buy worthless articles because a blind person made them, but for many years kind-hearted people have been buying useless and often ugly things for no other reason. Quantities of beadwork, to take only one example, which could appeal to no eye but the eye of pity have passed as specimens of what the blind can do. Yet with a lovely design and a little supervision the blind can do as beautiful beadwork as the seeing.

Even in the matter of books the seeing have shown that they consider us a group apart. They have often contributed books of a rather gloomy, preachy character to our reading rooms, apparently supposing that our books must be in keeping with our misfortune. But it is worth while to notice that the cheerful books are well-thumbed while the mournful ones stand unmolested in stern dignity on the upper shelf.

The number of books we have is far greater than it was when I was in school, but in comparison with those of the seeing we have few indeed. I have been told that for the seeing more than 10,000 titles a year are published. We have in all, outside of textbooks, 3150 titles. We are grateful for them, but we are hungry for more and more variety.

Much is being done to assuage this hunger. Formerly the fact that a book was in raised print did not mean that all the blind could read it, but since the

Uniform Type Committee of the American Association of Workers for the Blind has brought about the adoption of one system of embossed print throughout America, everything henceforth will be easily read by all the blind. This was done through the generosity of Mr. Migel, who financed the work of the committee. The head of the committee was Robert B. Irwin, our beloved comrade in the dark who is now head of the Bureau of Research and Information of the Foundation. Congress gives an annual appropriation for the embossing of books and many states have chapters of Red Cross transcribers. After provision was made for the reëducation of men blinded in the War many women throughout the country took up the transcribing of books. Not only have the blinded soldiers benefited by this service, but sightless high school and college students have been helped. Learning to write braille is not more difficult, and there are still hundreds of women who might brighten the dark hours of the blind by copying stories or poems for them.

There are among the blind to-day many with intelligence enough to share the responsibilities and rewards of our common humanity. The worst period that most of them go through comes when they graduate from school. No matter what their hopes may have been they are likely to see them fade away.

The prejudice of the seeing to whom blindness means inefficiency is such that the blind, confronted with the practical problem of making a living, turn away from competition in the open market to the workshop. Not infrequently they escape the workshop only to find themselves street musicians. The street life pays them better, but those who follow it deepen the public prejudice against the blind.

To-day no blind person can succeed in any of the higher professions unless he possesses a fighting spirit and a personality that attracts attention. Even then he needs a strong helping hand. I have known students to spend ten years and more in schools for the blind, receive a thorough training in piano, violin, organ, or voice, at a cost to the state of thousands of dollars, and after leaving school full of hope and ambition, find themselves back in their own homes with their uneducated families without a piano, without money, without friends, the institution which educated them having left them to shift for themselves as best they might. I am thinking of one young man who was considered a virtuoso who is now earning his livelihood tuning pianos. He cannot play any more; his hands are so stiff from carrying his bag of tools. There is a young lady not far from my own home with a beautifully trained voice who earns a meagre wage folding circulars. I can think of many others with various talents who might be musicians, writers, editors, statesmen and ministers if they had been given assistance when they left school.

Until the Foundation came into being there was only one national organization at work on the problems of the blind. That was the National Committee, which is now the National Society for the Prevention of Blindness. It was, and still is, doing one of the most important pieces of work in this country. It is not only helping conserve the sight of large numbers of children who have defective vision which, if neglected, will develop into blindness, it is establishing sight saving classes in the public schools and it is investigating the causes of blindness in industry and elsewhere, and is getting laws passed to lessen the danger from preventable causes.

It seems hard to believe now that twenty years ago the leading cause of blindness in the new-born, *ophthalmia neonatorum,* could not even be discussed in public. Massachusetts, as I have said in an earlier chapter, was one of the leaders in this campaign. She passed a law which was immediately followed in other states. The law required that every case of disease of the eye in the new-born should be reported and investigated. The remedy was provided gratuitously, with a statement from the highest medical authorities as to its purity and safety. To-day twenty-nine states have passed similar laws. I

think it was the happiest moment of my life when
Mr. Allen, director of the Massachusetts School for
the Blind, told me only a few months ago that the
day nursery for blind babies which was once full of
little sightless ones, with a long waiting list, is now
almost empty. The work of prevention is close to
my heart, and I am sorry that it is not possible for
me to take a more active part in it. I have been
greatly encouraged by the interest the Lions have
shown. In various places extending from Black-
well, Oklahoma, to Tsing Tao, China, they have
opened free clinics for eye correction among children. To-day in New York and indeed everywhere
thousands of oculists are spending their lives to make
people see better and to ward off blindness in the
eyes of the new-born. A great hospital has just been
opened in connection with Johns Hopkins Medical
School in Baltimore under Dr. William Holland
Wilmer, one of the leading ophthalmologists in the
world, who has retired from private practice in order
to devote himself to teaching and research in connection with diseases of the eye. This is a great step
in the right direction.

The doctors in New York are flanked by an army
of nurses who teach the patients how to carry out the
doctor's directions. Many of the patients are not
only poor; they are ignorant, and numbers of them can
neither speak nor understand English. This work in

the homes is very important, very necessary, and very costly, but it is work that has to be done, and I wish that those people who picture New York as a selfish city grabbing all things and making no return could see how marvellously she handles this tremendous task.

What the Foundation proposed to do was to correlate the scattered and disorganized work for the blind, to prevent duplication of effort, to see to it that each class of the blind receives the particular help it needs, and to give direction and effectiveness to the local commissions.

When we started on the campaign for the Foundation four years ago the public received us with open arms. For three years we covered the country from coast to coast. We addressed over 250,000 people at 249 meetings in 123 cities. Through attending innumerable luncheons and receptions and paying endless calls on persons likely to be interested in our work we came to understand what must be the exhaustion of campaigning political candidates. But we had an advantage over the politicians: they met divided support while our cause appealed to all parties.

The wiseacres say that after forty we cannot expect many pleasant surprises. I have not found this true. Some of the most joyful surprises I have known in my life have come since my fortieth birthday, many of them in connection with my work for the blind. Dr. Henry van Dyke is one.

When the time came to select a national chairman for our campaign, I remembered Elbert Hubbard's advice, "When you want to get something done, go to the busiest man you know. The other kind hasn't time." My mind leapt at once to Dr. van Dyke. I knew he was a busy man. I recalled the things he had been doing the past twenty-five years—teaching in Princeton, preaching and lecturing about the country for several years, three years in the diplomatic service, a year in the navy during the World War, many years of writing books that people loved, still more years of making the acquaintance of the great out-of-doors, and bringing up a family of five children and nine grandchildren. Even if I passed over the hours Dr. van Dyke spent fishing in many waters, I still felt that he was the man to launch a new project and to see it through.

I could not have picked a better one. Dr. van Dyke is the kind of a friend to have when one is up against a difficult problem. He will take trouble, days and nights of trouble, if it is for somebody else or for some cause he is interested in. "I'm not an optimist," says Dr. van Dyke, "there's too much evil in the world and in me. Nor am I a pessimist; there is too much good in the world and in God. So I am just a meliorist, believing that He wills to make the world better, and trying to do my bit to help and wishing that it were more."

The generosity and enthusiasm of Mr. Otto Kahn was a great help to us in the beginning. The far-reaching beams of his benevolence have illuminated the world of the dark not only in this country but in England as well.

Throughout the country newspapers opened their pages to us. Churches, schools, synagogues, women's clubs, the Junior Leagues, the Boy and Girl Scouts and the service clubs, especially the Lions, have assisted us in every way, holding meetings, soliciting funds, giving luncheons, and making contributions. The Lions, in particular, have made the work for the blind their major activity, just as the Rotarians have made crippled children their special charge.

Nearly everywhere we met with a spirit of coöperation that made our hearts glad. In the winter of 1926 I spent a week in Washington. Dr. van Dyke came from Princeton to assist me, and our hopes were high when we knew that the cause of the blind was to be heard in the First City of the land. It was there that the National Library for the Blind was established, and an annual appropriation granted for embossing books; there, too, that the work of rehabilitating our blinded soldiers had begun. Our hopes were not disappointed.

One morning at twelve o'clock my teacher and I

called upon President Coolidge at the White House. He received us most kindly. I had always heard that he was cold, but there was not the least coldness in his hand. He had only a few minutes to spare from a strenuous day, but he listened attentively to what I told him about the Foundation, then, placing my fingers on his lips, he said, "I am greatly interested in your work, and I will coöperate with you in every possible way."

He proved he was sincere by becoming our Honorary President, and by sending me his private check for a generous donation. I found in Mrs. Coolidge one whose heart is responsive to every whisper of sorrow. She told me she had always been interested in the deaf—she had taught the deaf at Northampton many years ago—and added that she would be happy to help brighten the dark world of the sightless.

I also called up Senator Borah, Thomas Schall (the blind Senator), and Mr. and Mrs. Lansing. They all did what they could to make my visit to Washington a success. Many other people in Washington helped with money and sympathy, among them Mr. Gilbert Grosvenor and his wife, Elsie, Dr. Bell's daughter, my playmate of long ago, Phil and Lenore Smith, Mrs. Frederick C. Hicks, the German Ambassador, Herr von Maltzan, and Mrs. Wadsworth, the daughter of John Hay. Mrs. Wadsworth gave a beautiful tea in her home, and her kindness will ever be a part of my most affectionate memories of Washington.

In Detroit my friend of many years in the work for the sightless, Mr. Charles F. F. Campbell, director of the Detroit League for the Handicapped, was indefatigable in his efforts to capture that city for my cause. One night at a mass meeting sponsored by the Junior League we raised forty-two thousand dollars before we left the auditorium. Nor did the interest of Detroit stop after my departure. Only within the last few days I have received checks ranging from one dollar to fifty-five hundred dollars. Among those who have made Detroit the banner city of my crusade are Mr. and Mrs. Henry Joy, Mrs. Seyburn, Mr. Warren, Mr. W. O. Briggs, the six Fisher brothers, and Mr. and Mrs. Edsel Ford.

Next to this meeting in Detroit comes one which we held in Philadelphia. It was the second meeting of the campaign, when very little was known of the Foundation and its purposes. Mr. Edward Bok presided, and Dr. van Dyke poured a flood of golden words into the responsive hearts of the people. We raised twenty-two thousand dollars that Sunday afternoon.

In two large cities, St. Louis and Chicago, workers for the sightless requested me not to speak, and we have respected their wishes. Only one city invited us and then gave us the cold shoulder. For some reason I am unable fully to understand Buffalo refused to be interested in the national aspect of the work for the blind. When I arrived at the auditorium where the meeting was to take place, and found only about twenty persons present, I thought there must have been a mistake in the date given out; but alas! there was not even that salve for my bruised feelings. The people were simply not interested. In five days I collected only about three thousand dollars, while in Rochester, which has about half the population of Buffalo, more than fifteen thousand dollars was given in less time. No doubt part of my success was due to the enthusiasm and generosity of Mrs. Edmund Lyon whom I had first met many years before, when my teacher and Dr. Bell and I visited the Rochester School for the Deaf where she was teaching. Two other friends in Rochester whom I remember with gratitude are Mr. and Mrs. Harper Sibley who held up the work for the blind with both hands.

I had thought that the stars in filmland might be especially sensitive to our appeal, since the breath and substance of their life was light, but I found that I was mistaken. I wrote letter after letter which I left at the studios, but never an answer did I receive, except from Mary Pickford. The silence that came back penetrated even my deaf ears. Naturally my heart thrilled at the responsiveness of Mary Pickford and her husband, Douglas Fairbanks.

I had, of course, known Mary Pickford as a child knows the characters of fairyland. I did not think this shadow acquaintance would ever become a reality, but fairy tales do sometimes come true and I have a bright memory of the day when the shadow Mary was transformed into a smiling little girl wearing a faded gingham frock and patched shoes and two long braids of golden hair. She had invited us to the studio grounds for lunch. She rushed out of a tiny cottage to greet us. I was accompanied by Mrs. Macy, Miss Thomson, and Mr. Charles Hayes of the American Foundation staff. She said that Mr. Fairbanks would be in soon, but we would not wait for him. "When we are working," she said, "we can't be regular about anything. That is why we live here most of the time when we are making pictures." She was working on "Little Annie Rooney" at the time, and Mr. Fairbanks was just finishing "Don Q." While we were eating lunch, I told Mary (I simply cannot call that slip of a girl in faded gingham and patched shoes Mrs. Fairbanks) the object of my visit to California. She listened intently and made intelligent comments while I talked. She said that before she became a motion picture actress, she had been on the stage, and in her first play had taken the part of a blind girl. She said that it had been in her mind a long time to make a picture with a young blind girl the central figure. She gave an attractive sketch of the story and asked me if I would offer suggestions when the time came. I promised to come out to Hollywood and see to it that her blind girl did none of the absurd, impossible things which the sightless are usually made to do on the stage.

Douglas Fairbanks came in, just as we finished lunch, with his director, Donald Crisp. Mr. Fairbanks was limping slightly, as he had sprained his ankle in one of the episodes in the picture, and there was a long gash on Mr. Crisp's face where Don Q had cut him with a whip. Mary told him what we had been talking about and said that she wanted to give a percentage of the proceeds of the picture to the blind. He replied, "That's splendid, Mary," but the picture has not yet been made. I believe there was some difficulty about the plot she had in mind then, but I still hope that she will carry out her beautiful plan.

We spent the afternoon watching Mary work. She seated me within the "location," so that I could feel her and her hoodlum gang running past, and sense their yells and the commotion when the two hostile gangs encountered each other. Several times a scene had to be repeated because the boys were so interested in seeing Mrs. Macy spell to me that they fumbled. When we said good-bye I realized with new poignancy how good Mary was to see me when she was working on a picture. I carried away in my heart an image of a little body tense with exertion, a sweet, warm face, and the touch of hot, dirty little hands that were full of good will.

One of the pleasantest contacts that I made on this trip was with Carrie Jacobs Bond. We dined with her delightfully, and afterwards, in the drawing room, she sang her poems which she had set to music. The songs were so sweet and intimate one felt that if one could sit there a while longer one could sing the songs oneself.

It was on this trip also that I visited Luther Burbank's experimental gardens in Santa Rosa and saw plants and fruits and flowers that never were found on earth before. The man who guided me had created these miracles. Very gently he put my hand on the desert cactus which no living creature could touch without pain. Beside it he showed me the thornless cactus he had made from it—smooth and pleasant and good to eat.

It is not only because of my charming visits with them that I treasure the memory of these friends, but also because of the warmth of their interest in the blind. Another friend who was zealous for the work in Southern California was Dr. John Willis Baer of Pasadena. He is a yea-sayer, and his lips were touched with fire when he pleaded the cause of America's hundred thousand blind.

For two years now I have not been able to continue

my lectures for the campaign owing to the necessity of keeping a promise of some years standing by writing this book, but I have written many letters, and when the book is finished I shall go on the road again. We have still a million and a half dollars to raise.

Nothing has made me happier during these two years than the way the gifts have kept coming in. Last year Mr. John D. Rockefeller, Jr., who has made of his millions a weapon to shake ignorance out of its citadel, contributed fifty thousand dollars. A few days ago he added an equal amount to his original donation. Mr. M. C. Migel, without whom the Foundation could scarcely have lived through those first hard years, has made a further contribution of fifty thousand dollars. Mr. Felix Warburg has given fifty thousand, and Mr. William Ziegler, the son of the Mrs. Ziegler who founded the *Matilda Ziegler Magazine for the Blind*, gave ten thousand. Mr. Samuel Mather of Cleveland, Harry Goldman, Mrs. Felix Fuld of Newark, and the Nathan Hofheimer foundation have given five thousand each. Mr. Graselli, who established a home for the adult blind in Cleveland, put his generous donation into my hand with such sweet trepidation that it seemed as if he, not I, was the beggar at the gate. It is with an especially grateful heart that I write the name of Mrs. Fuld. Her kindness to me personally is a lovely thing in my life. The contributions have become so numerous as to make it impossible to mention each by name. While I am praising the large givers my heart is remembering those whose names cannot be written for multitude, yet the fund has been built up of their mites, and the work of the Foundation has been made possible by their generosity. As Miss Thomson opens the mail checks tumble out of envelopes from school children and Sunday school classes, from Germans and Chinese and Japanese, from old soldiers, from the deaf and the blind. This morning's mail brought a donation of five thousand dollars from a group in Detroit, and another of one dollar from a poor working girl.

The way children have responded has been very touching. They bring their little banks and empty them into my lap and they write dear letters offering the money given them for soda water and candy. At a meeting in Endicott, N. Y., a fifteen-year-old boy who was an invalid, Bradford Lord, sent me a wonderful bouquet of roses and a contribution of five hundred dollars towards the Endowment Fund. The roses have withered long ago, and the young heart that stirred to that fine impulse has ceased to beat, but the lovely deed will blossom forever in the garden of my soul.

Chapter XVI

MUTED STRINGS

IT IS seldom now that I think of my deprivations, and they never sadden me as they once did when I had bitter moments of rebellion because I must sit at life's shut gate and fight down the passionate impulses of my nature. I know that a great many people pity me because I can show so little visible proof of living. They are often supercilious and sometimes contemptuous of the "poor thing" who is so shut out from everything they know. Meeting me in one of the noisy arenas of commerce they are as startled as if they had encountered a ghost on Broadway. At such times I smile inwardly and gather my dreams about me. My reason for living would be lost if the reality they think they see did not hide her cruel face from me under a veil of pleasant illusions—if they are illusions. One will not quarrel over definitions if one has the substance, and I feel that, since I have found existence rich in happiness and interest, I have the substance.

It would be wonderful to find myself free from even a small part of my physical limitations. It would be wonderful to walk around town alone with the key of the house in my bag to let myself in and out, to come and go without a word to anyone, to read the newspapers without waiting, and pick out a pretty handkerchief or a becoming hat in the shops.

Oh, the weariness of sitting hours upon hours in the same attitude as I have to do sometimes, not daring to look around or move an arm lest I be stared at or my uncertain movements misconstrued! I cannot see people staring at me; but I am always accompanied by persons who can see, and it is embarrassing to them. I am told that in the Orient people avert their eyes when a blind man passes, and the Arabs cover their eyes with their hands when they enter his dwelling. I wish this sensibility were more prevalent here. I understand perfectly the state of mind which caused Lafcadio Hearn to go to Japan, where the people were too courteous to notice his ungainly appearance.

I seem now to be complaining, but sitting here in my study, surrounded by my books, enjoying the intimate companionship of the great and the wise, I sometimes try to realize what my life might have been if Dr. Samuel Gridley Howe had not had the imagination to realize that the immortal spirit of Laura Bridgman had not died when her physical senses were sealed up. When Dr. Howe began her education those afflicted as I am with blindness and deafness were referred to in legal treatises as idiots.

Dr. Howe frequently quoted from Blackstone's *Commentaries* the following passage:

A man is not an idiot, if he hath any glimmerings of reason so he can tell his parents, his age, or the like matters. But a man who is born deaf, dumb, and blind is looked upon by the law as in the same state with an idiot; he being supposed incapable of any understanding, as wanting all those senses which furnish the mind with ideas.

I remember Laura very well. My interest in her began almost with my first word. My teacher knew her intimately. She had lived in the same cottage with her at the Perkins Institution; and it was Laura who taught her the manual alphabet. Miss Sullivan has told me how excited Laura was when she learned that her friend was going to Alabama to teach a blind deaf child. She had much advice to give as to my training. She admonished Miss Sullivan not to spoil me by letting me become disobedient. She made the clothes for a doll which the blind girls at the Institution sent me, and this doll was the object selected for my first word. She wrote to Miss Sullivan frequently in the early days of my education.

Laura was one of the first persons whom Miss Sullivan took me to see when I visited the Institution. We found her sitting by the window in her room crocheting lace. She recognized my teacher's hand instantly, and seemed very glad to see her. She kissed me kindly; but when I tried to examine the lace, she instinctively put it out of my reach, spelling rather emphatically, "I'm afraid your hands are not clean." Her hands were beautiful, finely formed, delicate, and expressive. I wanted to feel her face; but she shrank away like a mimosa blossom from my peering fingers, for the same reason, no doubt, that she would not let me touch the lace. Laura was extremely dainty in all her ways, and exquisitely neat. My strong, impulsive movements disturbed her greatly. She said to Miss Sullivan, "You have not taught her to be very gentle." To me she said, emphasizing each letter, "You must not be forward when calling on a lady." After that I decided to sit on the floor; but Laura jerked me up and spelled, "You must not sit on the floor when you have on a clean dress. You will muss it. You must remember many things when you understand them."

In my eagerness to kiss her good-bye I trod on her toes, which greatly annoyed her, and made me feel like the bad little girl of the Sunday school books.

Later she told Miss Sullivan I was "vivacious, but not blunt." To me she seemed like a statue I had once felt in a garden, she was so motionless, and her hands were so cool, like flowers that have grown in shady places.

My experience and Laura's were so closely parallel in their outward aspects that we have often been compared. We were about the same age when we lost our sight and hearing. We were alike in that although our parents and friends were exceedingly kind to us we both grew restless, willful, and destructive because we had no adequate means of expressing our desires. It was when Laura was about seven years old that Dr. Howe came to her rescue. He says that he found her a well-formed child with a nervous, sanguine temperament, a large and beautifully shaped head, healthy and active. In her letters Miss Sullivan describes me in almost these same words; oddly enough we both had blue eyes and light brown hair. And I, too, was seven years old when my education began.

Here the resemblance ends. We were educated in a different manner. This is a subject into which I should like to enter more fully, but obviously I am not the person to compare the methods of my own education with those employed in teaching Laura Bridgman and other deaf-blind children; I leave the task to those who are more detached. From what I have read of Laura I am sure that she was bright and eager, and I believe that if she had had my teacher she would have outshone me.

Of all the blind-deaf people I have known the one closest to me in temperament and sympathy of ideas is Madame Berthe Galeron, a French woman with whom I have corresponded for over twenty years.

We both find our chief delight and freedom in books. We both feel the impediment of deafness far more keenly than that of blindness. Both our lives have been made beautiful with affection and friendship. As my teacher is ever by my side, making the way straight before me, so has Monsieur Galeron watched over his wife for thirty years, guarding her against every hardship. On the other hand Madame Galeron has always been content to dream and sing while I have ever been impatient for the utmost activity I could compass.

Madame Galeron lost her sight completely when she was ten years old, and her hearing partially a few weeks later. At first this deafness was not serious; for with a little effort she could still understand what was said to her, and enjoy music. She was educated with care and devotion by her father, a distinguished French professor, who fostered her taste for literary work. She wrote several plays, two of which were acted in Paris. During the years that followed she wrote the book of poems, *Dans Ma Nuit,* by which she is best known. Among her father's friends were great men in whose intellectual talk she delighted. One of them, Victor Hugo, addressed a poem to her in which he called her "La grande Voyante." And truly; for with her wonderful powers of imagination and memory she penetrated deeply into the intimacies of life.

It was when her hearing finally failed that she tasted the real bitterness of affliction.

She and her husband had been out for a little while, and on their return they sat down to read together. She has told me in her letters how she used to love his voice. "When he read to me," she says, "we were most completely together, and our spirits met in exquisite feeling." But when they settled down on this fateful day to enjoy Pierre Loti's *Au Maroc,* something strange happened. M. Galeron had hardly begun to speak when she experienced a buzzing in her ear. The syllables kept repeating themselves and clashing like discordant echoes. After a few minutes she was obliged to give up in despair. In a day or two she could hear neither voices nor noises of any kind. Her ear died, as she expressed it, and for the first time she was quite shut out from the music and the brilliant intercourse she so passionately loved.

Fortunately, Monsieur Galeron knew the braille system, and from that time he and the writing frame were inseparable. He wrote everything he could to amuse, comfort, and encourage her. At the end of each day she waited for his return from work as the shipwrecked wait for aid, and his wonderful affection always roused her out of her nightmare. Madame Galeron declares that no one can ever imagine their efforts to prevent the cruel barriers of silence from separating them until they read in *The Story of My*

Life that I could read the lips. This was the beginning of our friendship. Madame Galeron asked me many questions about this means of communication. The first time she tried it she was able to read from the lips of a friend a sonnet of Heredia. In a letter full of delight she wrote to me, "What joy this success brought me. I was saved! Now I know I shall always enjoy sweet communion with my loved ones."

I have received a letter from Mme. Galeron today with a copy of her poems in braille. These poems offer to posterity a precious example of courage and sweetness. I think that perhaps when the generals and statesmen of France are forgotten the poems will remain a testimony to the energy of a spirit unconquered by the disaster which overwhelmed its outward life.

I saw more of Theodocia Pearce than of any other deaf-blind person. She was a sweet girl from Brantford, Canada, with whom fate had dealt cruelly. Besides losing her sight and hearing at the age of twelve, she suffered from spinal curvature and had to be strapped to her bed for three years. For several years she wrote me letters in the form of dainty poems. Then she came to New York, urged, she said, by a tameless desire for adventure. Four years later she died, worn out by her fight against forces she had not the physical strength to resist. She wrote a book of poems which she called, *Lights from Little Lanterns,* which she dedicated to me.

Helen Schulz is another deaf-blind girl who proves that the spirit can sing in spite of limitations. She was adopted fourteen years ago by Miss Lydia Hayes, a blind woman who is the head of the New Jersey Commission for the Blind. Miss Hayes has often told me, her fingers a-tremble with emotion, that when she saw Miss Sullivan's beautiful work with me, she resolved that she, too, would bring the light of joy into the life of a deaf-blind child. It is a touching story how under her loving care the wistful lonely child has grown into a happy young woman. A similar case is that of Helen Martin who, though she has not heard a sound or seen the light since her childhood, plays the piano. Those who go to her concerts express surprise at her delicacy of touch. It was through Miss Rebecca Mack, my friend whom I call the champion of the deaf-blind, that a fund was raised which gave her freedom to develop her musical talent.

There used to be at the Nebraska School for the Blind a merry girl of thirteen who wrote me letters so full of delight in her studies that I could feel the mischievous, joyous spirit laughing out of her dotted pages. She said she was so busy learning new things every day that she had no time to think of her misfortunes. When I met her a few years ago during my visit to Detroit in behalf of the blind I found that she had married a man who worked at the Ford plant. She told me how cleverly he had contrived to make "the dearest little home you can imagine—a home I keep myself." She threw up her little hand eagerly and hurried on, "That isn't all. I have a beautiful, healthy darling boy, seven years old. I have everything any woman can want! There's no incompleteness in my life!"

Another interesting blind-deaf woman is Katie McGirr, who for a number of years earned a living for herself and her mother at the office of the *Matilda Ziegler Magazine for the Blind*. She read the proofs of the magazine each month as they came off the press, and she copied on the typewriter the hundreds of letters which Mr. Holmes, the editor, received in dotted type, and which he could not read himself. Since he did not know the manual alphabet he used to communicate with her by writing script in her hand or on her arm or back. I am happy to say that Katie now has a small pension from the state of New York.

Every now and then I have had the pleasure of meeting again Tommy Stringer, whom I first knew when we were both children. The last time was when a vaudeville engagement took me to Syracuse, New York, where he lives with some friends. He told me proudly that he made crates and lettuce frames for a living, and he described his room full of tools and things he tried to invent "out of his own head." As he spelled into my hand, I remembered the little boy who once lay in a hospital bereft of light, neglected by his family, no one near to love him, and I was more glad than ever that my teacher and I had persuaded Mr. Anagnos to let Tommy come to the Kindergarten for the Blind.

I could go on writing page after page about the deaf-blind. Naturally this class of the handicapped appeals to me more strongly than any other. It distresses me to think that though forty years have passed since I was restored to my human heritage, the question of providing for those who dwell forever in silence and darkness remains unsettled to this day.

Many problems present themselves. One of the greatest needs is of a census of the blind-deaf in the United States. Rebecca Mack has for the past two years been engaged in making such a census. Thus far she has three hundred and seventy-nine names. Father Stadelman thinks there may be as many as two thousand, including the old and infirm. Fifteen of those whose names Miss Mack has are of school age and should be taught.

I have often been asked for suggestions as to the best way of caring for such children. They are widely scattered over the country. Very few of the parents are able to afford a private teacher, and even those who can have difficulty in finding one who is willing to go to the place where the child lives. It is too much to ask the teachers in either the schools for the blind or for the deaf to look after these doubly unfortunate ones. Such an arrangement does not do justice either to the teacher or the pupil. Moreover, the problem is not for the average teacher, but for the one who has special training, ability, and imagination. Each deaf-blind child is different from every other, and should, therefore, receive individual attention.

I have never favoured a special school for these children, but perhaps in the end it will be the wisest way to help them. I would rather see each state make a special appropriation for each child, and place him in the state school for the blind with a special teacher. In this way the child will have the companionship of other children, and will be much nearer to his own home than he would be if a national school were established. I say a school for the blind rather than for the deaf because the blind have a better command of language. It has been the experience of the Perkins Institution that blind children are quick to learn the manual alphabet and talk to those who cannot see and hear.

The importance of the early education of the blind-deaf cannot be over-emphasized. It was most fortunate for Madame Galeron, for instance, that she had acquired the use of language before her affliction came. It was also fortunate that there was no gap in her education. If the education of one who has seen and heard is begun as soon as deafness and blindness come, a large number of sense impressions may be retained. If the child has learned to speak the voice may be preserved. In cases where instruction is deferred too long, the blind-deaf lose initiative and desire to learn.

Very few of them are especially gifted. The causes of their affliction have often affected their minds adversely, but not always. And, from what I know of tests which have been conducted among them, I think their sensory equipment is in no way remarkable. Mine is certainly not.

All my life I have been the subject of tests. People in the possession of their physical faculties seem to have a great curiosity to find out how those who lack one or more senses inform themselves of their surroundings.

The playmates of a blind child love to test his ability to locate them, to orientate himself in a strange place and to distinguish objects which they put into his hands. Children, as a rule, are very matter-of-fact in their observations. They have not the inclination, so strong in adults, to exaggerate. They quite frankly announce that the blind child didn't hear them when they tiptoed quite close, or that he didn't know Mary from Dorothy at first, or that he ran into Jimmy when he stood in the middle of his path. Their observations may be crude; but certainly they are unprejudiced.

There is a tendency in the grown-up investigator to believe that a missing sense is compensated for by a superior capacity of the other senses. The only superiority there is comes with use and intensive training. When the eye is empty of light, a greater necessity is laid upon the remaining senses, and through the natural process of education they are strengthened.

I think people do not usually realize what an extensive apparatus the sense of touch is. It is apt to be confined in our thoughts to the finger-tips. In reality, the tactual sense reigns throughout the body, and the skin of every part, under the urge of necessity, becomes extraordinarily discriminating. It is approximately true to say that every particle of the skin is a feeler which touches and is touched, and the contact enables the mind to draw conclusions regarding the qualities revealed by tactual sensation, such as heat, cold, pain, friction, smoothness, and roughness, and the vibrations which play upon the surface of the body.

This sense is the chief medium between me and the outer world. The hand is the most highly developed organ of sense. The finger-tips are supplied with nerves more abundantly than the rest of the body. But it is not altogether the rich endowment of nerves that gives the hand its efficiency. The arrangement of the thumb and fingers, also the motions of the wrist, elbow, and arm enable the hand to accommodate itself to many surfaces and contacts.

The exercise of the sense of touch covers a wide field of sensation. The effort to determine with scientific accuracy the nature of these sensations was the object of some experiments which Dr. Frederick Tilney, professor of neurology at Columbia University, conducted with me recently. I wonder if any other individual has been so minutely investigated as I have been by physicians, psychologists, physiologists, and neurologists. I can think of only two kinds of tests I have not undergone. So far I have not been vivisected or psychoanalyzed. To scientists I am something to be examined like an aërolite or a sunspot or an atom! I suppose I owe it to a merciful Providence that I have not been separated—actually separated into ions and electrons. I suppose it is only a matter of time until they will turn an alpha particle of charged helium into the dull substance of my body, and knock the nucleus into a million particles. The only consolation there is in such a possibility is that it will be very hard for a taxicab to hit those miniature me's.

My scientific tormentors bring all kinds of instruments with long Greek names and strange shapes and appalling ingenuity. Like diabolical genii they check off one's faults and little idiosyncrasies, and record them, so that any gossip may learn them by rote, and cast them into the eyes of all the world. Like Cassius, I could weep, thus having my slight equipment displayed, until "they do appear as huge as high Olympus!"

When the moment of the test arrives you screw your courage to the sticking point, and await the assault of a score of little fiends which alight upon your body. With mechanical precision they pinch, prick, squeeze, press, sting, and buzz. One counts your breaths, another counts your pulse, another tries if you are hot or cold, if you blush, if you know when to cry and laugh, and how fear and anger taste, and how it feels to swing round and round like a large wooden top, and if it is pleasant being an electric battery, and shooting out sparks of lightning—for fun. Resignedly you permit them to bind your wrists with rubber cuffs which they inflate, asking, "Is it tight or loose?" "Oh, no," you answer, "it doesn't hurt, my arm is quite paralyzed."

Then comes a procession of vibratory tests, tuning forks, and clashing cymbals. A twin sister of a vacuum cleaner climbs your back. An orchestra bellows vibrations of the nth degree of pandemonium. Then comes the little Pallas-æsthesiometer to measure the number of high, thin vibrations you can feel.

Then your head is screwed into a vise-like instrument, and your fingers and joints are moved up and down rapidly. You are asked which finger, which joint is moving, and whether the motion is up or down. You say whatever comes into your head, and trust to the instrument to tell the truth.

The tests continue hour after hour, and always a sense of the untrustworthiness of your sensations is borne in upon you. There is a monotonous murmur as the results are read that keep you informed how short you are falling of what was expected of you. You are confident before the tests begin that you will win by a generous margin over people who see and hear. But the instruments, like your playfellows of long ago, tell the truth—your sensory capacities are just like everybody else's. There is nothing extraordinary about you except your handicap. Ruefully you try to save your face by explaining to your inquisitors that your impressions of the world do not come through the senses alone, but through the magical medium of imagination and association of ideas which enter your mind as detached, chaotic physical experience, and are synchronized into harmonious entity which is your conception of the universe.

The kind of instrument I want to see invented is one which will show what takes place in the mind when we think. Although my account of experiments I have undergone from time to time is somewhat flippant, yet I regard them as of great importance, and I am glad I have had ever so small a share in researches which are pregnant of results. I believe that the nature of sensory experience and the concepts derived from them and the process of uniting these mental ideas with the external world will ultimately be determined with considerable, if not complete, accuracy. If it shall turn out that Dr. Tilney's experiments with me add a jot to the sum of the world's knowledge on this important subject, I shall be abundantly repaid for the time and slight physical discomfort I have contributed. Even if there were no increase of knowledge, I should still be the gainer, since the experiments have given me opportunity to know Dr. Tilney.

I have tried to show in this book that it is possible to make delightful days out of one's own impressions and adventures though debarred from the audible, visible life of the world. My life is "a chronicle of friendship." My friends—all those about me—create my world anew each day. Without their loving care all the courage I could summon would not suffice to keep my heart strong for life. But, like Stevenson, I know it is better to do things than to imagine them.

No one knows—no one can know—the bitter denials of limitation better than I do. I am not

deceived about my situation. It is not true that I
am never sad or rebellious; but long ago I determined
not to complain. The mortally wounded must strive
to live out their days cheerfully for the sake of others.
That is what religion is for—to keep the hearts brave
to fight it out to the end with a smiling face. This
may not be a very lofty ambition, but it is a far cry
from surrendering to fate. But to get the better of
fate even to this extent one must have work and the
solace of friendship and an unwavering faith in God's
Plan of Good.

As I look back over my life, I have the satisfaction
of knowing that I have "done my little owl." In a
letter to a friend Edward Fitzgerald wrote, "My
grandfather had several parrots of different sorts
and talents: one of them, Billy I think, could only
huff up his feathers in what my grandfather called
an owl fashion; so when company were praising the
more gifted parrots, he would say, 'you will hurt poor
Billy's feelings—come, do your little owl, my dear.'
And so I do my little owl," he concluded, referring
to *Tales of the Hall,* which he had just completed.
That is how I view my life—I have done my little
owl.

Chapter XVII

VARIED CHORDS

I HAVE to smile when people lament the few contacts I have with life, remembering the prodigality of interests that is mine through my friends, my books, through magazines, through travel, through letters. I have become consciously proud of my rich possessions because my friends are so prone to pity me.

Whatever is not in braille I depend upon others to read to me. Miss Thomson spells out the headlines in the newspaper at breakfast, between bites, and I choose what I want to hear. Magazines are read to me in the same way, either by Miss Thomson or Mrs. Macy or a friend who happens to be present who is familiar with the manual alphabet. In this way I have enjoyed the *American Mercury,* the *Atlantic Monthly, World's Work, Harper's,* and *Punch* and many others.

My teacher reads me a large part of the *Nation* each week. Its editor, Mr. Oswald Garrison Villard, is a man for whom I have the warmest admiration. He is one of the last editors in America whose name is as well known as that of his paper. He gives out light as well as heat. He is never tongue-tied by authority, nor does he gild the injustices of society to placate anyone. He never departs from the realities of love, faith, and personal liberty. I like to think what a high standard American journalism would have if there were more editors like Mr. Villard.

Articles in all these magazines are constantly being reprinted in our braille magazines, which I sometimes think are superior to the magazines for the seeing. The editors of the ink-print magazines are most generous in giving permission for the use of their material. Not once has it been refused, and since our editors are able to choose the best, our magazines are freer from trivialities. But they are, of course, subject to the same limitations as those of the seeing. They are limited by the capacity of the readers.

Besides my braille magazines I have many friends who write to me in braille and other friends who have their letters copied for me. I especially enjoy reading letters with my fingers. They seem more my own than when people spell them to me. When I was a member, the Massachusetts Commission for the Blind used to have all its reports embossed for me, and the American Foundation for the Blind has its bulletins, special letters, and communications transcribed now.

One of my friends, Edna Porter, took a braille tablet on a cruise around the world so as to send me word pictures of places and people she thought would interest me. Using a braille tablet, for one who is not accustomed to it, is a laborious process, and exasperatingly slow. Every letter must be pricked out with a stiletto—not an occupation for a tourist, one would think.

Most of her missives came in the form of postcards, on which she punched snatches of song, stories, witty descriptions of funny situations she encountered. Thus I have been able to share her adventures.

I shiver with her when she hears the crunching of icebergs in the Atlantic Ocean. I stand with her in Kensington Gardens. I fly with her across the Channel, "a tiny black dot high, high in the blue sky."

I walk through Paris. I stand before the statue called "Blind" in front of the Luxembourg. I bow my head in Notre Dame at a special mass for the Unknown Soldier.

I visit Sarah Bernhardt's granite monument on the isle of her whaler ancestors. I skip through Germany. I dawdle through Venice "with a full moon and the gondolier singing, and the houses gliding past."

I stand in the Coliseum. I stand before Vesuvius. I journey eastward.

At last I reach the Ganges and listen to the weird

notes, "Om, om, om," of the song of hallowed waters. I visit the Taj Mahal. I am off to China where I watch the Mandarins riding past. I reach Japan in time for the Cherry Blossom Dance! "How the petals fall like cascades of snow, while the temple bell rings sweet and low, and people go to the shrines to pray. Oh, look! there go women with babies on their backs and men in kimonos down the street klop-klop-klop, in wooden shoes with heels four inches high."

Whether she is writing or talking Edna seems always to be saying, "I'm glad I love the human race. I'm glad I like the silly way it talks, and I'm glad I think it's jolly good fun."

The friend who does more than any other to keep me in touch with the world of science is Edward L. Holmes. I have known him since I was at the Gilman School for Young Ladies in Cambridge and he was a student of architecture at the Massachusetts Institute of Technology. He was the first Californian I had met, and it seemed to me that he was talking to me over the Golden Gate. Afterwards I visited in his home in California and had many delightful trips with him around San Francisco. Now he lives in New York and I see him very often.

Ships and lighthouses have always had an irresistible lure for him. For more than twenty years he has had in mind a master mariner's compass electrically harnessed to operate automatic navigation

apparatus, and for ten years he has worked unceasingly in developing it.

The brotherhood of the sea tell us that no man
may touch the magnetic compass aboard ship, yet
throughout the ages men have wanted to do this
because it is in man's nature to strive to do that which
other men say he shall not do. The navigators declared that anyone who meddled with the magnetic
compass would destroy the governing spirit of the
ship, for it is the divine shepherd of ships—the hand
that drives them in ocean channels and brings them
safe to the harbour. Mr. Holmes thought otherwise.
Long years he studied the duties and idiosyncrasies of
compasses and decided that the magnetic compass
could be induced to look at an electric current without losing its head. The brotherhood of the sea looked
at my friend with supercilious disdain. Some of them
said, "Other fools have thought they knew more than
their creator." My friend looked at the compass and
the compass looked back at him, each gauging the
other's capacity for overcoming and resisting. He
has told me many times how he learned the secret of
getting the magnetic compass to act naturally in the
presence of an electrically charged wire. Patiently
he talked down to my level until he became convinced
that I really wanted to know about his compass.
Then we talked as men together, each too interested

to think about anything except the subject in hand,
and that subject was compasses—the Kelvin compass,
the Ritchie compass, the gyro compass, and his master magnetic compass. In connection with his compass
Mr. Holmes has developed an instrument which he
calls a path and position indicator. It is an uncanny
contrivance to keep a check upon the usual method
of ascertaining a ship's position in relation to its
course. It possesses the attributes of a super-watch-
dog. It gives instant warning to the man on the bridge
if the ship strays the least bit from the set course and
enables him to bring the vessel back to that course.
Tirelessly it watches every movement of the great
ship. This clever instrument, in addition to saving
time and fuel, does away with all guessing on the
part of the helmsman and increases the safety of
navigation as well.

In these days when the names and sayings and
doings of millionaires, titled foreigners, and criminals are dinned into the public ear, a man of real
achievement like Mr. Holmes is likely to be passed
over by the ministers of publicity. It is reassuring,
however, to know that Mr. Holmes, the inventor of
the Holmes Master Compass and Position Indicator,
is safe in the impregnable stronghold of time.

With such friends as Edna and Mr. Holmes I have
no sense at all of limitations, but when I am with a
group, especially if strangers are among them, I very

much miss not being able to join in their conversation.

During the gaps when I am left alone I amuse myself by observing the callers. There is nothing about me to put them on their guard, and I find I can, or imagine I can, substitute myself for the visitor. If he is dull I know it by the parts of his conversation that are repeated to me. If he is fidgety I can tell by the behaviour of his feet and hands and by the small vibrations that come to me when he laughs to cover his embarrassment.

I know when callers are pleasant by a sort of spiritual freemasonry. If a woman is sitting beside me, and I read her lips, I at once notice the friendliness or the animation of her face and the little nameless motions of head and hand that give colour and emphasis to her words, and I observe her mood, gay or grave. If she is seated at a distance from me, Mrs. Macy or Miss Thomson interprets for me, and the alertness of their spelling, (and they do not always spell what people think they do) enables me to form an impression of my caller. If she smiles, I am told; if she speaks of something with much feeling, a quick pressure on my hand prepares me to fall in with her mood. Usually, however, after her first or second call she talks to me herself.

My life has been rich in friends. I can hardly mention anything I have done without bringing in the name of one. A friend who all through my life has held out a helping hand to me whenever I came to a special difficulty is Mrs. William Thaw. She was overburdened with claims on her benevolence, yet she never failed to contribute generously to every movement in which I took part—the saving of human eyes, the raising of funds for the European soldiers blinded in the World War, and the work of the American Foundation for the Blind. Even when she learned I had become a Socialist, she did not withdraw her friendship and financial help. She used to plead with me not to let fanatics preach their crazy theories through me; but the temper of her mind was such that while she abhorred my radicalism she cherished me. It was at Mrs. Thaw's that Dr. John Brashear used to tell me of his work—how the great telescopes were made. He showed me how they were polished with the palm of the hand, and showed me his hands scored with many arduous endeavours! He would talk of his goings and comings among the observatories where his glasses were, and the stars he had seen through the lenses he fashioned. "In my thoughts there are obscurities," he would say, "but the lenses I have wrought are as transparent as light."

Mr. Frank Doubleday, or Effendi, as he lets me call him, has been a friend of mine since my college days. Twenty-five years ago, when the House of

Doubleday was just starting out, he published *The Story of My Life*. It is pleasant to realize that he has continued his interest in my literary work all these years. More than anyone else he is responsible for this book. For more than a decade he has urged me to bring the story of my life up to date, and I am vividly conscious of his kind hand and friendly encouragement as I write.

John Morley says in his *Recollections* that "the great publisher is a sort of Minister of Letters, and is not to be without the qualities of a statesman." These qualities I think Effendi has. A publisher's life is colourful of the past, rich in memories of noted people who were his friends. Effendi's life, in retrospect, must look good to him, full of hard work and fine achievement, of success and friends, of public honour and affection and happiness.

Effendi's brother, Mr. Russell Doubleday, is another whose name it is delightful to associate with the writing of this book. With what charming kindnesses he has put fresh zest into my tasks when I called loud and long for my thoughts, and they would not come! On one occasion when I had waited long for an idea he invited me to visit the beautiful gardens which surround the plant in Garden City where this book is to be printed. After I had wandered a while among the roses and evergreens my thoughts came bounding to me like a dog at call.

Greatly refreshed, I returned home and finished a chapter that evening.

For twenty years I have missed the warm handclasp of my *Pflegevater,* Mr. Hitz. His footfall is death-muted, but other Swedenborgian friends walk with me, Mr. Paul Sperry, Mr. Clarence Lathbury, Mr. C. W. Barron, and Mr. George Warren of Boston. There are radiant moments when I feel the beams of spiritual kinship that occasionally shine upon the yearning soul. I had this experience last May when I spoke at the convention of the New Jerusalem Church in Washington. I shall always be deeply moved when I recall how beautifully they welcomed me—the fragrant flowers they showered upon me, the lovely music that floated around me while the hymn was played, "O Love That Will Not Let Me Go," and the affection with which the people surrounded me, like one family.

I have already spoken of Mr. and Mrs. Charles White. It was through them that I met Max Heinrich.

Mr. White had often spoken of him. "Max is a romantic figure," he would say. "He has been one of the greatest favourites of his time in the musical world. He is old now, but interesting still. If he likes you, his charm is irresistible."

"Do you think he will like us?" I ventured. "Max's likes are not predictable," Mr. White answered; "but send him an invitation to come out with me, and see what happens."

Max came, and liked us so well he spent several days at our house, and came afterwards many times. Frequently I lunched or dined with him in New York at Lüchow's.

I fell immediately under his spell. He was an old man, but I felt as if he were a princely youth, so chivalrous was his homage. He has been dead for years, and in the interim my life has been crowded with friendships, but I have not forgotten his imperious, intense, lovable, whimsical personality.

Like a great book he created a new world wherever he went. Max was not a happy man, yet he had known all the happiness mortals can experience. His unrest, charm, and wilfulness were temperamental, and the source of his joy and his misery. More than most men, he seized for himself the privilege of doing as he liked, and others less audacious got out of the way of his magnificent impudence.

He had been a dazzling success on the concert stage but sang very little when I knew him, being sensitive, and realizing that his voice was no longer what it had been. But sometimes he would take me into the sitting room and sing for me some of the songs that had made him famous. He would half sing and half recite "Enoch Arden" to a beautiful accompaniment, while I kept one hand on the piano, and the fingers of my other hand on his lips. He used to say cynically, "I still have my triumphs, Charlie. The blind and deaf find me magnificent." Every time he went away, I felt the disappointment of a child who finishes a book and cries for something more to follow.

It was a cold day in February, 1912, that Georgette Le Blanc (Mme. Maeterlinck) came out to Wrentham to bring me, she said, greetings from Maurice Maeterlinck. She was singing "Pelléas and Mélisande" in the Boston opera that winter. She was animated and confiding, and to my touch beautiful. Her gayety of heart and her lively interest in many subjects carried us over the difficulties of communicating in French. After she returned to France she sent me a card on which Maeterlinck had written "My greetings and love to the girl who has found the Bluebird."

I met Signora Montessori on two occasions while she was lecturing in America. The first time was in Boston, the second in San Francisco during the Pan-American Exposition when a great meeting was held to celebrate educational achievement. Signora Montessori and Mrs. Macy and many others spoke, and Signora Montessori paid my teacher a beautiful tribute, the memory of which thrills me with happiness.

In conversation Signora Montessori talked with

charming vivacity in Italian and a lovely young lady interpreted what she said. She was interested to learn that her system and Mrs. Macy's were much alike. She spoke of the attitude of the Church in Italy towards education and freedom of thought, and the blighting effects of poverty upon childhood. She declared that school life should be an adventure, the child spirit must be free. "I would not bind it even to the feet of God."

Another worker among the children of the poor whom I like to recall is Miss Margaret Macmillan of London. She told me that my teacher's method had been a wellspring of beneficence to thousands of unfortunate children in England. She herself had made use of it among the children in her care.

It is many years now since Judge Lindsey first greeted me in Denver. He had just come from a meeting where he had advocated a mother's pension law. He was very much excited and poured out his indignation at the stupid indifference of society. "Here we are, huddling children into homes and nurseries and paying strangers to look after them, while the mothers take care of other people's children and homes. Wouldn't you think any intelligent citizen would see that it would be more sensible to pay the mothers for taking care of their own children?"

He said he knew he had a hard fight ahead, but I

doubt if Judge Lindsey himself knew just how hard it was going to be. People said he was crazy when he took the part of bad boys against the police and said that they should have a court of their own. But he established such a court, and people came from all over the world to see how it was managed. Public playgrounds and public baths came as a result of his dreams. Old laws were changed and better ones made, as he recommended, and these things are only a small part of what he has done for the good of his country.

I cannot help wishing that so many of my friendships did not have to be conducted by correspondence. I have letters that I treasure from John Burroughs, William Dean Howells, Dr. Richard Cabot, Carl Sandburg, and others. The only personal contact I had with Eugene Debs was through letters. I heard of him first in connection with the Great Northern Strike in 1894, but it was not until I was a woman of thirty that I began to understand the significance of the liberating movement for which he stood.

He needs no defence among those who know his work, but there are many who have not yet learned to appreciate him justly. He was a working man, but he succeeded in making himself master of the culture of the dominant class. Gentle, modest, refined, a lover of books and of beauty, he chose to be the champion of the despised cause of the poor. He attacked the rule of the strong and the system of private property, and always he was in earnest, terribly in earnest. He never doubted the righteousness of his mission, or that his cause would win in the end, as surely as the sun lights the sky. He summed up the whole philosophy of life in these words, which are inscribed on my heart:

Your Honour, years ago I recognized my kinship with all living beings, and I made up my mind that I was not one bit better than the meanest of the earth. I said then, and I say now, that while there is a lower class, I am in it; while there is a criminal element, I am of it; while there is a soul in prison, I am not free.

Most of my contact with La Follette was with letters to him or his family. I met him—I think it was in the spring of 1905—when my mother and I were in Washington, and Mr. Hitz was showing us the Capitol. He saw the Senator coming out of one of the committee rooms, his hands full of papers. Mr. Hitz knew him only by sight, but, thinking it would be pleasant for my mother and me to meet him, spoke to him and introduced me. Mr. La Follette greeted us in gentle perplexity, wondering who we were. When, however, Mr. Hitz repeated my name, he responded, "Yes, yes, I know," and shook my hand again saying, "When people meet you, I am sure they always shake hands twice."

When he had said good-bye, Mr. Hitz remarked, "That's a fighter. They say here in Washington that if there were two ways of getting a man to cross the street, one to invite him over and the other to take him by the collar, La Follette would take him by the collar."

When I came to know Senator La Follette better, I regarded him as Woodrow Wilson did, "a lonely figure climbing the mountain of privileges," steadfastly serving the interests of the American people. Yet in another sense he was not lonely. Never did a man have a more devoted family. His wife fought side by side with him in his political battles. His son, who is now in the Senate, told me recently that from their earliest years he and his sisters were permitted to be present at the family councils. As they grew up they joined their father's forces and upheld his noble principles.

Shortly after I began campaigning for the American Foundation for the Blind I received a contribution for the work inclosed in a delightful letter signed Jedediah Tingle. I did not know until last year that Jedediah Tingle was Mr. William Harmon. In the second letter, which was signed with his own name, he wrote that he would open to the blind a series of awards for creative achievements in the various fields of education, craftsmanship, art, public endeavour and industrial relationships. "I want to do this," he said, "for those who are handicapped so that they may know the ambition and joy which come, not only from achievement itself, but also for the occupational effort to achieve." Out of his generosity and sympathy Mr. Harmon radiated the beneficence that really helps because those whom it assists are enabled to help themselves.

Many people whose visits it is delightful to remember have called upon us here in Forest Hills. Sir Richard Paget, who sees in the science of phonetics a way of improving speech; Mr. Akiba, who is head of the School for the Blind in Tokio; Miss Betty Hirsch of Berlin, a sightless worker in the rehabilitation of blinded German soldiers; Dr. James Kerr Love, a distinguished aural surgeon of Glasgow, greatly interested in the education of deaf children; Countee Cullen, the negro poet, whose poems Edna Porter has copied in braille for me.

A comrade in the dark who lives far away now but used to visit me often is Elizabeth Garrett. When books began to appear about the thrilling adventures of Elizabeth's father, Pat Garrett, the famous sheriff of New Mexico, and the hairbreadth escapes of "Billy the Kid," I felt as one might if somebody took liberties with his family. For Elizabeth has told me so much about her father and "the kid" that they seemed to belong to me somehow.

Elizabeth has been blind since she was born, but

she has her father's free spirit. Even as a child she was perfectly fearless. She rode horses bareback without anyone to accompany her, and gave her family many anxious moments, especially when she took it into her wilful head to ride wild horses. One day she swung herself to the back of an unbroken pony which belonged to one of her father's young deputy sheriffs. The pony flew down the road. No one could stop him. Miles and miles he ran until he was worn out. When he slowed down Elizabeth slipped off and sat calmly down by the roadside and waited for her father. With the same unconquered spirit she is still seeking adventures in the dark. No danger or hardship can hold her back. She is one of the few blind people who travel about the country alone. When she goes to a city where she is likely to have difficulty, she writes to the station master telling on what train she will arrive, and asking him please to have a porter meet her. Not once has the porter failed to be on hand.

Elizabeth has a lovely voice and a talent for composing her own songs. She has written the state song of New Mexico, which is my favourite among her compositions. It breathes of the wild flowers she has gathered, the mountains she has climbed, and the unconfined frolic of the winds upon the mesas of her romantic homeland. She used often to spend the week-end with us while she was studying singing in

New York, and there was no happier hour than when we gathered about her in the twilight. She always asked me to stand beside her with my hand on her throat. "I can't bear to have you left out, dear," she would spell, "and I feel I can sing better if you 'hear' me." Sometimes we accompanied her when she gave recitals in towns around New York, and she always insisted that I listen to her just as I did at home.

She is ever ready to go wherever she might bring cheer to the sick, the sorrowful, and the lonely. One day she visited Sing Sing prison and sang for the men. Not long afterwards I was deeply touched to read in the *Ziegler Magazine for the Blind* a poem which one of the prisoners addressed to her. I will quote the first verse:

> Fools, they! They call her blind!
> They call her blind, yet can she lead
> A thousand soul-sick men
> From cold gray stones and make them heed
> The song of wind and rain,
> From gloomy cell to dewy mead,
> To sun and stars and sky,
> And show the message all can read
> Of love and peace and hope.

I met Elizabeth through another blind friend, Nina Rhoades, whose father, John Harsen Rhoades, used to try to teach me a little practical sense in my young days. I was not a very apt pupil; but he was always patient with me.

I very often visited the Rhoadeses at their home in New York and their country house at Seabright, N. J. Miss R. knew the manual alphabet, and we had many long talks about books and people we knew, or would like to know. She had many delightful books which her friends copied for her in N. Y. Point that could not be obtained from any library. With what delight I read Goethe's *Iphigenia, Daniel Deronda, Nathan the Wise* and *The Casting Away of Mrs. Lecks and Mrs. Aleshine.* Nina Rhoades herself is a writer of charming stories for girls. She used to write them out in Point, and sometimes I had the pleasure of reading them before they were published.

She has a captivating personality, and I loved the way we used to laugh and argue the summer hours away on the upper piazza of her Seabright home. Every now and then our discussions were interrupted by great breakers which leapt the bulkhead and flung wreaths of white spray in our faces.

It was through her also that I met Sir Arthur Pearson, founder of St. Dunstan's Hostel for the blinded soldiers in London.

When Rabindranath Tagore visited America, he came out to see me, accompanied by a number of friends and admirers. He was tall and stately. His long gray hair and beard mingling together gave him the appearance of an ancient prophet. Serene, gracious, he saluted me in a monotone, almost like a prayer. I told him I was pleased to meet him because I had read his poems, and I knew that he loved humanity. "I shall have cause for rejoicing," he said gently, "if my writings reflect my love of man. . . . The world is waiting for men who love God and their fellow creatures and not themselves."

After the Stately One had seated himself in the centre of a circle of friendly and reverent listeners, he talked of poetry, of India and China and the power of the spirit that alone can bring freedom. He spoke sadly of the war clouds hovering over the world. "The West is trying to thrust opium down the throat of China, and non-compliance by the Chinese means taking possession of their country, and Asia doth prepare weapons in her armouries, and her target is to be the heart of Europe, and nests are being built on the shores of the Pacific for the vulture-ships of England. Japan, the farthest East, is already awake. China will rouse herself when the robbers break through her walls. . . . Yet love of self can have no other destination than self-destruction. Love of God is our only fulfilment. It has in it the ultimate solution of all problems and all difficulties."

I could not help thinking of Gandhi, who not only

hears this message of love, but also teaches it and
lets it shine in his deeds before all men.

It was not until we came to Forest Hills to live
that I made the acquaintance of Art Young, though
for years Mr. Macy had described his cartoons to me
as they appeared in *Life,* in *The Liberator, The
Nation,* and *The Masses.*

One day when we were returning from a camping trip in New England, we passed through Bethel,
Connecticut. Edna remarked, "Art Young lives near
here." We easily found his quaint little house on the
side of the road, with a giant pine tree in front of it,
and morning glories running wild everywhere; and
we found Art Young in the living room, drawing pictures of "trees at night" for the *Saturday Evening
Post.* I told him that Mrs. Macy also saw things in
trees at twilight—animals and human beings. After
supper we sat on the doorsteps in the semi-darkness
and they searched the trees for the goblins and dry-
ads that inhabit them.

It was my privilege not long ago to have a call
from Dr. Watson, Dr. Bell's assistant in the invention of the telephone. The nobility of his character reveals itself in every movement. I believe there
is a parallel between a man's accomplishment and his
character. His work is a visible sign of his spirit.
Some such thoughts passed through my brain as I
talked with Dr. Watson. There was the consciousness

of a self unified as in a work of art. There was the strong, skilful hand that had subdued the electric current and won a victory over matter; and there he sat, modest, gentle, radiating kindly interest and heightening the effect by reciting Browning's noble words:

> "He fixed thee 'mid this dance
> Of plastic circumstance,
> This Present, thou, forsooth, would fain arrest:
> Machinery just meant
> To give thy soul its bent,
> Try thee and turn thee forth, sufficiently impressed."

Every Sunday since I have been in Forest Hills a number of little neighbours run in after Sunday school. They bound into my study like a burst of sunshine. One of them kicks the big stone which keeps my door from slamming; another spoils the letter I am writing by pushing down the keys of the typewriter at random; they scatter my braille notes all over the floor. They open my file and rummage among the papers. They are mischief incarnate, but I adore them. Their teasing, their laughter, and their sprawling affection keep me young for the springtime of Heaven.

Many artists whose appeal is directed to the eye or ear have tried to project their art beyond the dark curtain of sense for my entertainment. When I was a young girl Ellen Terry, Sir Henry Irving, and

Joseph Jefferson assumed for me characters which they had made famous and I followed with breathless interest their gestures and changes of expression. My fingers have traced the mobile lines of David Warfield's face and felt the youth and charm of Jane Cowl's Juliet. With my fingers on his lips, Caruso poured his golden voice into my hand. Chaliapin shouted the Russian folk song with his strong arm encircling me so that I could feel every vibration. I knew his tone of defiance, the great peasant laugh, and the passion of the multitude. He also sang the Volga Boat Song, and I sensed its sad, haunting notes, the resignation and sustained effort of strong men who believe we must pull together.

I was present in Detroit at one of Gabrilówitsch's concerts. I sat so close to the orchestra and the vibrations carried so wonderfully in that resonant auditorium that I seemed to swim on a flood of harmony.

Two blind men who have played for me, they tell me, are gifted violinists, Abraham Haitovitch and Edwin Grasse. Mr. Grasse accompanied me in the campaign for the American Foundation for the Blind, and audiences everywhere received him with glorious enthusiasm. Recently the Brooklyn Institute of Arts and Sciences chose Mr. Grasse as its organist, guaranteeing him good remuneration, and in October he will begin giving three recitals a week.

When we were in Denver during one of my

vaudeville tours Heifetz played for me. My fingers rested lightly on his violin. At first the bow moved softly over the strings, as if the master were questioning the Spirit of Music what he should play for one who could not hear. The bow fluttered. From the sensitive instrument there came a tremulous, far-away murmur. Was it the faint rumour of the wings of birds? Each delicate note alighted on my fingertips like thistledown. They touched my face, my hair, like kisses remembered and love-lit smiles. Immaterial, transient as the sigh of evening winds, the violet breath of dawn. Are they rose petals dropped from a fairy's hand, or wordless desires born in the heart?

There is a change of mood. The bow is lifted to the point of radiant flight. The melody rises like Shelley's skylark climbing the air with voice and wing challenging immensity. One is sad without knowing why. The song is joyous, and yet nowhere is there a loneliness so great as the little bird in that vast dome of light, for the moment the only actuality in the universe, yet so slight a thing, a glimmering echo of thought, a passionate prayer, a dauntless faith in things unseen.

I think it was Schumann's "Song of Moonlight" that Heifetz played.

Godowsky, too, has played for me. With my hands on the piano while he played one of Chopin's

Nocturnes, I was transported on a magic carpet to a tropical island in one of Conrad's mysterious seas.

Sometimes I have listened to concerts over the radio, placing my fingers lightly on a resonant board. Lovely to my touch is the music of different instruments—the harp, the cornet, the oboe, the deep-voiced viola, the violin in all its singing moods and the triumphing, blending harmony of all in a chorus of sweet vibrations! Always one voice seems to leap from the deep surge and fling its notes like flower petals blown by the wind.

The fire music in "The Valkyrie" spreads exultant flames through the orchestra, now curling upward swift and shrill, now clamouring against the sky and now rolling back to earth Brunhilde's bitter fate.

Jazz has a bombarding sensation not pleasant to the touch, and it is disturbing to the emotions. When it is continued for some time, I have a wild impulse to flee from something sinister that is about to spring upon me. I suppose it wakens primal emotions— quenchless fears of things wild-eyed and savage . . . shadow memories . . . gigantic creatures . . . sons and daughters of the jungle . . . the cry of dumb souls not yet able to speak.

I have several times been presented at the American Court of Industry. I have talked with men who have more power than almost any monarch of history. Some of these men have been my friends, others I have only met in passing. One of the first of my friends among the Kings of Industry was Mr. John Spaulding, about whom I have already written. Another who came early into my life was Mr. H. H. Rogers, who made it possible for me to go to Radcliffe College. I first met him one afternoon at Mrs. Lawrence Hutton's when he called with Mark Twain. Shortly afterwards Mrs. Rogers invited Miss Sullivan and me to dinner at their beautiful home in New York. We saw both Mr. and Mrs. Rogers frequently up to the time of their death. Whenever we passed through New York we saw them, they both called upon us when I was in college, and Mr. Rogers came to see us at Wrentham.

One of the most delightful visits we ever had with him was after my teacher's marriage, when he invited the three of us to Fairhaven, where he was spending the summer with his daughter, Mrs. Coe, and his grandchildren. We took a glorious sail on his beautiful yacht, the *Kanawha,* and I loved the steady, swift motion and the flying spray. Most interestingly Mr. Rogers described the coast and islands we passed. He was so pleased that Mrs. Macy could see more distinctly through his field-glasses that he presented them to her. A delicious luncheon was served on board, after which Mr. Rogers insisted that we must take a nap; but bless his heart! we could not sleep when there was so much to see. We had never been on a private yacht before. I had to pinch myself every little while to see if I was awake or dreaming. Just as the sun went down the *Kanawha* floated up to her pier like a huge white swan. Mr. Rogers's automobile was waiting for us. There were to be other guests at dinner, and it was a scramble to get dressed in time.

After dinner we sat round the fire and chatted. Mr. Rogers talked naturally and simply on whatever subject came up. At that time Mr. Lawson was attacking him in *Everybody's Magazine*. Mr. Rogers denied that the reported conversations between himself and Mr. Lawson had any foundation in fact. We talked of Mark Twain, and Mr. Rogers chuckled over some of his drolleries. We also spoke of Mrs. Rogers, who was at Dublin, New Hampshire, at the time. Mr. Rogers said she had one fault, she was always giving his old clothes away, so that when he wanted to go fishing he had nothing suitable to wear. Frequently Mr. Rogers and I did not agree on subjects of public interest, but I always liked to talk with him. He was always noble in bearing and winning in manner. Mark Twain said that he was "the best-bred gentleman I have met on either side of the ocean in any rank of life from the Kaiser of Germany down to the bootblack."

Next to Mr. Spaulding and Mr. Rogers, Mr. Carnegie did most to uphold my hands in what I wanted to do. It was the year that I met Mr. Carnegie that I met another royal personage in the kingdom of industry—Mr. Thomas A. Edison. He asked me to visit him when I was lecturing in East Orange, New Jersey.

He seemed to me a man of many idiosyncrasies and moods. Mrs. Edison told me that he often stayed all night in his laboratory. When he became interested in a problem nothing else existed for him and he was annoyed when someone interrupted him to tell him it was dinner time.

He asked me very particularly what I could feel when I placed my hands on a victrola. When I told him that I could not make out words he tried to focus the sounds under a high silk hat. Vibrations were stronger under the hat, but the sounds were not defined.

He told me he thought deafness was an advantage to him. "It is like a high wall around me which excludes distractions and leaves me free to live at peace in my own world."

I said, "If I were a great inventor like you, Mr. Edison, I would invent an instrument that would enable every deaf person to hear."

"You would, would you?" he retorted. "Well, I

think it would be a waste of time. People say so little that is worth listening to."

I tried to make him understand me by putting my mouth close to his ear. He said my voice was very unpleasant—like steam exploding, and that he got only the consonants. "Get Mrs. Macy to tell me what you have to say," he commanded, "her voice is like velvet."

"The trouble with people is," he remarked, "they are all alike. I doubt if their parents could tell them apart when they grow up."

"They are not alike to me," I said. "Everyone has a particular person-odour different from everybody else's."

"That may be," he said, "I never noticed it."

It was on a lecture tour also that I first met Mr. Ford. We stopped for a few days in Detroit on our way home from Nebraska, where I had been speaking against preparedness. I expressed a wish to visit the Ford motor plant, and if possible to meet the great organizer of that industry. Accordingly, we went to the plant in the afternoon. We had to wait some time before Mr. Ford could see us, but when he did appear, the pleasure I had in making his acquaintance was worth waiting for. His handshake was quiet and full of what I call reserve energy. Mr. Ford showed us over the plant, and I shall never forget the alertness of his hands that seemed eyes as he guided my awkward fingers through the intricacies of the huge dynamo which runs the plant.

He talked with pleasant simplicity about his success. He told how he had conceived the idea of a car that the farmers could afford to buy, and then found out how to make it. "The trouble with many people who have ideas," he said, "is that they don't know what to do with them. It is all well to have ideas; but what are they worth if one doesn't know how to go about embodying them in actual service?"

A visit to the Ford plant gives one much to meditate upon. I have tried to imagine what the world would be like if it were all run like the Ford plant, with Mr. Ford as world dictator. Many things would be better. There would be a shorter working day and higher wages. Mankind would have leisure undreamed of now. Men would spend a part of the day providing food, clothes, and shelter, and insurance against old age, and still have four or five hours to devote to their families, to education, or to recreation. It would give the workers the economic freedom which is the starting point of all other freedom.

At first flush the Ford idea looks wonderful. It seems as if this "hard-headed" business man had found the high road to Utopia. But memory flashes a picture on the mind of the thousands of men at the Ford plant working in perfect unison, like a marvellous mechanism, each man a tiny cog or screw or shaft in the machine, and one wonders if, when the machine is dismembered, the human parts will be capable of enjoying the blessings of Utopia, or will their brains have become so mummified that they will prefer to remain parts of the machine?

The year after this visit to Detroit Mr. Ford invited me to be his guest on the *Oscar*. I declined, because if I went, I should be obliged to cancel a number of lecture engagements, and I felt that the service I might render on such an expedition would not justify me in disappointing my audiences. It seemed to me Mr. Ford's significance lay in what he had accomplished in the field of industry rather than in international diplomacy. I felt that, had he brought the same engineer-mind to the affairs of the world that he did to affairs of his workshop, the "Peace Ship" would never have sailed.

My next connection with the Ford family came ten years later, when I was again in Detroit. When I was speaking for the blind at the memorable meeting which I have already described, Mr. and Mrs. Henry Ford and Edsel Ford contributed ten thousand dollars each. I had another pleasant surprise when Mr. Ford informed me that he employed seventy-three blind men in his plants, not because he pitied them, but because they were capable of doing their work efficiently.

It is pleasant to record the Fords' interest in the blind, for sometimes during our campaign we have been greatly disappointed at the unreadiness of certain extremely rich people to respond. Mingled with the fragrance of blossoms, the sweet strains of music, the gracious hospitality and expressions of kindness there were tears of regret at the strange contradictions of human nature. Grotesque things sometimes fall out of fat pocketbooks, but if I went into that I should stir up a hornet's nest indeed!

Chapter XVIII

I GO ADVENTURING

CUT off as I am, it is inevitable that I should sometimes feel like a shadow walking in a shadowy world. When this happens I ask to be taken to New York City. Always I return home weary but I have the comforting certainty that mankind is real flesh and I myself am not a dream.

In order to get to New York from my home it is necessary to cross one of the great bridges that separate Manhattan from Long Island. The oldest and most interesting of them is the Brooklyn Bridge, built by my friend, Colonel Roebling, but the one I cross oftenest is the Queensborough Bridge at 59th Street. How often I have had Manhattan described to me from these bridges! They tell me the view is loveliest in the morning and at sunset when one sees the skyscrapers rising like fairy palaces, their million windows gleaming in the rosy-tinted atmosphere.

I like to feel that all poetry is not between the covers of poetry books, that much of it is written in great enterprises of engineering and flying, that into mighty utility man has poured and is pouring his

dreams, his emotions, his philosophy. This mate-
rializing of his genius is sometimes inchoate and
monstrous, but even then sublime in its extravagance
and courage. Who can deny that the Queensborough
Bridge is the work of a creative artist? It never fails
to give me a poignant desire to capture the noble
cadence of its music. To my friends I say:

> Behold its liberal loveliness of length—
> A flowing span from shore to shore,
> A brimming reach of beauty matched with strength,
> It shines and climbs like some miraculous dream,
> Like some vision multitudinous and agleam,
> A passion of desire held captive in the clasp of vast utility.

New York has a special interest for me when it
is wrapped in fog. Then it behaves very much like a
blind person. I once crossed from Jersey City to
Manhattan in a dense fog. The ferry-boat felt its
way cautiously through the river traffic. More timid
than a blind man, its horn brayed incessantly. Fog-
bound, surrounded by menacing, unseen craft and
dangers, it halted every now and then as a blind man
halts at a crowded thoroughfare crossing, tapping his
cane, tense and anxious.

One of my never-to-be-forgotten experiences was
circumnavigating New York in a boat. The trip took
all day. I had with me four people who could use
the hand alphabet—my teacher, my sister, my niece,
and Mr. Holmes. One who has not seen New York

in this way would be amazed at the number of people who live on the water. Someone has called them "harbour gypsies." Their homes are on boats—whole fleets of them, decorated with flower boxes and bright-coloured awnings. It is amusing to note how many of these stumbling, awkward harbour gypsies have pretty feminine names—*Bella, Florodora, Rosalind, Pearl of the Deep, Minnehaha, Sister Nell.* The occupants can be seen going about their household tasks—cooking, washing, sewing, gossiping from one barge to another, and there is a flood of smells which gives eyes to the mind. The children and dogs play on the tiny deck, and chase each other into the water, where they are perfectly at home. These water-babies are familiar with all manner of craft, they know what countries they come from, and what cargoes they carry. There are brick barges from Holland and fruitboats coming in from Havana, and craft loaded with meat, cobblestones, and sand push their way up bays and canals. There are old ships which have been stripped of their majesty and doomed to follow tow ropes up and down the harbour. These ships make me think of old blind people led up and down the city streets. There are aristocratic craft from Albany, Nyack, Newburg. There are also boats from New London and Boston, from the Potomac and Baltimore and Virginia, from Portland, Maine, bringing terra cotta to Manhattan.

Here comes the fishing fleet from Gloucester hurrying past the barge houses, and crawling, coal-laden tramps. Tracking the turmoil in every direction are the saucy ferry boats, bellowing rudely to everyone to get out of the way.

It is a sail of vivid contrast—up the Hudson between green hills, past the stately mansions of Riverside Drive, through the narrow straits that separate Manhattan from the mainland, into Harlem and the East River, past Welfare Island, where a great modern city shelters its human derelicts, on to the welter of downtown docks, where longshoremen heave the barge cargoes ashore, and the crash of traffic is deafening, and back to your pier in the moonlight when the harbour gypsies sleep and the sense of peace is balm to the tired nerves.

As I walk up Broadway, the people that brush past me seem always hastening toward a destination they never reach. Their motions are eager, as if they said, "We are on our way, we shall arrive in a moment." They keep up the pace—they almost run. Each on his quest intent, in endless procession they pass, tragic, grotesque, gay, they all sweep onward like rain falling upon leaves. I wonder where they are going. I puzzle my brain; but the mystery is never solved. Will they at last come somewhere? Will anybody be waiting for them? The march never ceases. Their feet have worn the pavements unevenly. I wish I knew where they are going. Some are nonchalant, some walk with their eyes on the ground, others step lightly, as if they might fly if their wings were not bound by the multitude. A pale little woman is guiding the steps of a blind man. His great hand drags on her arm. Awkwardly he shortens his stride to her gait. He trips when the curb is uneven; his grip tightens on the arm of the woman. Where are they going?

Like figures in a meaningless pageant, they pass. There are young girls laughing, loitering. They have beauty, youth, lovers. They look in the shop windows, they look at the huge winking signs; they jostle the crowds, their feet keep time to the music of their hearts. They must be going to a pleasant place. I think I should like to go where they are going.

Tremulously I stand in the subways, absorbed into the terrible reverberations of exploding energy. Fearful, I touch the forest of steel girders loud with the thunder of oncoming trains that shoot past me like projectiles. Inert I stand, riveted in my place. My limbs, paralyzed, refuse to obey the will insistent on haste to board the train while the lightning steed is leashed and its reeling speed checked for a moment. Before my mind flashes in clairvoyant vision what all this speed portends—the lightning crashing into life, the accidents, railroad wrecks, steam bursting free like geysers from bands of steel, thousands of racing motors and children caught at play, flying heroes diving into the sea, dying for speed—all this because of strange, unsatisfied ambitions. Another train bursts into the station like a volcano, the people crowd me on, on into the chasm—into the dark depths of awful forces and fates. In a few minutes, still trembling, I am spilled into the streets.

After the turmoil of the city it is a joy to rush back to my little garden. My garden is a humble place—a rustic nook, a hut of green. One friend says it is more like a nest than a garden. Another calls it "the philosopher's garden," because it is so walled in on all sides and so narrow, but at the same time so high that it reaches the stars. For me it is a shelter from the bustling world, a place to meditate in, a sweet, tranquil haunt of birds, bees, and butterflies, a realm of peace where a restless spirit often escapes from the buffetings of life, a secret confessional where my besetting sins are repented. It matters not at what hour I enter my garden, whether in the cool pure dawn when the golden gates of the sun open, and the first rustle of leaves stirs to consciousness the bird in its nest, disperses the mists and dews from the sleeping flowers, and each flower uncurls its petals and lifts its face to the beauty of the day; or in the noonday, when all the banners of life are unfurled and the sun's rays turn everything to splendour; or in the magical stillness of evening when shadows steal across my path with soundless feet, and I sense "a folding of a world of wings" and down in the dusk of the grass fireflies light their glow-lamps, I am filled with infinite gladness, and my heart sings the praise of the Creator who out of space and eternity made this little place for me, and sent the flowers to be my comforters.

I enjoy my garden in all weathers. Even wintertime has its own sport and charm for me. As I walk briskly along, the wind shakes the snow down upon me from the hedge. Every few minutes I pull off my gloves to revel in the touch of congealed loveliness on the trees and bushes—wondrous forms which God has

> Insculped and embossed
> With His hammer of wind,
> And His graver of frost.

Usually I find the green circle of trees which surrounds my walk without the slightest difficulty by going from the steps along a cement path that turns off abruptly at the right, but when the snow is deep all paths are obliterated, so that there is no unevenness of the ground to guide my feet, and I get completely lost; but the adventure of blundering into every place but the right one gives me a good laugh or two before I successfully orientate myself beside the hedge, and Mark Twain's felicitous words form a sprightly accompaniment to my steps. For I feel like Sandy when the Connecticut Yankee asked her, "Whereabouts does the castle lie? What is the direction from here?" and she replied, "Ah please you, sir, it hath no direction from here; by reason that the road lieth not straight, but turneth evermore; wherefore the direction of its place abideth not, but is sometimes under the one sky and anon under another, whereso if ye be minded that it is in the east, and wend thitherward, ye shall observe that the way of the road doth yet again turn upon itself by the space of half a circle. . . . It were woundily hard to tell [the leagues I have walked], they are so many, and do so lap the one upon the other, and being made all in the same image and tincted with the same colour, one may not know the one league from its fellow, nor how to count them except they be taken apart."

It is when the book of the year opens at the page of June that I want to drop my work, whatever it may be, and enter the Kingdom of Delight. It is then that Nature receives the spring flowers at her Court, and each perfect day brings new beauties to grace the fête.

June-time within the circle of evergreens that shields my garden is a wondrous woof of odours —evergreens and marsh-grass threaded with the scent

of lilac and laurel. Bright-hued flowers march beside me and hold up lovely faces to me. Where the
grass grows softest, the violets open their blue eyes
and look at me wonderingly. I call them dream
flowers, because I always see them growing in the
Garden of Sleep—violets and lilies of the valley.
The honeysuckle trails over the privet wall, blessing
every breeze with its fragrance. The weigelas reach
out wraithlike arms to embrace me. When I push
them aside to pass, how the wingéd plunderers of
their sweets scatter in the sunshine! Tall irises from
Japan and Germany display their exquisite gowns
across the ribbon-like trails which the gardener has
made around the summer house. In one corner of my
garden there is a clump of old-fashioned lilacs. In
June the boughs are weighted with loveliness, and
heart-penetrating odour—oh, nobody has ever put
it into words!

All through May and early June a flaming tide of
tulips spreads over the lawn, with here and there an
island of daffodils and hyacinths. If I touch one of
them, lo, a lily is born in my hands! As far as my
arms can reach, the same miracle has been wrought.
Love, which fulfils itself in giving life, has taken
possession of my Eden.

One day a few summers ago two robins decided
to live in my dogwood tree, which was all tremulous
with white blossoms. It is one of the trees which bor-

der my green circle. Morning and evening, as I pass
it again and again, I reach up to touch the branches.
The robins went about the business of life with
singleness of purpose. They did not seem to mind me.
At first, when I put up my hand to touch the
branches, they would fly off to a near-by tree and
watch me attentively, but they soon became accustomed to me. I brought them food and in my awkward human way tried to tell them I was a friend,
and had no evil intentions toward them. They seemed
to understand; anyway, they came and were quite indifferent to my doings. I would stand perfectly still
for a long time with my hand on the branch, and
often I was rewarded by feeling the leaves quiver
and the twigs bend ever so slightly. Once I sensed
a commotion very close to my hand, and a few days
later I felt a tiny claw pinch my finger. It was not
many days before the male bird lit squarely upon my
hand, and after that there was perfect understanding
between us. A bird doesn't stay long on one's hand
without saying something. My new bird-friend began to twitter; he hopped back and forth on the
branch, telling his mate about me, I suppose. When
the eggs were hatched, she came way out on the
branch to take a good look at me. She must have concluded that I was harmless, for she flew away on a
foraging expedition, leaving her little ones at my
mercy.

Toward the end of the summer Elizabeth Garrett came to see me. We were chatting in my study. A thunderstorm came up suddenly, and the rain began to beat in. Elizabeth went to close the windows. As she did so, she heard a plaintive bird-cry, and, catching my hand, drew me to the window. "I believe," she said, "a bird is beating its wings against the screen." It was difficult in the rain to raise the screen; but we succeeded, and there, clinging to the vines which had clambered over the sill, was my little Robin Hood! He fluttered into my outstretched hand. He was limp and dripping wet. After he dried off a bit, he began to fly about the room, scrutinizing everything with his inquisitive little eyes. When the shower ceased, we took him to the window, but he did not seem to want to leave us. His sharp claws pinched my finger, he tilted his body. as though he would say, "I am satisfied, why do you want me to go?" I put him down on the sill, and he flew back into the room. We managed to catch him, and again I put him outside the screen, and again he flew back into the study. This time he hid under the couch, and we could not find him. We had to get someone with eyes to dig him out. He hopped on the windowsill from one side to the other, cocking his head this way and that, soliloquizing, I thought. "Oh, which do I prefer? Do I prefer you or yonder tree? Shall I stay here, or go on and on, away, away, away? Oh.

my heart reaches out both ways with such contrary desires!" At last he slowly spread his wings and unwillingly sailed away on the freshly washed air. He has never returned to the dogwood tree or my hand.

Of all things that grow in my garden I love best the evergreens. What a beautiful way they have of entering into relations with human beings! How readily they harmonize the wild nature of their forest kindred with our domestic habits, and how subtly yet powerfully they influence us while we set bounds to their growth. Always beautiful, they seem to draw out of us spiritual loveliness akin to their own.

The evergreens which grow on one side of my garden walk seem to know me as I know them. They stretch out their branches like hands to me and tease me and pull my hair whenever I pass them. In the springtime, when the world swims with odours of life, they bend toward me like friends full of glad news. They try to tell me what it is but I cannot always make out what they are saying. I imagine they are asking each other why human creatures move from place to place, unstable as water, and as the wind that is always in motion. "Look!" they say, pointing their sharp little fingers, "look how she is going in and out among the flowers, like the moths the wind is blowing away out of sight."

If I could fathom that murmur, that sigh, I should fathom the depths of consciousness of my evergreens.

I do not know whether they speak of the future, but I am positive they could reveal the past. I should find out the whence and the how of things that happened centuries ago. They could tell me what they have fared through in the immortality that lies behind them. I have felt the rings buried in trees—rings of the many seasons of births and deaths they died to reach this life. Why this thirst to rise higher? Why this love of stars and sun and clouds? Why this sense of duty to the earth, this fixity of purpose, this inward soul that remembers and sighs? As I stand beside my evergreens they whisper "All that is you has always been, and will always be. Every atom and every impulse of you began in eternity with us, and with us will return into eternity."

Oh, when my spirit is sore fretted by the thought of the unhappiness in the world, it soothes me to walk back and forth beside my evergreens. I feel like a flower after a night's frost, when it steadies itself on its stem and looks up again to the sky with brave hope. And ever as I walk round my green circle, I seem to hear the song of the roots down in the ground, cheerily toiling in the dark. They never see the lovely work they have wrought. Hidden away in darkness they bring forth flowers of light! Little and despised are they; but oh, mighty is their power to create flower and tree! I think of them no less lovingly because they are out of reach of my hand.

As I walk round and round the green circle, rain-wet winds fleck filmy spray in my face. From far-off shores come sweet memories which surge and sigh like surf breaking on invisible sands. They send a spray of whispers through my mind—"Home! South-land!" "Mother." "Father." My heart gropes in the throbbing darkness for the dear hands that long ago caressed me and guided my faltering steps. Words spelled by tiny, irresolute hands make me smile. They are so real, I almost feel my baby sister pressing against my knee.

The warm winds of Alabama flit between me and the years. My brother Phillips is lisping, his baby voice tapping lightly against my finger-tips, "Sis Helen, please play horse with me." So many years I sleep and wake and sleep again; but memory gives back the kisses that brushed my cheek and the hands that brought me violets and the first ripe strawberry. O the preciousness of all things that are "beautiful for being old and gone." O the young days wreathed in jessamine and rose-scented, full of frolic and the din of mocking birds beating at the gates of Paradise!

O south winds, blow leagues and leagues beyond the bars of night, or you'll have the heart out of my breast with your sighs over the changes and the distances! The world is wide to roam, yet my thoughts are all for taking the path the south winds have come. At the end of that path my loved ones are waiting for me—Mildred and Warren, Phillips and Ravia, Katherine, Patricia and little Mildred, Brooks and baby Katherine. Names—names, yet how sweet they sound in the ear of my heart! I am coming home, children dear, to hide myself from work and cares behind the arras of your gay laughter! You shall do with me as you will in merry wise, and I shall forget for a brief space the cares of the grown-up world!

Winds of the South, you have brought me pain and joy in one breath! But you have poured your changeless sweetness upon my weary head and quieted the restless roaming of my mind.

All of us need to go often into the woods alone and sit in silence at the feet of Nature. A few years ago I persuaded my conscience to turn its back upon prosaic tasks and go pleasuring in the open for two months. Mrs. Macy and Edna Porter went with me. Our automobile was equipped with a tent, a small gasoline stove, an ice box, and last but not least, Sieglinde, whose business it was to strike terror into the hearts of wandering Robin Hoods and other intruders. One of our camping spots was a pasture in the Berkshires where a brook laughed and romped. We were awakened in the morning by a herd of cows. I touched their glossy coats and wet noses as they investigated our bivouac, and if they objected to this familiarity they kept their thoughts to themselves. Another spot I loved was a pine wood near Lake Champlain. One night we pitched our tent in a great hay field out of Montreal which we called Stormfield because just after we had settled for the night a tempest burst upon us. We followed the St. Lawrence from Montreal to Quebec, from Quebec we came down through Maine and camped on the Kennebec River. Logs were being floated down from Moosehead Lake to sawmills farther along. In order to get a sense of what the river was like I crawled into it, keeping my body out of the reach of the logs and clinging to the rocks. The current turned me over and over like a leaf, but I managed to touch some of the logs as they shot past, and the sense of adventure was delightful.

We returned home slowly by way of the White Mountains and the Adirondacks. In New Hampshire we camped on the top of a hill near Lake Winnipesaukee because the other members of the party liked the view. But before the night was over we discovered that a fine landscape does not make a fine camp. A demoniacal wind sprang up which was soon reinforced by a whole army of marauding winds which seemed bent on tearing the tent to shreds. Finally they did lift it, and would have carried it off bodily if we had not each grasped a rope and held on with might and main. Sieglinde howled like the winds themselves. At daybreak we wrapped ourselves in blankets, chucked the tent into the car and made our escape, with never a backward look at the beautiful view that had lured us into that battlefield of the winds. When we reached a sheltered spot we made coffee, rested a little, dressed, and continued on our way.

The most wonderful camp of all was in the very heart of the Adirondacks, where the shade was so dense that noonday seemed like midnight. We slept on a bed of firs, by the side of a log fire which burned all night. From the Adirondacks we dropped into the Catskills and down the Hudson back to New York.

People sometimes express surprise that I enjoy the out-of-doors. But God has put much of his work in raised print. The sweet voices of the earth reach me through other avenues than hearing and sight. When I am in the woods I love to put out my hand and catch the rustling tread of small creatures in the leaves.

I love to follow dark roads that smell of moss and wet grasses, hill roads and deep valley roads so narrow that the trees and bushes touch me as I pass.

I love to stand on a little bridge and feel the brook flowing under it with minnows in her hands.

I love to sit on a fallen tree so long that the shy wood-things forget it may be imprudent to step on my toes, and the dimpling cascade throws water-spray in my face. With body still and observant, I hear myriad sounds that I understand—leaf sounds, grass sounds, and twigs creaking faintly when birds alight on them, and grass swaying when insects' wings brush it, and the thistle's silvery flutter. These sounds I hear, yet my way is still.

Chapter XIX

ENCHANTED WINDOWS

MORE than at any other time, when I hold a beloved book in my hand my limitations fall from me, my spirit is free. Books are my compensation for the harms of fate. They give me a world for a lost world, and for mortals who have disappointed me they give me gods.

I cannot take space to name here all the books that have enriched my life, but there are a few that I cannot pass over. The one I have read most is the Bible. I have read and reread it until in many parts the pages have faded out—I mean, my fingers have rubbed off the dots, and I must supply whole verses from memory, especially the Psalms, the Prophets, and the Gospels. To the Bible I always go for confidence when waves of doubt rush over me and no voice is near to reassure me.

In *My Religion* I have written of how Swedenborg deepened my sense of the Lord's presence on earth. His books have given me a richer understanding of the Bible and a precious sense of the Lord's nearness. They have kept burning within me a desire to be of use and to help prepare the way for the second coming of our Lord in the lives of men. I still have *The Divine Love and Wisdom, Intercourse Between the Soul and the Body,* and many volumes of extracts from his other books which were copied for me when I was a little girl by Mr. Hitz, who was the first to open that wonderful window into the spiritual world for me.

It was while I was still a little girl that I made the acquaintance of three great American writers who are inseparably linked in my mind. All three opened for me magic windows through which I still look upon the universe and find it "many splendoured." I mean Emerson, Thoreau, and Whitman. Of the three Whitman is my best beloved. He has been an inspiration to me in a very special way. I began to read his poetry years ago at a time when I was almost overwhelmed by a sense of isolation and self-doubt. It was when I read "The Song of the Open Road" that my spirit leaped up to meet him. For me his verses have the quality of exquisite physical sensations. They wave like flowers, they quiver like fountains, or rush on like mountain torrents. He sings unconquerable life. He is in the middle of the stream. He marches with the world's thought, not against it. To me he seems incomparably our greatest poet. He is a prophet, a voice crying in the wilderness, "Prepare ye the way for the new day." *Leaves of Grass* is the true American epic in the vastness of its scope, in the completeness and beauty of its execution. As the sea reflects the sky's immensity, so *Leaves of Grass* reflects the glowing, potential soul of America. He portrays America as a young giantess subduing a continent, and sings of her vastness, of her resources, her multitudinous activities, her unparalleled material development, her commercialism, her restlessness, turmoil, and blindness, her dullness and drudgery, her dreams and longings, her tireless energy, her limitless opportunity. She is lawless, rushing onward, always at extremities. She is anarchic—she does not walk, she runs—she does not run, she flies—she does not fly, she falls; all this Whitman has pictured in a way that, so far as I know, no one else has approached.

I did not know Whitman personally, but I knew his friend, Horace Traubel, editor of *The Conservator*. When I came to live in New York, I met him occasionally at meetings in memory of Whitman. Later he came to see us here in Forest Hills, and we had some delightful talks together. One of the things he said about Whitman that I remember was, "He's an age. As a man he has exhausted his vitality, but as an age he is exhaustless. The world will go on thinking about Whitman and getting new lights on him as long as men continue to think about the age he lived in. The mystical predominates in him. That is why you get so near him. Many people miss him altogether because they lack that sense, but you could set your net anywhere in Whitman and catch something worth taking home."

Next to Whitman in the American trio I love Thoreau. When I read Thoreau, I am not conscious of him or the book or the words which flow under my finger-tips, I am There. Through him Nature speaks without an interpreter. He puts his ear to her breast and hears her heart beat; and she speaks to me in her own voice. I am a part of the river, the lake, the field, the woods—I am a spirit wild and free. I see everything for myself, no one interprets for me. I have the illusion of being free of my deprivations—I live my life in my own way.

Another naturalist whose books are to me a harbour of content is John Burroughs. They are what he was when I met him—drenched in the sunshine and sweetness of the out-of-door world. I love all that he loves—birds, bees, and everything that blooms and ripens, snow, ice, rain and wind, and the restful simplicity of a life freed from the complex trappings of modern society.

An American who is somehow connected in my mind with Plato and Francis Bacon is Professor William James. When I was a little girl he came to see Miss Sullivan and me at the Perkins Institution for the Blind in South Boston. He brought me a beautiful ostrich feather. "I thought," he said, "you

would like the feather, it is soft and light and caress-
ing."

We talked about my sense perceptions and he
wove a magic web into his discourse. He said then,
and afterwards when I sent him a copy of *The World
I Live In,* that in our problems and processes of
thought we do not greatly differ from one another.
He was not surprised to find my world so much like
that of everyone else, though he said he was "quite
disconcerted, professionally speaking," by my account of myself before my " 'consciousness' was
awakened by instruction."

His thought was clear like crystal. His body, like
his mind, was quick and alert. In argument his
tongue was like a rapier, but he was always ready to
listen to the other side, and always made me ashamed
of my cocksureness about many things.

He was not a mystic—his mind could not thrive on
air as mine does—but I think he was something of a
poet as well as a philosopher.

As a young woman I was extremely fortunate in
having John Macy to counsel me with regard to
books. He was a great reader and an enthusiastic admirer of all that is beautiful in poetry
and prose. Whenever in his own reading he found
anything particularly impressive he read the passage to me. He read long passages from William
James's books as they came out, and many of Steven-

son's letters. He suggested that Mr. Hitz put *Virgini-bus Puerisque,* and E. V. Lucas's *The Open Road,* and *The Friendly Town* into braille, and he read other books for me which later were printed in braille, *Huckleberry Finn* among them. And it was he who had Shelley's "The Cenci" embossed for me.

One of the most stimulating adventures I ever had occurred when Mr. Macy became absorbed in the question of the authorship of the Shakespeare plays. We read books on the subject by Reed, Greenwood, Begley, and our friend, Mr. William Stone Booth. I cannot go into details here. I can merely comment on the confused, breathless wonder of that delightful time. Mr. Furness himself had told me that only three facts had been ascertained with regard to England's greatest genius—he was born, he married, and he died! I was human enough to experience a lively sense of gratification when Mr. Booth's arguments convinced me that Bacon had left his signature upon the plays in the form of acrostics. I could look behind them not to an uneducated rustic, but to a man of mighty intellect. One not without grave faults, but one who was "a memorable example to all of virtue, kindness, peaceableness and patience, one who stood cool and composed before a thousand universes." Whether this was right or wrong, the vigorous discussion shook my mind into more independent thinking, and taught me not to be afraid of established opinions. Such experiences add many years to one's biography; for a thousand thoughts spring up where there was one.

I am constantly surprised at the slight things which have influenced me. A casual acquaintance, an article in a magazine or a book, has caused me to discard opinions I had held with a dogged faith. When Mr. Macy first introduced me to H. G. Wells's *New Worlds for Old*, the kingdom which was my mind became a Social Utopia. With confidence I exchanged my old world for his new one. How simple he made everything! His eloquence changed the selfish old world into a fair City of God. Was not this the fulfilment of the hope of youth? Mr. Wells was a glorified prophet until I saw that he stopped at every altar to revise his articles of faith. Then I gave him up but he had already made a lot of trouble for me—God forgive him!

It was Mr. Macy who introduced me to Tolstoi, Romain Rolland, Hardy, Shaw, Kropotkin, Anatole France, Brieux, and Karl Marx. I had the pleasure of meeting M. Brieux some years later when I was lecturing in Northampton and he was lecturing at Smith College. He could not speak English, and my French was atrocious, but by some miracle of intuition we understood each other: I read his lips, and he was so delighted when I repeated his words correctly, his tears fell on my hand. I managed to tell him I liked his brood of heresies, and that I was grateful to him for breaking the cowardly silence of the world on social evils. I told him how my eyes had opened to those evils in my work for the blind. I tried to say in French that we must use the lever of plain speech to pry at the underpinnings of a social system which ruins human bodies and minds and covers the disaster with false blushes. I could not think of the words for lever and pry, so my high sailing sentiment went on the rocks. I managed better with my offering that M. Brieux and Mr. Shaw were true reformers, and both were assuredly destined to drive people out of their refuge of pretended ignorance. "But," said M. Brieux, "according to the critics we are not artists, and should be cast out because art has nothing to do with social or political reform—it is an expression of beauty for beauty's sake."

I think he assented to this view; but he said beauty meant something different to him. "All things are beautiful to me if they are a real part of human life. Sad, terrible things must be shown also. To realize ugliness is to suffer and to long for beauty."

After he returned to France he wrote to me, and I was glad to learn through an article he inclosed that he was taking an active part in the rehabilitation of blind soldiers.

I encountered another distinguished author from a foreign shore when I was in vaudeville. Mr. G. K. Chesterton happened to be in Cleveland when I was there. We were stopping at the same hotel. One evening he and Mrs. Chesterton called on us in our rooms. He was exactly what I expected after reading *Father Brown, Trifles,* and *Three Diamonds,* only more delightful. He was a formidable personage, with an Englishman's honest prejudices against nearly everything American, and a scintillating vocabulary in which to parade them. As our faults passed before us they were so brilliantly illuminated by Chestertonian rays of wit, aphorism, and invective that we were glad we had them.

I find that my mental constitution is unlike that of most modern writers. I am thinking especially of Mr. Mencken, Mr. Sinclair Lewis, and Mr. Eugene O'Neill. I enjoy being credulous, while they seem to abhor it. I am aware of a subtle connivance with my folly. I keep the windows of my soul open to illusions. Like the saints of early years, I am constantly on the lookout for miracles. The unexpected may happen at any odd moment, and I want to be on the spot.

Of all the writers that have come to me in recent years Joseph Conrad stands preëminent. I did not really make his acquaintance until 1920—I did not have any of his books in braille before then. I cannot define the peculiar fascination he has for me, but he took possession of me at once. I had always loved books of the sea, and the days I have spent along the shore have been happy ones. I love the dunes and the sea weeds that drift in and crawl up on the sands, the little waves that creep through shells and pebbles, like fingers seeking to spell a message to me. "We used to be friends when you were the beginning of a fish—do you remember?" I love winds and storms and sailors, tropical dawns leaping out of the east, and billows that like mighty tusked mastodons crunch the land. It may be that I am especially alive to the spell of the sea because it is so much like the darkness that is my element. The dark, too, has its deep silent currents and dangerous reefs, its monsters, its creatures of beauty, its derelicts and ships. In the dark, too, there is a star to steer by, and no matter how far I travel there are always before me vast oceans of experience that I have not yet explored.

It seems to me, the picture most constantly in Conrad's mind is that of bits of humanity adrift upon a dark sea, trying to save themselves. Some think they can reach shore by swimming, some fashion rafts, some keep bobbing up and down, declaring that there is no shore, yet they go on fighting, driven by some incomprehensible urge to self-preservation. While they seek to reach an invisible shore, they see themselves as eventually safe, triumphant heirs of immortal happiness. What matter the loneliness, the hardships, the loud beating of the billows and solemn moan of fathomless waters? What counts is the inner vision, the brightness and blessedness of the dream.

Mr. Frank Nelson Doubleday, Conrad's friend and publisher who is also my friend and publisher, has given me *Chance, Victory,* and the *Life and Letters* by Jean-Aubry. My teacher had the *Life and Letters* put into braille as soon as they came. While I have been writing they have been reposing tantalizingly on the shelf, and my fingers have ached to get hold of them.

I like books that bring me close to elemental things —books like Willa Cather's *My Antonia,* Knut Hamsun's *Growth of the Soil,* Edgar Lee Masters' *Spoon River Anthology,* and Olive Schreiner's *The Story of an African Farm.* Two years ago Miss Thomson gave me *The Story of an African Farm.* It was the first time I had read anything of Olive Schreiner's. I do not know of another woman writer who has the power and vision of the author of this book. It is now fifty-three years since it was written and it is still as terrible as a primal force of nature.

Thomas Hardy came to me first with *Tess of the D'Urbervilles* in his hand. The intensity of his dark vision fascinated me. He is the greatest pessimist in English letters, I think, with the exception of Dean

Swift, but his disheartening realism stimulates while it depresses. Like Job, he is a poet, and one cannot escape the feeling that he revels in his dark sorceries, or the wish that a few gentle fairies had made their abode in Dorsetshire.

Bernard Shaw came to me first accompanied by Candida and her poet lover. I cannot imagine anyone dozing when Shaw is around. There is a mischievous imp in him which brings the dullest of us to attention. He is the gadfly of the absurdities of our time. He has packed into two short sentences the causes of unhappiness in the world. "What is the matter with the poor is poverty," he says. "What is the matter with the rich is uselessness."

A recent book that I have enjoyed immensely is *Microbe Hunters,* by Paul de Kruif. It was most comforting to learn that great scientists are human like ourselves. I could have shouted with glee over their quarrels, jealousies, and mistakes. How like mere mortals they are in their weaknesses! But how like gods in their imagination, patience, and nobility of purpose! I have read few books relating to science so entrancing as this one.

At times when I have not been able to get books I wanted embossed over here because our braille presses were so busy with other matters I have appealed to my friend, Sir Arthur Pearson, in England. It was he who had Turgenev's *Smoke* done for

me and *Value, Price, and Profit,* by Karl Marx.
Several of Conrad's books were also transcribed for
me in England.

Publishers of books are as generous in giving
reprint permission to the blind as publishers of
magazines, but the publishing of braille books is
expensive, and many of the most important works
by the greatest authors are not available for the blind.
Very few of the blind can own any books at all,
not even a Bible. The cheapest Bible in raised print
costs sixty-five dollars.

Through the generosity of the Lions International
the blind are enjoying a great many more books
than they ever had before. We are indebted to them
for *The Forsyte Saga.* Galsworthy opens a wide
window for me. Like William Blake, he feels that a
bird in a cage puts out a light in Heaven, and that
the cry of a hunted animal tears a fibre out of the
brain of an angel, and that beggars' rags are toad-
stools on a prince's throne. "As he caresses the heads
of his own dogs, an aching tenderness runs from his
finger-tips to the human under-dog—to tramp, and
prostitute, and hungry workingman." He knows
that compared with the spiritual experiences life
has to offer, "property" is nothing, nothing, nothing!

I wish I could express what poetry means to me.
I have always loved it. For many years I have had
beside me Palgrave's *Golden Treasury,* Keats, Shel-

ley, Whitman, Browning, and Burns. In all of these books there are pages which I have worn out. Keats's "I Stood Tip-toe on a Little Hill" is quite flat. Shelley's "Prometheus Unbound," "To a Skylark," and "The Cloud" are very thin. So is Browning's "Saul," and the whole of *The Golden Treasury* is in a sad state of dilapidation.

Poetry is to me the Mystic Trumpeter of which Walt Whitman says,

At thy liquid prelude, glad, serene,
The fretting world, the street, the noisy hours of day withdraw,
A holy calm descends like dew upon me,
I walk in cool refreshing night the walk of paradise,
I scent the grass, the moist air and the roses;
Thy song expands my numb'd, imbonded spirit, thou freest,
    launchest me,
Floating and basking upon Heaven's lake.

Next to Whitman my favourite American poet is Lanier. It is given to poets and blind people to see into the Unseen, and together Lanier and I have gazed into the "sweet-within-sweet" mystery of flowers and corn and clover, and the sweep of marsh and sea has revealed to us the liberty beyond the prison bars of sense.

As I read the poems which Francis Thompson seems to put into my hands as a child brings "some fond and fancied nothings," all I touch becomes more significant—the rustle of the leaves, the shy ways of children, the fugitive winds that come and go among the flowers with trackless feet; and always there is the undertone of ineffaceable sorrow and tenderness.

I have not said much about the poets who are singing to-day because their music is not in raised letters. I only catch tantalizing notes now and then when some good Samaritan who is also a lover of poetry reads to me. In this way I have enjoyed poems by Yeats, Padraic Colum, and others. The brooding Celtic note grips my heart. Yeats makes me want to visit the Isle of Innisfree and know the Danaan people and gather "the golden apples of the sun" and "the silver apples of the moon." For a time our house in Wrentham was vibrant with Synge's tragic laughter. My mother read me "Riders to the Sea" and "The Well of the Saints." I also go with Douglas Hyde into the cabins of Connaught where he finds songs on the lips of old women spinning in the sun. I should like to see more of the shining ones George Russell (Æ) finds dwelling among the hills of old Ireland. And more of Lord Dunsany, who seems in the poem or two I have read to penetrate into the realms of twilight wonder where the incredible is tangible, and the Irish little folk make music that enthralls the unwary.

John Masefield is the most vital of the English poets I have met of recent years. Poetry is not for him, as for the Irish, an escape from life, but his slums and peasants and sailors and taverns interest me.

Perhaps it is true of everyone, but it seems to me that in a special way what I read becomes a part of me. What I am conscious of borrowing from my author friends I put in quotation marks, but I do not know how to indicate the wandering seeds that drop unperceived into my soul. I am not even extenuating my appropriation of fine thoughts. I prefer to put quotation marks at the beginning and the end of my book and leave it to those who have contributed to its interest or charm or beauty to take what is theirs and accept my gratitude for the help they have been to me. I know that I am not original in either content or form. I have not opened new paths to thought or new vistas to truth, but I hope that my books have paid tribute in some small measure to the authors who have enriched my life.

Chapter XX

THOUGHTS THAT WILL NOT LET ME SLEEP

I HAVE already said that people are not interested in what I think of things outside myself, but there are certain subjects about which I feel very deeply, and this book would not be an honest record of my life if I avoided them. I realize that I am apt to be too dogmatic when I write of things that mean much to me. I know it would be an advantage to express disapproval with captivating grace. If I could deliver my indictments with an urbanity so exquisite that every reader would feel himself implicitly exempted from the charge, and free to relish the strokes administered to the rest, this chapter would be more enjoyed. Even the accused like to be taken into their enemy's confidence, and invited as a personal favour to look on while execution is being done on the host without. While they laugh, no doubt they resolve privately to be less like those "others" in the future. But delicate banter is not one of my strong points. I ask nothing for myself. I am not among the victims of unjust laws. The struggle I have gone through is no worse than, indeed, it is not so grinding as, that of the majority of men and women who are enmeshed in economic problems which they are incapable of solving.

When I look out upon the world, I see society divided into two great elements, and organized around an industrial life which is selfish, combative, and acquisitive, with the result that man's better instincts are threatened, while his evil propensities are intensified and protected. My knowledge of the conditions that this system imposes is not vicarious. I have visited mill towns in Massachusetts, Georgia, the Carolinas, Alabama, Rhode Island, and New Jersey. I have visited mining towns in Pennsylvania, Utah, Alabama, Tennessee, West Virginia, and Colorado. I have been in foundry towns when the men were on strike. I have been in packing towns when the men were on strike. I have been in New York when the longshoremen were on strike. I have been on the New York Central when the railroad men were on strike, and stones went flying through the windows. I have spoken in cities where feeling was so intense because of the conflict between capital and labour that when I was asked questions about the dispute part of the audience hissed, and the manager came on to the stage to ask me not to answer.

I have gone through ugly dark streets filled with small children whose little grimy faces already look old. Many of them are defective in body or mind or both.

All over America I have been appalled by the number of young children who spend the greater part of the day in stuffy, overcrowded rooms, looked after by old people or by children only a little older than themselves, while their parents work in factories or in other people's houses. This seems to me the most deplorable tragedy of our modern life. A nation's first and last responsibility is the welfare of its children. No nation can live if its children must struggle not to die; no nation can decay if its children are healthy and happy. These children who have neither health nor happiness, who were born in ill-smelling, sunless tenements, whose hunger drove them early to the sweat-shops and mills and mines—these children, who in body and soul have become dwarfed and misshapen, are not fit citizens for a republic. They are at once a danger and a reproach.

We bar the children of Europe's slums at our gates. Our immigration laws do not permit the weak and unfit to come into our country, but a singular change of sentiment occurs when mothers wish to restrict another kind of immigration far wider and more fateful. Anyone who advocates the limitation of families to a number which their parents can care for in health and decency is frowned upon as a law-breaker. It is not illegal to bring defective children into the world to grow up in soul-destroying poverty, but it is criminal for a physician to tell a mother how to protect herself and her family by birth-control! It is a strange, illogical order that makes it a crime to teach the prevention of conception and yet fails to provide decent living conditions for the swarms of babies that come tumbling into the world.

O America, beloved of my heart! The worst that men will say of you is this: You took little children out of their cradles, out of the sun and dewy grass, away from play and their toys, and huddled them between dark walls of brick and cement to work for a wage, for their bread. For their heart-hunger you gave them dust to eat, and for their labour you filled their little hands with ashes!

I love my country. To say that is like saying I love my family. I did not choose my country any more than I chose my parents, but I am her daughter just as truly as I am the child of my Southern mother and father. What I am my country has made me. She has fostered the spirit which made my education possible. Neither Greece nor Rome, nor all China, nor Germany nor Great Britain has surrounded a deaf-blind child with the devotion and skill and resources which have been mine in America.

But my love for America is not blind. Perhaps I am more conscious of her faults because I love her so deeply. Nor am I blind to my own faults. It is easy to see that there is little virtue in the old formulas, and that new ones must be found, but even after one has decided this, it is not easy to hold a steady course in a changing world.

One of the painful consequences of holding to one's course, if it is unpopular, is the division it causes between friends. It is not pleasant to feel that friends who have loved us no longer care to see us. One says defiantly, "I don't care! I'm perfectly happy without their friendship"; but it is not true. One cannot help feeling very sad about it at times. We are all complex. I wish I were made of just one self— consistent, wise, and loving—a self I should never wish to get rid of at any time or place, which would move graciously through my autobiography, "trailing clouds of glory." But alas and alack! Deep within me I knew nothing of the kind would happen. No wonder I shrank from writing this book.

It is no use trying to reconcile the multitude of egos that compose me. I cannot fathom myself. I ask myself questions that I cannot answer. I find my heart aching when I expected to find it rejoicing, tears flow from my eyes when my lips were formed to smile. I preach love, brotherhood, and peace, but I am conscious of antagonisms, and lo! I find myself brandishing a sword and making ready for the battle.

I think that every honest belief should be treated with fairness, yet I cry out against people who uphold the empire of gold. I am aware of moods when the perfect state of peace, brotherhood, and universal love seems so far off that I turn to division, pugnacity, and the pageant of war. I am just like St. Paul when he says, "I delight in the Law of God after the inward man; but I see another law in my members, warring against the law of my mind." I am perfectly sure that love will bring everything right in the end, but I cannot help sympathizing with the oppressed who feel driven to use force to gain the rights that belong to them.

That is one reason why I have turned with such interest towards the great experiment now being tried in Russia. No revolution was ever a sudden outbreak of lawlessness and wreckage incited by an unholy brood of cranks, anarchists, and pedagogues. People turn to revolution only when every other dream has faded into the dimness of sorrow. When we look back upon these mighty disturbances which seem to leap so suddenly out of the troubled depths we find that they were fed by little streams of discontent and oppression. These little streams which have their source deep down in the miseries of the common people all flow together at last in a retributive flood.

The Russian Revolution did not originate with Lenin. It had hovered for centuries in the dreams of Russian mystics and patriots, but when the body of Lenin was laid in simple state in the Kremlin, all

Russia trembled and wept. The mouths of hungry enemies fed on new hopes, but the spirit of Lenin descended upon the weeping multitude as with cloven tongues of fire, and they spoke one to another, and were not afraid. "Let us not follow him with cowering hearts," they said, "let us rather gird ourselves for the task he has left us. Where our dull eyes see only ruin, his clearer sight discovers the road by which we shall gain our liberty. Revolution, he sees, yea, and even disintegration which symbolizes disorder is in truth the working of God's undeviating Order; and the manner of our government shall be no less wonderful than the manner of our deliverance. If we are steadfast, the world will be quickened to courage by our deeds."

Men vanish from earth leaving behind them the furrows they have ploughed. I see the furrow Lenin left sown with the unshatterable seed of a new life for mankind, and cast deep below the rolling tides of storm and lightning, mighty crops for the ages to reap.

It is not possible for civilization to flow backwards while there is youth in the world. Youth may be headstrong, but it will advance its allotted length. Through the ages in the battle with the powers of evil—with poverty, misery, ignorance, war, ugliness and slavery, youth has steadily gained on the enemy. That is why I never turn away from the new generation impatiently because of its knowingness. Through it alone shall salvation come.

Yet the prospect of the millennium does not seem to me as imminent as it once did. The process of the emancipation of mankind from old ideas is very slow. The human race does not take to new ways of living readily, but I do not feel discouraged. Personally, I am impeded by physical difficulties which generate forces powerful enough to carry me over the barriers. This is true of the world's problems, too. It is for us to work with all our might to unite the spiritual power of good against the material power of evil.

It is for us to pray not for tasks equal to our powers, but for powers equal to our tasks, to go forward with a great desire forever beating at the door of our hearts as we travel towards the distant goal.

Man is unconquerable when he stands on the rights of man. It is inspiring to see against the background of our ignorance an old ideal or a discarded truth flash forth new-created. The tragic deaths of Sacco and Vanzetti were a fiery sign to the friends of freedom everywhere that the powers never slumber which seek to subject the weak and unbefriended. Now and then a Juarès, a Liebnecht, a Debs, a Rolland, a Lenin, or a Tolstoi startles the dormant souls of a few men and women with the thunder of his words. The veil of the temple is for a moment rent in twain; Truth, piercing as lightning, reveals the hideous thing we have made of our humanity.

Then the veil is drawn, and the world sleeps again, sometimes for centuries, but never as comfortably as it did before.

This need not discourage us. We can still keep our faces towards the dawn, knowing that with God a thousand years are as a watch in the night. There is always a new horizon for onward looking men.

The world which my imagination constructs out of my philosophy of evolution is pleasant to contemplate. It is a realization of everything that seems desirable to us in our best moods, and the people that live in it are like those we sometimes meet whose nobility is a prophecy of what we shall be when we have reached the state in which the different parts of our bodies and souls, our hearts and minds, have attained their right proportions. This state will not be attained without tribulation.

The clatter of a changing world is not pleasant, and those who have enjoyed the comforts and protection of the old order may be shocked and unhappy when they behold the vigorous young builders of a new world sweeping away their time-honoured antiquities. I look forward to the time when the most atrocious of these antiquities—war—will be as much shunned by mankind as it is now glorified. The voice within us that cries so passionately for peace cannot lie.

"The great God," said William Penn in his address

to the Indians, "hath written His Law in our hearts, by which we are taught and commanded to love and help do good to one another. It is not our custom to bear hostile weapons against our fellow creatures, for which reason we come unarmed. Our object is not to do injury, but to do good. We are now met on the broad pathway to good faith and good will, so that no advantage may be taken on either side, but all is to be openness, brotherhood, and love, while all are to be treated as of the same flesh and blood."

If the experience of the other colonies of the Atlantic seaboard was any criterion, Penn and his followers were preparing themselves for destruction. Any wise militarist of Massachusetts or Maryland or Virginia could have told him of the treacherous Indians, of their bloodthirstiness, of their unexpected raids with tomahawk and torch, and the necessity, therefore, of being armed. But the Quakers did not know, or if they did know, they did not believe, and so they came to this wilderness without so much as a sword or a rifle, to establish a "City of Brotherly Love," and they succeeded. While other settlements were attacked and burned, and slaughtered or carried off into captivity, the little Pennsylvania colony enjoyed uninterrupted peace and prosperity. The Quakers had no forts, no soldiers, no arms. They lived in the midst of a savage people who knew that they were defenceless; and yet, in spite of this fact, or shall we say because of it, they knew no war for seventy years. "Whatever were the quarrels of the Pennsylvania Indians with others," says one of the Quaker historians, "they respected and held, as it were, sacred the territories of the Quakers. The Penn colony never lost a man, woman, or child by the Indians. The flowers of prosperity and good will smiled in the footprints of William Penn."

I should like to see all the energy that is going into preparation for war express itself in ideals that we should be proud to cherish—that would make us ashamed of the sordidness which prevails at the present time. Work should be joyous. Everyone should go to his labour singing as Whitman hears America singing "the varied carols," the mechanics singing blithe and strong—the vitality of America voiced in building for a race of free men and women. There is a passage in Whitman which expresses my desire for America with such sympathy I shall quote it here:

This moment yearning and thoughtful, sitting alone,
It seems to me there are other men in other lands, yearning and
    thoughtful;
It seems to me I can look over and behold them, in Germany,
    Italy, France, Spain—or far, far away, in China, or in
    Russia, or India—talking other dialects;

And it seems to me if I could know those men, I should become
    attached to them, as I do to men in my own lands;
Oh, I know we should be brethren and lovers,
I know I should be happy with them.

I believe that we can live on earth according to the teachings of Jesus, and that the greatest happiness will come to the world when man obeys His commandment "Love ye one another."

I believe that every question between man and man is a religious question, and that every social wrong is a moral wrong.

I believe that we can live on earth according to the fulfilment of God's will, and that when the will of God is done on earth as it is done in heaven, every man will love his fellow men, and act towards them as he desires they should act towards him. I believe that the welfare of each is bound up in the welfare of all.

I believe that life is given us so we may grow in love, and I believe that God is in me as the sun is in the colour and fragrance of a flower—the Light in my darkness, the Voice in my silence.

I believe that only in broken gleams has the Sun of Truth yet shone upon men. I believe that love will finally establish the Kingdom of God on earth, and that the Cornerstones of that Kingdom will be Liberty, Truth, Brotherhood, and Service.

I believe that no good shall be lost, and that all

man has willed or hoped or dreamed of good shall exist forever.

I believe in the immortality of the soul because I have within me immortal longings. I believe that the state we enter after death is wrought of our own motives, thoughts, and deeds. I believe that in the life to come I shall have the senses I have not had here, and that my home there will be beautiful with colour, music, and speech of flowers and faces I love.

Without this faith there would be little meaning in my life. I should be "a mere pillar of darkness in the dark." Observers in the full enjoyment of their bodily senses pity me, but it is because they do not see the golden chamber in my life where I dwell delighted; for, dark as my path may seem to them, I carry a magic light in my heart. Faith, the spiritual strong searchlight, illumines the way, and although sinister doubts lurk in the shadow, I walk unafraid towards the Enchanted Wood where the foliage is always green, where joy abides, where nightingales nest and sing, and where life and death are one in the Presence of the Lord.

Chapter XXI

MY GUARDIAN ANGEL

I HAVE already spoken of the memorable passage in Gibbon's *Autobiography* in which he says,

> Between the hours of eleven and twelve at night I wrote the last page of it (*The Decline and Fall*), in a small house in my garden. I laid down my pen and took several turns in a berceau, or covered walk of acacias, which overlooked the country, the lake, and the mountains. The night was calm, the sky was serene, and the silvery orb of the moon was reflected from the waters.

He goes on to describe his mingled emotions of joy and pain,

> . . . my joy on the recovery of my freedom, and perhaps the establishment of my fame—and whatsoever may be the fate of my history, the life of the historian must be short and precarious.

I have written the last line of the last autobiography I shall write, in my little study, not in Lausanne but in Forest Hills. I lift my tired hands from the typewriter. I am free. There are no acacias in my garden, but there are spruce and firs and dogwoods. However, I am using the acacias symbolically. To me they represent the life path on which

I have walked while the love of countless friends has shone upon me. I am conscious not only of those who walk the earth but also of those who dwell on the heaven side of life. My books, too, I like to think of as friends smiling upon me along the winding pathway. It would require more genius than I have to paint in felicitous words even a small part of the multitudinously hued light that has given beauty and meaning to my life, but through the distance and darkness I fling those who have given it the best wishes of my heart and my gratitude.

My autobiography is not a great work. Whatever value is in it is there not because I have any skill as a writer, nor because there are any thrilling incidents in it, but because God has dealt with me as with a son, and chastened me, and muffled His beams that He might lead men in the path of aid to the deaf and blind. He has made me the mouth of such as cannot speak, and my blindness others' sight, and let me be hands and feet to the maimed and the helpless. And because I could not do this alone, being imprisoned in a great darkness and silence, it was necessary that another should liberate me. That other is Anne Sullivan, my guardian angel.

I have been frequently asked what I should do without her. I smile and answer cheerfully, "God sent her, and if He takes her, His love will fill the void," but it terrifies me to face the thought that this question brings to my mind. I peer with a heavy heart into the years to come. Hope's face is veiled, troubling fears awake and bruise me as they wing through the dark. I lift a tremulous prayer to God, for I should be blind and deaf in very truth if she were gone away.

The day that I hold the dearest of the year is the day she came to me. She was a young woman, alone. She had been blind from childhood, and her sight had just been partially restored. Everything before her was unfamiliar. She was fifteen hundred miles away from her friends in a strange little town that had been almost wrecked by the Civil War. With little equipment except an extraordinary mind and a brave heart, handicapped by imperfect vision, with only the training she had received from Dr. Howe's reports of his work with Laura Bridgman, without help or counsel or previous experience in teaching, she struggled with some of the most complicated problems in one of the most difficult of all fields of education.

There were gaps and deficiencies in her own instruction that she had the wisdom herself to see. Perhaps it was because of them that she brought so much freshness to her work. She was a delightful companion, entering into all my discoveries with the joy of a fellow explorer, and to this youthful interest she added a smiling tact and endless ingenuity in explaining what I did not understand. And in those days there was scarcely a thing in the world I did understand. Above all she loved me.

The stimulating contacts of life that had been denied me she strove to supply. She was ever at hand to keep me in touch with the world of men and women, and did everything she could to develop ways by which I myself could communicate directly with them. During the four years I was in Radcliffe College, she sat beside me in the classroom and with her supple speaking hand spelled out the lectures to me word by word. In the same way she read many books to me in French, German, Latin, Greek— philosophy, history, literature, and economics—and she has continued to bring me day by day, through the years, the best thoughts of men and the news of their achievements. In spite of repeated warnings from oculists she has always abused her eyes for my sake. Now she is able to read only with the aid of a powerful lens which was prescribed for her by Dr. Conrad Berens, who has stood near while this book has been struggling into existence to keep the flickering light in her eyes that she might spell the typed pages into my hand and thus direct the stream of my thought within the bounds of a conceived plan.

I often wonder what my life would have been like if she had not come into it. I cannot picture anyone else in her place. There seems to me nothing accidental in the circumstances which made her my teacher. The conditions of her childhood were so harsh that from her earliest years she had to take thought of life or perish. Wellington said that the battle of Waterloo was won on the cricket fields of England. So I say my education was accomplished in the tragedy of my teacher's life. She understood the void in my soul because her childhood had been so empty of joy. It is when I think of how often I have disappointed her with work I have done ill that I cannot imagine what she saw in me that has kept her at my side all these years.

She could have lived her own life, and had a better chance of happiness than most women. Her power of clear, audacious thought and the splendour of her unselfish soul might have made her a leader among the women of her day. The freshness and lucidity of her writing would have won distinction. But she has closed these doors to herself and refused to consider anything that would take her away from me. She delights in the silence that wraps her life in mine, and says that the story of her teaching is the story of her life, her work is her biography. She has given me the best years of her womanhood, and she is still giving herself to me day by day. She has done much for me that cannot be defined or explained. By the vitalizing power of her friendship she has stirred and enlarged my faculties. She has made my good impulses more fruitful, my will to serve others stronger. Slowly, slowly, out of my weakness and helplessness she has built up my life. No one knows better than she and I how that life falls short of what we should like to make it. But, such as it is, she has built it.

Out of the orb of darkness she led me into golden hours and regions of beauteous thought, bright-spun of love and dreams. Thought-buds opened softly in the walled garden of my mind. Love flowered sweetly in my heart. Spring sang joyously in all the silent, hidden nooks of childhood, and the dark night of blindness shone with the glory of stars unseen. As she opened the locked gates of my being my heart leapt with gladness and my feet felt the thrill of the chanting sea. Happiness flooded my being as the sun overflows the earth, and I stretched out my hands in quest of life.

THE END

INDEX

INDEX